AF270943

A Call to Courage

M. K. Eddleman

in collaboration with

Sheryl J. Williams

BRIGHTON PUBLISHING LLC
435 N. HARRIS DR, MESA, AZ 82303

A Call to Courage

M. K. Eddleman

in collaboration with

Sheryl J. Williams

Brighton Publishing LLC
435 N. Harris Drive
Mesa, AZ 85203

www.BrightonPublishing.com

ISBN: 978-1-62183-556-1

Copyright © 2019

Printed in the United States of America

First Edition

Cover Design: Tom Rodriguez

Acknowledgments

M K. Eddleman is a mother daughter writing team. M stands for Martha, the mother of the team. K stands for Katherine, her daughter.

Sheryl Williams and MK Eddleman would like to address the issue of race before readers begin *A Call to Courage*. A white woman writing about a black woman's experience in 1967 Mississippi raises questions. How could any white person know the accumulated indignities, angst and fear resulting from centuries of segregation? The answer is, she couldn't.

Martha: My husband, son, six-year-old daughter Katherine and I lived in Mississippi during the Civil Rights movement. For years, I have wanted to write about our enlightening and sometimes frightening involvement with the Head Start program and the newly integrated public schools. As I started to write, I had to find a way to recall accurate details of events that forever shaped my life. I watched countless hours of interviews recorded by the Library of Congress/Smithsonian *Voices of Civil Rights* project of black men and women who worked and fought for justice. I realized the story I had in mind was so much deeper than what my family and I experienced.

Slowly, a new fictionalized version of events, with a heavy emphasis on the struggle to achieve full voting rights, took shape. But I knew if I were going to write about the courage it took to fight for rights, I needed the perspective of

I

someone who had lived the experience, someone who fully understood all the nuances of the physical threat, psychological anxiety and emotional trauma associated with bigotry and violence. Cole Powell, a friend of mine, suggested his cousin Sheryl Williams, a 72-year-old African American who lives in Florida.

The moment I connected with Sheryl, a collaboration was in the making. Daily we talked on the telephone. In time, she embraced the concept and began adding to the storyline from personal experiences. As we talked about our understandings of past events, we created *A Call to Courage*. At the end of each day of writing, I sent rough drafts to Sheryl. She would read the day's work, then accept, add or correct the manuscript. She made sure the characters and tone representing black culture in 1967 were authentic. Though the book references real events and details from many diverse lives, the characters in *A Call to Courage* are fictionalized. Once we were finished, I sent our work to Katherine who edited with a discerning eye for detail and imaginative understanding of storyline. She spent many hours adding her insightful perspective to each event before she gave her final approval.

Sheryl: I'd like to thank my cousin Cole Powell for recommending and introducing me to Martha Eddleman. I never envisioned having such an opportunity to be a part of a novel that I helped create. I initially approached the work with questions of commitment from the author. Why did a white woman hold onto the negative experiences? I had tried to put similar experiences or events away somewhere. This story really hits home for me. Some events happened and even worse. A friend of mine and her parents, her dad a minister, had to leave Mississippi after her dad was accused of touching a white woman inappropriately. They were terrified, afraid of their shadows, even in Manhattan. They were receiving death threats. A woman I met had to leave South Carolina after being impregnated by a law officer. He threatened to kill her if she stayed. She found refuge with my neighbor, who was her sister, until she gave birth to a baby boy. Recalling some of the indignities I personally was privy to (as well as my grandparents and other persons I've known) these were expected to be normal, part of a brown skin person's life, with no complaints. Complaints could cause cross burnings or house burnings or even loss of life.

During my many conversations with Martha, I discovered though our skin color was different, our souls were held together by a common thread. Our self-expressions were worded differently, but her passion was greater than mine. I was so accustomed to accepting a degree of bigotry without a fight, I've lived a great part of my life as isolated as the world would or will allow, oft times being termed a hermit. I love everyone; however, I truly enjoy being left alone.

Katherine: Mom and I are collaborative by nature. We approach each project differently. In this book, Sheryl and Mom are the creative entities; I am the bricks and mortar. When Mom came to me with this concept, I encouraged her to move forward, as I knew our experiences in Mississippi, both mutual and distinct, impacted our perspectives on life. I believe conversations about difficult subjects need to be held both privately and publicly. This story is the result of private conversations between two deeply creative women who took a risk to write *A Call to Courage.* I strive to be as courageous as they.

We would like to thank all our readers - Tom Anderson, Linda Berzok, Doris Bobo, Bob Drach, Ro LaFrancesca, Georgia Lambert, Karen McClave, Cole Powell, Beverly Preslik-Gerbracht, Myrna Loy Riles, Carol Shaw, David Silberman, Linda Starnes, and Claudia Wanlin.

All were fearless in their reviews and suggestions yet generous with their encouragement and time.

Finally, thanks to Donald McGuire and Brighton Publishing for their confidence in the book and Tom Rodriguez for designing the perfect cover.

We hope the story resonates with all readers.

⟨Prologue⟩

hat's that smell? Smoke. Not the warm, woody smell from burning logs in a fireplace. More an acrid smell from something not meant to burn. The terrifying whoosh of air being sucked out of the room issued a final warning. For a moment, I stood paralyzed, unable to comprehend what was happening. Suddenly, a terrifying realization dawned on me as I watched wispy tendrils of smoke circle up from around the door. Someone had set fire to our home. Fear, hidden deep in my brain, tumbled out, overriding any good sense I might have had. *Think. What did they say to do? Oh, Lord, why can't I remember?*

Flames licked at the door scorching the white paint until it bubbled and hissed. I tried to calm myself by breathing deeply, but the heat seared my lungs. *Where was Dessie? I have to save Dessie.* Instinctively, I reached for the brass doorknob. Like a hot iron, it scorched my hand adding the smell of burning flesh to the sickening stench of danger. I had to think of a different way to save my daughter.

Stumbling through the blinding smoke, I held my breath, reaching out to find the end, then side of the bed. Using it to guide my way, I made it to the window. Pushing the sill upward, I gasped for air. That's when I saw him. Wrapped in the white garb of the Klan, a figure raced across the lawn, whooping in the joy of his fiery success, until the billowy drape of his gown ensnared his legs, throwing him to the ground. He kicked and squirmed like a fish flopping on the bank of a river, swearing at his mistake. Untangling himself, he staggered to his feet. In a final gesture of loathing, he swore words of condemnation at my daughter, and then dove into the safety of a waiting pickup truck. As he and his gang sped off into the veil of darkness, I could hear their shrill laughter pierce the night air. *"Cowards,"* I hissed.

⊙⊱Chapter One⊰⊙

SUNDAY, MAY 14, 1967 (MOTHER'S DAY)

To say it had been a busy week at the mortuary was an understatement. Shirley, the wife of a popular barkeep in our community, had died suddenly when she slipped and fell, hitting her head on the corner of a table as she went down. The folks who witnessed her death were traumatized. She was a kind woman who made everybody feel at home in her bar no matter how much money they might have had. Her death was a terrible loss to the community.

The expectation was my husband Marvin and I would put on a fitting send-off for a woman who had been so dearly loved. We did just that. At one o'clock on a humid Saturday afternoon, we turned our humble mortuary into a sanctuary for mourners from all walks of life to come pay their respects. Marvin made sure Shirley looked peaceful and beautiful. Not muddy like some morticians made black folks look. And I made sure the service was a true celebration of her life. More than two hundred people showed up to sing praises to her memory.

You would have thought with all those folks being occupied at a funeral, there would have been nobody left in town. But, right in the middle of the service, Dessie, our sixteen-year-old daughter, quietly approached her father and whispered in his ear that old Mr. Williams had had a heart

1

attack in the parking lot outside of the local grocery store. He died right there on the spot. None of the white folks in town wanted anything to do with him. They insisted Marvin come right away. So, he left in the middle of Shirley's service leaving Dessie and me to take over handling the rest of the funeral.

By Sunday, all we wanted to do was go to church in the morning, then come home and relax. Maybe watch a little TV, catch up on napping and eat leftovers. We had even let Dessie spend the night with her best friend, Josey, so we could take a break from any routine or demands. I was so excited to do nothing, I almost forgot it was Mother's Day.

While we were fixing to go to the First Primitive Baptist Church that Sunday morning, Marvin said, "After service. I'm gonna come home, get in my relaxin' clothes and watch the Braves kick the Pirates out of their own park. They're on the move—only one game ahead in their division, but they're on the move. Hank Aaron's gonna have another great year. I can feel it in my bones."

"Who's Hank Aaron?" I teased as I poked my best dangly pearl earring through my left ear lobe and pushed on the back. Marvin rolled his eyes, but I saw him smiling.

Marvin was good to me. I liked him the first time I saw him in mortician school. Marvin had inherited his Papa's business. His family had been the morticians for black folks for over fifty years. Through the years they'd built a beautiful mortuary with a big old house right next door. Marvin said by the time he was ten years old, he knew how to comfort a family in mourning, drain the blood from a deceased, and fill out a death certificate. But I'm rambling. The point was, what we wanted to happen and what did happen were two different things.

If Pastor Turner had gone on for any longer, I think I would have melted right down to a puddle on the floor. It was only May and already so hot I started thinking about going to that Hell Pastor warned us about just to cool off. Being Mother's Day, the ladies were decked out in their special outfits, looking crisp and clean at the start but, about halfway into the choir's second hymn, they were looking limp and damp. Far more fans were waving in the air than hands praising the Lord. Even the flowers on the lectern started to droop.

During hot weather, Pastor Turner really should have paid more attention to his sweltering flock. In the cool weather, his sermons were inspirational persuasions. Not so much in hot weather, more like robust ramblings. I will admit, I got cranky in the heat. I knew that was why Marvin forked out the money to buy air conditioning units for the mortuary and our home. I was so blessed. Not everyone in this congregation got to go home to a cool house. Maybe that was a consideration when Pastor Turner stopped us as we exchanged pleasantries in the vestibule.

"How would you like Helen and me to come to your house for dinner tonight? I got somethin' I want to talk to you about," Pastor Turner asked, placing one hand on Marvin's shoulder and shaking his hand with the other. He held Marvin like that until he got an answer.

Marvin hesitated, but what could he say? He blurted out, "We'd love it. We eat at half past four." Then he added, "Say, why don't you come watch the baseball game with me?"

I almost jabbed him in the ribs. What was he thinking?

"I was hopin' you'd ask," Pastor Turner said. "What can we bring?"

"Just yourselves. We're honored havin' you," Marvin answered.

He could have said, "Bring a dessert." No, he should have said, "Bring a dessert." Instead, I only had two hours to rush home, straighten up the house and cook a proper Sunday supper. So much for a relaxing day.

"Why'd you do that?" I asked as we climbed in our big old, dark grey 1964 Ford Econoline we used to carry bodies to the mortuary. It was not the prettiest or the easiest vehicle to drive around, but we would have been lost without it.

"Do what?" Marvin asked.

"Humph." Do what? Men didn't have a clue about what women had to do to get a supper ready. There weren't any stores open on Sundays. Only ingredients I had were those in my cupboard and garden. When I finally answered, only thing I said was, "Pull on over to that payphone right there. I got to call Dessie, let her know we're coming for her. I need her help." The rest of the way we drove in silence, me planning all I had to do. I came to look back on this day as easy.

My spirits picked up when I saw Dessie was waiting for us on the porch outside of Josey's house. Pulling up to the curb, I hardly recognized the child I had given birth to sixteen years earlier. Dessie was taller than I was, which was saying a lot because I was five foot six. But the big change was her emerging womanly body. She had lost the baby fat around her middle and had found it in all the right places. She was beautiful. And, her lovely rose brown skin simply glowed. It

4

was like her daddy's, except, by forty-three years old, his had become a little tarnished. Truth be known, over the years, Marvin and I had put on a few pounds we could have afforded to shed. We were not fat, nothing like that. You might say we were of generous proportions.

"Mama, you promised I could stay 'til supper. We were makin' ice cream for dessert. They were countin' on me to help," Dessie complained as she climbed into the back seat of the van. "This car is ugly," she grumbled, "It's embarrassing drivin' around in somethin' meant for haulin' dead bodies."

Lately, my daughter had been testing my patience. Along with her womanly body, she had gained an attitude.

Already in a mood from having to change my plans, my temper was running thin.

"Don't start. This isn't the way I wanted to spend my Mother's Day either," I warned, hoping to make her feel a little guilty for forgetting what day it was.

When I was Dessie's age, I went back to living with my mother after spending my entire childhood growing up with Big Mama and Big Buddy. My mama had me when she was fourteen. No way could she take care of me, so her mama and papa took me in. As far as I was concerned, they were my real parents. I especially loved Big Buddy. I loved his big calloused hands that had known so much misery and so little joy. Sometimes when his strong hands picked me up and set me on his lap, he made me feel like nothing could ever hurt me. Big Buddy was the one who got me interested in being a mortician.

One Memorial Day, when I was six, he took me to the black cemetery in town. He knelt down before a grave, said a prayer of thanks, and then showed me how to plant little flags next to the simple grave markers.

As he picked weeds from around a grave, he said, "Millie, child, always remember the black folks who gave their lives for you. Memorial Day was actually started by former slaves to honor dead Union soldiers who had been buried in a mass grave in a Confederate prison camp way back in 1865. The ex-slaves dug 'em up and gave 'em a proper burial in gratitude for fightin' for their freedom. Same thing happened during the Great War. I lost so many friends. That's why I come here every year—to remember and to honor."

I couldn't get my head around there being dead people under all those crosses until we came upon a hole some critter had dug...went real deep. I peered down into that hole and saw what looked like a hand or something.

"What are those?" I asked.

"Those are bones," Big Buddy said. "They belong to a person buried down there."

"There's a person down there?" I asked, fascinated but confused. "That person don't have no skin."

"He used to," Big Buddy said. "He probably wasn't embalmed right."

"Embalmed? What's that?"

"It's what special people do to help the dead look good," Buddy explained.

"That's what I'm gonna do. I'm gonna make sure you always look good, Big Buddy. Your hands are always gonna have skin on 'em," I said with the assurance and innocence only a child could have.

But I meant it. From then on, even though I went back to live with a mama who resented me from the day I was born, especially around her new husband, I knew I was going to be a mortician. And when Big Buddy died, I kept my promise. I took good care of him. He went to heaven looking mighty fine. Everyone said so. I bet his hands will look good as new a hundred years from now.

Thinking about Big Buddy calmed me down. By the time the three of us drove up to the house, I was ready to start cooking.

"You go out and pick two onions and enough collards for five people," I told Dessie as the van came to a halt in the driveway. She stormed out of the vehicle, slamming the sliding door shut with a bang.

"That's enough, Dessie," Marvin called out the window in his sternest fatherly voice.

"She'll be fine," I said with a reassuring pat to his knee.

Marvin was absolutely right. Normally, I would not tolerate her storming and slamming, but I had too much to do. I got out of the van and headed up the stairs to the porch. Stepping inside to the coolness of the hall, I took off my hat and hung it on the antique mirrored hat rack that had welcomed family and guests for decades. Something about the tall ceilings and highly polished wood floors of the house calmed my nerves and settled my spirit. I was home.

Walking into the kitchen, I donned my apron and got to work deciding how to make a meal from whatever ingredients I could muster up. Smothered chicken turned out to be my only choice. I made a roux from bacon grease, flour and broth. I kept adding liquid until it was bubbling nice and thick, finally seasoning it with salt and pepper. Once it was the perfect consistency, I tossed in pulled chicken pieces until they were evenly coated with the savory sauce.

I looked through the kitchen window and saw Dessie out in the garden working on the collard greens just as I had taught her. She picked leaves from the bottom of the stalks, leaving smaller ones towards the top of the plant to grow for another day. She laid them on screens perched on cinder blocks. The screens made for easier cleaning. She went through each one picking off bugs and getting rid of as much dirt as she could. Collard greens were a messy business, but done right, mmm-mmm, they were good.

She walked in from the garden loaded with the collards ready for round two of the cleaning process. Young as she was, she knew what to do.

"Ooh wee, it's hot out there," she said as she plopped the collards in the sink, half-filled with cold water, and wiped her forehead with the hem of her shirt.

Actually, she was a good cook. And like all good cooks, she quieted down as soon as she started the final wash to get rid of any remaining dirt. Satisfied the greens were clean, she pulled off the stems and tossed the leaves into the simmering cauldron.

"Don't forget the grease," I said, nodding my head to the jar filled with bacon drippings perched on the edge of the stove.

"I won't," she said, annoyed with my interference. Squinting her eyes at me, she spooned two heaping tablespoons into the already boiling pot with a deliberate splat that sprayed enough water onto the hot stove to hiss and sputter. The smile on her face showed she took pleasure in the sound of her rebellion.

Not wanting to engage in that particular battle, I shifted my focus to my famous gingerbread cake. I knew the recipe so well, I didn't have to measure. Same with the cornbread. Just came natural over the years. They were mixed and ready for the oven in no time.

I almost upset my calmness when I realized I had forgotten to make the strawberry jello. A proper jello needed time to sit before it bloomed into a colorful, sweet delicacy. Serving a runny dessert was unacceptable, so I quickly chopped the strawberries, added some sugar and put them on the stove to boil over a medium heat. While that cooked, I prepared the gelatin then let it stand to absorb all the water just like Big Mama had taught me to do. Once done, I mixed the gelatin with the puree I made from the strawberries, spooned it into a mold and put it in the fridge to set.

As the food was cooking, we set the table with my best and only linen tablecloth and napkins. We finished right on time. I liked that it looked like we hadn't been sweating bullets to get everything done. I also knew the house smelled inviting—a combination of spice, onion, and bacon.

In the living room, Marvin had just finished adjusting the rabbit ear antenna on our tabletop Motorola TV, so the game would come in loud and clear. At two o'clock on the dot, when the doorbell rang, we were ready. Pastor Turner and Sister Helen were still in their Sunday clothes, but we insisted they get comfortable. Pastor took off his jacket and loosened his tie. A little overweight, he suffered terribly in the heat. Beads of sweat collected on the trim grey beard framing his umber toned face. After Pastor pulled his handkerchief from his pocket to wipe his brow, he almost had to wring it out.

Helen was the opposite. Café-au-lait skin, chiseled face and beanpole thin, she appeared cool as a cucumber. But I could tell she was relieved to be in an air-conditioned house because once she took off her hat and jacket, she pinched the damp blouse away from her body and proceeded to refresh herself by waving it in a fanning motion.

"It's so nice to be in your lovely home. We've been socializin' all morning, what with Mother's Day and all. Takes a lot of energy," Pastor Turner confessed.

"I can't thank you enough," Sister Helen added. "My girls being grown and gone, I was feelin' a little down today. They did call, but it's not the same as being around family. And, as you know, we consider you family."

I glowed at the compliment. Maybe it wasn't totally true, but I liked hearing it anyway. What she was saying was they were hankering for a few hours of downtime. So that's what we gave them. The men watched the Pirates beat the Braves five to two. They coached from their comfortable chairs, groaning when players struck out, cheering when they scored. They talked a little about the growing unrest over the escalating war in Vietnam. At the end of the game, they were momentarily disappointed with the loss but reassured each other the Braves would win tomorrow. All the while, Helen and I quietly exchanged tips on cooking, clothes and hats, careful not to disturb the men's enjoyment of the game and each other.

By four o'clock, it was time to make sure the cornbread was ready to come out of the oven piping hot. Everything else was heated to perfection. We were ready to sit down to eat. For my final touch, I poured iced sweet tea into chilled glasses, adding a sprig of mint and slice of lemon to each. I admit I wanted to impress.

Standing at the table, holding hands as Pastor Turner said a lovely grace, making sure to thank mothers for their daily work to keep families together, all my effort seemed worthwhile. I smiled at Dessie and mouthed, "Thank you." She tucked her head in silent acknowledgment.

In no time at all, we devoured the chicken, collards, and cornbread. The gingerbread cake and jello disappeared just as fast. With the last bite, Pastor Turner leaned back in his seat, patted his stomach, and thanked me and Dessie for a spectacular supper. Then he started talking in his sermon voice. Something big was on his mind.

I nodded to Dessie, indicating she could leave the table, but Pastor Turner leaned back, putting his arm out to block her exit.

"No Dessie," Pastor said. "You need to hear what I'm going to say. It's going to affect you as much as anyone else in the family. Please sit back down."

He gestured to the seat she had just left. She looked over at me questioningly, but I shrugged in confusion. I tilted my head towards her chair letting her know it was okay for her to stay. She slid back down in her spot, keeping her eyes lowered.

"Dessie," Pastor Turner started, "How much do you know about all the civil rights activities going on over the past five years?" He stopped and looked directly at her.

I knew silence made her uncomfortable, but what she did next took me completely by surprise.

Dessie looked up and suddenly, with total confidence, said, "I know I go to an integrated school because of the Supreme Court case *Brown versus the Board of Education*. I know Rosa Parks started the civil rights movement by refusing to give up her seat on a bus. I know President Johnson passed a Civil Rights Act making everyone equal, declared a war on poverty to help the poor and signed a Voting Rights Act giving black folks the right to finally have a say. I know three civil rights workers were killed by the Klan just up the road. I know there was a big march in Selma led by Dr. King where people got beaten by state troopers, attacked by dogs and sprayed with fire hoses. I know there's been trouble with the Ku Klux Klan. And I know Steve Conrad has been eyeing me in a nasty way."

That last statement was like a punch to my stomach. I shot a look to Marvin who was staring directly at Dessie. The muscles in his jaw were so tight I could see them bulge on the side of his face. Even the Pastor sat up straight as a rod.

"You mean Steve Conrad of the Conrad family who owns the grocery store in town? Steve Conrad where our friend Mayola cooks and takes care of the family? That Steve Conrad?" Marvin asked.

"Yes sir," Dessie said, her chin set in defiance. "But he doesn't scare me."

"Dessie," Pastor Turner interrupted. "This is exactly why I wanted you to stay…"

I tuned out what Pastor Turner was saying. I was in such shock. I had no idea Dessie might have been a victim to some entitled white boy. Lord, this was not good. I could have spit nails at that family. They thought they were so high and mighty. Suddenly, I was worried about how I was going to protect her. I felt myself start to panic. I took a few deep breaths to calm my heart down. Then I thought of Mayola, and I knew where I would start. I would ask her about what was going on with that boy.

"Right?... Millie?... Millie?" Pastor Turner said, leaning forward to touch my arm and bring me back to the conversation.

"Sorry, Pastor. What'd you say?" I asked, suddenly aware I hadn't been listening.

"I was saying Dessie is an amazing young lady. I think she'll be fine with what I want to present to you." The Pastor sat up straighter in his chair looked at each one of us before he continued. "As part of Johnson's war on poverty he wants communities like ours to open preschools for disadvantaged children. Some of the poorest children across this country have never seen a crayon, much less words in a book. Johnson knows these children need various forms of enrichment to help them catch up to students who come from more privileged backgrounds. He even wants dental and health care for the children. He's calling his campaign Operation Head Start. And I can't think of anyone better than you, Millie, to be the director of our community program."

Tuning out again, I tried to get my head around what the good Pastor was saying. Did he just offer me a job? I got a job. Why would I want to give up what I loved? What I had been trained to do? For heaven's sake, I had a family to take care of.

Right when I was thinking I didn't know anything at all about teaching, I heard Pastor Turner say, "I have several teachers lined up. Millie, what I need you from you are your organizational skills. If it weren't for you, nobody in this town would have a proper funeral. You take care of everything. And you even have some medical knowledge. At least, I assume you had to take biology and anatomy to learn how to embalm. Am I wrong?"

"No, you aren't wrong Pastor, but I have a job. And …I can think of a hundred reasons why I am not the right person for your …"

"It's not for me, Millie. It's for the children," Pastor Turner interrupted.

Oh, he was good. Knew how to butter me right up. But me running a school was completely out of the question.

"Sorry, Pastor. Not two minutes ago I heard my daughter say some white boy was acting ugly towards her. And now you're asking me to head up a program the Klan is sure to hate? Thank you for your faith in me, but you need to find someone else. I do not want my family to be the Klan's number one target in town." I looked at Marvin and Dessie to back me up, but they didn't even glance my way.

"Yes, Millie, unfortunately you are correct. The Klan will not like these schools," Pastor Turner admitted. "They hate anything that helps black folks. But please think about it. Talk it over with your family. Take some quiet time to pray about it. I don't need an answer today. We have some time before the doors open."

"Pastor, I don't know a thing about running a school." I felt panic welling in the pit of my stomach. This was all too much for me to handle.

"Millie, don't you worry about running this on your own. We've got a board made up of myself, Father Bob from St. Michael's Catholic parish, Reverend Larson from St. Bartholomew's Episcopal Church and Rabbi Harvey Silberman from Beth Immanuel. We'll help you every step of the way."

Pastor Turner sure did his best to calm my nerves and persuade me to join him. But if that weren't bad enough, Sister

Helen piped up, putting her two cents into the pile of confusion building inside my head.

"Now Millie, before you make up your mind, I'd like you to come to one of our voter registration meetings at the parish hall. We meet every Tuesday and Thursday night. This Tuesday, Buddy Murray is comin' to talk to us. He's friends with James Meredith. They were together at the Ole Miss riots. His stories will make the hair on the back of your neck stand straight up. If his words don't inspire you to accept this callin', nothin' will," Sister said.

Looking at me, then looking at her husband, she added, "I think it's time we were on our way. The Howards have been more than generous with their Sunday afternoon, and Millie's got a lot to think about." She knew I was agitated.

She was right. I was reeling. First, Pastor Turner talked about the Head Start program then Sister Helen talked about voter registration. Did they expect me to do both? I didn't want to do either. I enjoyed working full-time at the mortuary with Marvin. And what about my sixteen-year-old daughter? Lord help me, I needed time to process. More than anything, I wanted them to leave before they came up with more jobs for me to do.

The Turners finally said their good-byes, leaving the three of us standing on the inside of our closed front door looking at each other, not saying a word. I wasn't ready to talk. I needed to ponder some, so I started cleaning up. Something about cleaning helped clear my brain. I gathered the plates left on the dining room table and headed into the kitchen. A little slice of cake, the only food left from our supper, was perched atop the stack of plates in my hands. Martin snatched that cake right off the plate as he headed into the living room to turn on the TV. He nearly toppled the entire stack by removing that one tiny piece. Same as life. Change one tiny piece and the whole thing could come toppling down.

The familiar sound of, "Good evening, ladies and gentlemen. Live from New York City. The Ed Sullivan Show," stirred me from my thoughts. The sound traveled through the hallways of our peaceful home and for an instant, I felt normal. Then, Dessie said, "I wanna go to that meeting on Tuesday night."

"Marvin. Turn off that TV and come in here," I called out.

Dessie saw she had fired me up. Avoiding eye contact, she put her head down and busied herself by washing the dishes in the sink... without being asked. Very unlike her.

"Can't it wait?" Marvin called back, knowing from my tone I was riled. When I didn't respond, he tried to guilt me. "The Turtles are going to be on the TV singing 'Happy Together.'"

"Turtles? Who are the Turtles?" I wasn't having any of his excuses. "I don't care if Aretha Franklin herself is singing R-E-S-P-E-C-T right here in our living room. We need a family meeting," I insisted. "Dessie, put those dishes down and come on over here and sit at the table."

Marvin huffed, pushing himself out of his chair. I noticed he didn't turn off the TV. Not only that, he took a position at the table where he could look past me to see it. I shot a warning look at him, but he ignored me. Dessie dried her hands on a dish towel as a slight smile crossed her lips with her father's resistance to my summons. For the first time in years, I felt alone.

"What is going on here?" I asked. "Marvin, your daughter wants to go to that meeting on Tuesday. Tell her that's no place for a sixteen-year-old girl who has some white boy acting ugly towards her. He finds out she's going to that meeting, he'll really get horrible. Are you willing to let your daughter walk into a dangerous situation?" I was satisfied I managed to squeeze in every bit of ammunition to make my point.

"Sorry Millie, I think she should go," Marvin said, taking my hands in his and holding me with a direct stare. Out of the corner of my eye I saw Dessie sit back, crossing her arms over her middle. A self-satisfied smile lit up her face as she delighted in her father's unexpected support.

"But Marvin," I sputtered, close to tears.

"No, Millie, this time you're wrong," Marvin interrupted. "Did you listen to your daughter tonight? Did you hear how much she knows about this world? She's the future. She needs to be at that meeting. I think we should go together. You. Me. And her."

I couldn't help myself. Tears welled up in my eyes and overflowed down my face. I was ready to explode with all sorts of reasons why we shouldn't go when the phone rang. I flinched. A phone call at eight o'clock on a Sunday night was never good news.

Chapter Two

Marvin answered the phone, "Howard's Mortuary. How may I help you?" He paused, listening for a long while to the person on the other end of the phone.

I stopped crying and listened too. Dessie didn't change her expression. She seemed to be in her own world, and it was making her smile.

"Where are you located?" Marvin finally asked. He picked up a pen next to the pad we kept on the telephone table and jotted down some instructions. "I'll be right there."

"Who died?" I asked.

"Ida Brown," Marvin said.

"Ida Brown? I don't think I know her." I was baffled because I thought I knew everyone. Searching my brain, I sifted through all the Browns I could think of, but none were named Ida.

"You wouldn't. Ida was only eight years old. Never ventured too far. Her family is from way out in the backcountry, and they're very poor. That was their neighbor who called. They don't have a phone," Marvin explained. "I'm supposed to meet the neighbor in half an hour at Buchannan's place. I'll never find the Brown's if he doesn't lead me. Dr. Starke will be there to help. They won't have enough money to pay for a fancy funeral, but we can do something for them. How much do we have in the memorial fund?"

"I think there's around $2,000. I'll check," I said distractedly. I was wondering why Dr. Starke was headed out there. Only time he worked with Marvin was under questionable circumstances. Dr. Starke was the only black doctor in the county and had to take care of all of us. Good thing he wasn't married. His family would have never seen him.

"No matter... I'll tell the Brown family we have a special going on. Either $100 or something from their smokehouse or garden," Marvin said. "That way they won't feel like they're a charity case."

"Marvin, you are the kindest person I know," I said, forgetting all the mean thoughts I had not fifteen minutes ago. Death had a way of putting things in perspective.

Marvin had seen so much over the years. He had always been sensitive to the family of a loved one who passed. He understood what a terrible time this was for the Brown's and wanted to ease their worries. He knew people in shock didn't think right. Often got taken advantage of. But Marvin respected people's grief and helped them maintain their dignity by being sensitive to their financial needs.

Marvin's papa, George, was the same way. In fact, he started Howard's Mortuary on account of when his parents died suddenly in a car accident. He wanted them treated properly but found his options were limited. Ended up doing everything himself. Lots of black folks did back then. Only difference, George turned his frustration into a business and passed his talent onto his son. That's why Marvin had spent his whole life around dead people. As good as he was at it, tending to the death of a child affected him profoundly. Said it was out of the order of things. I remember few years back, the Klan bombing of a church in Alabama killing four innocent little girls touched Marvin deeply. It seemed to awaken in him a need to do something more. At the time, he told me we might have to make great sacrifices someday to help secure the right for people of color to live without fear. I sensed the someday he talked about was upon us.

"I best be going. I got to collect some things from the mortuary before I head out. Don't wait up. It may be a long night," Marvin said, pulling me into the present as he kissed me on the forehead. He gave Dessie a hug and took off through the back door to the mortuary.

"Your papa sure is special," I said to Dessie who was standing with a puzzled look on her face prompting me to ask, "What's the matter?"

"I'm not sure. It's sad knowing a little girl died," she said.

"Death is never easy," I said, heading over to the sink to finish cleaning up the dishes. I handled difficultly best when I kept busy. "Always feels shocking, even when it's expected. But, you're right. The death of a child is different. People live their whole lives carrying the grief of having a child die."

For a long while, Dessie and I were quiet. I washed, she dried. Together we cleaned the kitchen until it was spotless.

As soon as we finished, Dessie said, "This is the first time I've ever heard you and Papa talk about money. What does a funeral cost?"

"They aren't cheap," I said, holding back on the truth of life. I felt she had heard enough for one day. "There are a lot of expenses. But lots of folks buy insurance policies to cover the cost."

"Mama, I asked what a proper funeral costs?" Dessie insisted.

I hesitated, wondering how honest I should be. But the look in my daughter's eyes moved me to be as straightforward as I could. "Average is $3,500."

"Dollars? What do poor people do?" she asked, genuinely shocked.

"It's not easy for them," I started.

"I heard you and Papa say something about a fund?" Clearly, she had been paying close attention to my conversation with Marvin.

"Yes. When we were first married, we agreed every full fee we got, we'd put some of it in a fund for the poor," I said.

I was getting ready to tell her that morticians always had food because even if a family didn't have the money to pay for a funeral or burial, they always had crops they had grown or meat they had hunted and smoked. More often than not, they would leave a basket of goods on the back porch until they felt our services were paid in full. But once again, Dessie surprised me.

"How did you meet Papa? I've never heard your story," Dessie said. She seemed to be responding to a curiosity driven by her new respect for her papa.

"You really want to know?" I asked.

"Uh-huh."

I told her how I got interested in becoming a mortician on that Memorial Day so long ago with Big Buddy. I explained how I worked hard to get good grades in high school and went to Saint Aloysius College in southern Georgia to get certified as a mortician. Just before graduation, Marvin came to campus as a guest lecturer. I was taken right away by his tall, strong figure and dark good looks. I didn't even notice his hair was thinning because I was so impressed by how he talked about being a funeral director. He said this job was more than simply taking care of dead bodies. He said it was a calling. He said he was often awakened in the middle of the night by a grieving family trying to make sense of their devastating loss, sometimes involving tragic circumstances. If the deceased died in a car accident, he might have to reconstruct the body. But Marvin captured my heart when he said he would tell distraught families, "Don't mourn because they're gone, be joyful because they were here."

"Did he really say that?" Dessie asked. "No wonder people want him to take care of their loved ones."

"I agree," I said. "I thought the same thing. After he finished his talk, I wanted to tell him how much I admired his philosophy. I stood in line behind other eager young students who were hoping to catch his attention when my mind went blank. As my turn came up, I blurted out, 'Do you think our class would benefit from visiting a coffin manufacturer?' I felt kind of embarrassed once the words came out of my mouth. But you know what he did? He said he was headed over to Georgia Caskets at three o'clock and asked me if I'd join him for lunch then visit the company with him. Of course, I accepted right away. We sat at a booth in a busy café and talked for nearly two hours. Almost missed the appointment at Georgia Caskets."

"Oh, Mama, that's so romantic," Dessie said. "How come you never told me this before? Did you know he was the one?"

I could tell she'd never thought about her parents being in love, so I admit, I added a little spice to my story. "Well, as we headed back to the school, I realized I didn't want my enchanting afternoon with this charming man to end. I had never believed in love at first sight, but that's exactly what happened. Your papa felt it too. Before he dropped me off, he asked if I would consider coming home to Mississippi to apprentice with him. He said he took one look at me and knew we'd make a perfect pair. I said 'yes' right then and there. We worked together for two years before I passed the state exam and earned my mortician's license. Then we got a different kind of license, a marriage license. I knew he was the one for me, and never once have I thought otherwise."

MONDAY, MAY 15

The next morning, I eased out of bed trying to not wake up Marvin and headed down the hall to the bathroom. He hadn't gotten home until close to one in the morning. When he crawled into bed, he smelled like pine Brick soap, like he had showered. Strange. I hadn't heard him in the bathroom. But I let go of the thought. I was just glad he was home safe. I knew he'd had a hard night. I pretended to sleep so he wouldn't feel obliged to run through the evening's sorrow. He must have been exhausted because he started snoring the minute his head hit the pillow. I decided I'd let him sleep in late if he wanted, but he was awake when I came back from the bathroom.

"We've got a lot to do today, Millie," he said, without the usual smile in his voice.

Something big was bothering him. I kept quiet. There were times a person wanted to talk, and there were times when they just needed quiet in order to think. I was pretty good at knowing the difference. This was a quiet time. I left him alone.

In the kitchen I set to making his favorite breakfast—bacon fried crisp, grits, biscuits 'n gravy, fried eggs (a little runny in the middle) and strong coffee. The smell of bacon cooking was maybe the best way to start a day, and that day he needed a good start. Even Dessie came shuffling out of her bedroom, barefoot, hair frizzed and going every which way, still in her pj's.

"Today ain't Sunday. How come you're fixin' bacon?" she asked.

"Isn't, Dessie. Don't say 'ain't.' Sometimes the way you talk, you'd think you were born in a barn," I said, compelled to correct her.

"Today i-s-s-n't Sunday," she said, rolling her eyes.

"Your papa had a hard night last night. He needs lookin' after this morning," I said. "What are you doin' still in your pajamas? You not plannin' to go to school anymore?"

"There's only one week left, and we don't do anything but sign yearbooks. It's boring. Besides, Josey is plantin' sweet potato slips at the plantation this week. I was wonderin' if I could go with her. They need help, and they pay some," Dessie said.

"Have you gone plumb crazy?" I asked, shocked by her request.

"Absolutely not. Not today, not ever," Marvin roared as he stormed down the hall.

I didn't expect Marvin to be ready so quick. I jumped a little when he appeared in the doorway, fully dressed in his work overalls and long-sleeved Henley shirt he usually wore in the preparation room. Unaccustomed to seeing her daddy in a temper, Dessie was shaken too.

"Last night I thought maybe you knew something about our history. But I guess not." Marvin said. "Don't you know those plantation folks keep people enslaved forever. You ask Josey why her family has to keep going back year after year. When the planting season's over, instead of getting their wages, they're given a list of what they owe. Lunches, water, transportation. Or maybe they didn't meet their daily quota. If that isn't another type of slavery, I don't know what is. Josey might not even realize what's going on yet. But someday she will. Why do you think all her sisters and brothers have to help out? Not only that, they don't want Josey or anybody else going to school. You think they want her learning about civil rights or protests of any sort? You best think about this again, Dessie."

By the time he was finished, I could see Dessie was almost in tears. I was pretty shocked too. The way he was acting, I knew something big was bothering him, but I'd talk to him about it later. Instead, I cracked the eggs in the skillet and fixed him a plate. We sat in silence, eating what I had thought would perk everyone up. Guess I was wrong.

As Marvin got up from the table, he said, "I don't want you comin' into the morgue today. I want you to take care of paperwork. Also, the medical examiner may call. Tell him to call Dr. Starke."

Soon as I heard "medical examiner," no more guessing. I was right. I knew something really bad had happened. Marvin was in such a temper, I figured I'd best not ask. I nodded and told him I'd be over to the office as soon as I could.

I turned my attention to Dessie.

"I've been thinking you could take the day off from school if you're sure nothing's goin' on. It'd be a big help for me today. I can tell your papa's bothered by somethin', and I don't want to be over here cleaning up if he needs me."

"I promise, Mama. I've taken all my exams and all we're gonna to do is sit around," Dessie said with such an earnest look on her face I gave in.

Rarely did I put my needs above Dessie's education, but something was in the air. I shivered, prickles running up and down my spine even though it wasn't cold. "Go wash up and get ready to work," I said, feeling a pang of guilt as I rattled off a long list of chores for her to do.

As I left her cleaning up from last night and this morning, I heard the TV blaring the sound of Ronnie Schell and Julie Parrish bantering on CBS's "Good Morning World." I glanced back at my daughter as I passed through the door and stopped dead in my tracks. Oh my, she was growing into a most beautiful woman. Her dark, curly hair framed her heart-shaped face, accented by high cheekbones and almond-shaped eyes. She looked at me and smiled, then tied her hair back and got to work. I could tell she was relieved she wasn't going with Josey to plant those sweet potato slips. She's not dumb. She knew what her father said was true. Besides, it was hotter than blue blazes outside and planting was back-breaking work.

Wearing a new summer dress I made from Simplicity's pattern 3559 and my favorite Air Step pumps, I walked out the back door, over the path covered by an arbor leading to the side door of the mortuary. Such a different feeling from our open, light-filled home. Low ceilings, beige walls, thick beige carpeted floors, the sweet smell of lilies, dim lighting and knick-knacks memorializing the departed decorated the rooms. Guests told me they never expected to feel so comfortable in the parlor of a mortuary as they did in ours. Made me proud to think we were doing right by them. It was what I trained for. Marvin and I, we were a good team.

What was Pastor Turner thinking last night? I didn't want to help run a school. I didn't want to leave my husband's side and let him deal with the dead all by himself. We were partners. We had worked together our entire married lives. So why hadn't Marvin backed me up?

By the time I finished rehashing the details of Pastor Turner's visit in my mind, I found myself standing outside the preparation room knowing Marvin was inside making Ida Brown look like she was sleeping the peaceful sleep of eternity. People thought their loved one lying in a casket looked natural, but that was not the case. They didn't know what magic Marvin did inside that room. Good thing, too. I doubted they would have felt the same sense of comfort in there as they did in the parlor. Grief needed healing time, not double sized freezers flanked by embalming tables where bodies were washed, and blood was replaced by formaldehyde. Or cold cement floors and stainless-steel sinks designed for easy sterilization. Or the smell. The smell of decaying bodies and formaldehyde was a stink that clung to your clothing and held in your nostrils until you either got used to it or quit. The preparation room was no place for survivors of the dearly departed.

I shuddered at my own thoughts, closed my mind to such ideas and walked into the office. I sat down at the simple pine desk Marvin's papa designed and crafted by hand fifty years ago. A large wooden cross, similar to the one gracing the wall of the main chapel down the hall, hung on the wall behind the desk. We placed it there, hoping it would help the grieving remember resurrection was ahead for their loved ones. On top of the desk was a telephone, a pewter cup filled with Bic ballpoint pens embossed with Howard's Mortuary and, today, a folder with the name Ida Brown on it. For a moment, I bowed my head and said a small prayer asking for strength to be of service to Ida's family. I opened the folder and saw what had been bothering Marvin.

There it was. Cause of Death—Suspected typhoid fever. And it was signed by Dr. Starke. No wonder Marvin's been agitated. If that family's water supply was contaminated, all the Browns were in danger. Marvin knew this. He was worried and rightly so.

Then, it dawned on me why I hadn't heard him take a shower last night. I reached for the phone to call him in the preparation room. Before I picked up the receiver, it rang, startling me.

"Howard's Mortuary," I answered, taking a moment to calm myself.

"Millie, that you?" Dr. Starke asked.

"Oh, Dr. Starke," I moaned into the phone. "I just read about Ida Brown. You sure it's typhoid?"

"As sure as I can be. I've seen it before out there. In this hot weather, the cows cool themselves by standing in the stream. You know the rest. Droppings and drinking water are a dangerous and often deadly combination. We, in town, take our water for granted because it comes from a tap. Out where this family lives, that's not true. She was sufferin' from malnutrition too. Probably contributed to her demise."

Poverty was a mean master. I felt sorry for her. I really did, but I was more worried about my husband, so I asked, "Is Marvin in danger? I mean, he's working on her right now." I didn't know that for sure, but I had to ask.

Since the doctor knew I was as tough as a pine knot, he told me the truth. "Millie, I got to be honest. Her body was leakin' pretty bad last night. We used gloves and wrapped her good in a tarp. We put her in a body bag before we loaded her in the van. But I can't promise we didn't get some of that leakage on us. We took showers in the prep room last night. By the way, that was one of the smartest moves you made, installing that shower last year. Anyway, he's goin' to have to be careful to contain the contamination. By the way, I don't think her family can afford..."

I broke in, thinking I was going to give him good news. "We talked about using our fund to help them out. Charge them only a pittance or food."

"Millie," the doctor said, fixing to correct me, "First, the Brown's don't have any money. I mean nothing. And, second, you'd be takin' food out of already starving mouths if you asked for any of their meager supply. No, you best think of leaving them with as much dignity as you can by wrapping the body good and telling the family to bury her at least one hundred feet from the stream."

"I didn't know these folks were in such a bad way, and in today's world. Shameful," I said. "Bless their hearts. I guess I've forgotten how bad some folks have it. Thank you for remindin' me."

"The reason I called," the doctor said, passing over my insensitivities, "I had to let the county know about the typhoid. They're sending the ME out to get a sample. Will you let Marvin know? The man's name is Warren."

After saying our goodbyes, I hung up and called Marvin to relay the information Dr. Starke had given me.

"I'm glad you know," Marvin said. "I didn't really want to talk about it in front of Dessie. Not that I don't trust her, but if this gets out before the ME does what he needs to do, things could get ugly for the family. Klan would like nothin' easier than to take out a poor black family, sayin' they're savin' white folks from the dreaded typhoid."

I hadn't thought of that. "Okay, honey. You take care. I'll bring Dr. Warren to you when he gets here."

"I still have the van to disinfect. I might be outside when he comes. Remember, I don't want you or Dessie near any of this. Okay?" Marvin said.

"Okay. I understand, Marvin. I get it," I said. Little did I realize how much more I was going to "get."

Chapter Three

TUESDAY, MAY 16

D r. Warren finally called the next morning to say he wouldn't be able to come for at least four days. But when Marvin explained the situation to him, he relented and came. He was a strange looking man. Stooped so bad, if he stood up straight, he'd be a foot taller. The combination of wild wiry hair, sickly looking white skin and a grumpy attitude made him hard to warm up to. I might have forgiven his looks because a person can't help what nature gave them, but I couldn't forgive the constant cigarette dangling from the side of his mouth creating a stink and trail of ashes that followed him wherever he went. I had to spray my special homemade orange oil and vacuum the carpet after he passed through the entry and shuffled down the hall to the preparation room. Marvin told me later the only time the guy didn't have a lit cigarette was when he put on a surgical mask. Couldn't imagine he was married. Who'd want to live with that?

You heard that old saying, never judge a book by its cover? Well, that applied to Dr. Warren. Marvin told me he was efficient, professional, and quick in his handling of the situation. Within minutes he pointed out signs of malnutrition and confirmed typhoid. He told Marvin to tell the Browns to bury the body as soon as possible. He said he'd go out to the site to get a sample of water from the stream and caution the family about risks, giving them no-cost ways to protect themselves. I swear, I hope his ears weren't burning from all my earlier bad talk. Dr. Warren turned out to be real professional. And kind too. Yet another one of life's reminders. Be careful with first impressions.

The rest of the day I was busy with the paperwork. A major part of my job was filling out death certificates and submitting them to the state so heirs could start the process of applying for benefits from insurance policies or veteran offices. I often applied for transfer of these funds for the survivors. Deep down, I suspected the forms were deliberately difficult and confusing to people so they would give up and the powers in control would keep their precious funds. Lots of money, not to mention our payments, depended on me doing a good job.

My next task was notifying the local newspaper of the brothers and sisters from the surrounding area who had passed in the last two weeks. Can't say I did a very good job here. Our local white paper didn't want to include "Negras" on their obit page, but money had a way of loosening up an editor's mind. Even so, dealing with them was challenging. Convincing the operator to put me through to an editor took the patience of Job. One time I got so disgusted, I went down to the paper to handle my business in person. I won't go into how I was treated, but I've never gone back. I had better luck with *The Weekly Digest*, the black paper in town. Still cost money, but about half the price of the white man's paper.

When I looked up, I was surprised to see it was four o'clock. Today was all the proof I needed to confirm I could not take on any other job. My place was here. But I had agreed to go to the voter registration meeting, so if we were going to get there by seven, I needed to get moving. I straightened up my desk, called Marvin to say I was leaving and scuttled back to our house. As I entered, I could hear giggling in the living room. I knew immediately who was there.

"Josey, when did you get here?" I asked, a little suspicious Dessie had disobeyed our very clear instructions she could not take off any days from school to help Josey at the plantation.

"Mama, I know what you're thinking, and I didn't skip school to work with Josey. I invited her to come to the meeting with us tonight. She wants to," Dessie protested. It was as if the child could read my mind.

"Josey, do your parents know where you're going?" I asked, wondering if she understood how dangerous this could be. "You do know if the plantation manager finds out you're at the meeting, he might fire your parents. In fact, your whole family, if he wants."

"Isn't it at the church?" she asked.

"Yes," I thought I knew where she was going with this.

"Well, those white folks like us going to church. Think it keeps us honest. Don't know why, it don't keep them honest," she said poking Dessie with her elbow. The two collapsed into giggles.

I couldn't take much more of their silliness. "I sure hope you two don't act like this tonight," I said and walked out of the room.

Marvin, Dessie and I, and now Josey walked into the parish hall of First Primitive Baptist church not knowing what to expect. My goodness. I could not believe all the people who were present. I had no idea so many people were committed to the cause.

A group of folks near the back were stuffing envelopes. Another was making *Sign Up to Vote* flyers complete with a final registration date of June 24, and instructions on how to fill out the forms. People were typing, folding papers, addressing envelopes, I mean, the room was buzzing with activity.

"I'm so glad you came," a voice from behind me chimed in as a hand touched my shoulder. I turned, happy to see Sister Helen. Giving her a big hug, I said, "You've got quite an army here."

"You know, that's one way of lookin' at it. But I like to think of it as a room of hope. Follow me. I'd like you and Marvin to meet some folks," she said taking my elbow, looking over at Marvin. I looked around to see where Josey and Dessie were, but I couldn't find them. Sister Helen redirected my attention and guided us to a group of men surrounding a nice looking older black man and a white preacher with a charming smile and kind blue eyes.

"Marvin and Millie Howard, this is Buddy Murray and Reverend Larson. They were with James Meredith when he enrolled at Ole Miss. Buddy's goin' to tell us about his experience tonight. Reverend Larson came to reminisce about their time together," Sister explained.

"Is this the Millie Howard who's turning us down for Head Start?" Reverend Larson asked, looking at Sister Helen.

"I'm afraid it is. I'm hoping tonight will change her mind," Sister said with a smile. "Maybe you talking to her will be more persuasive than I was."

They were talking about me like I wasn't there. Marvin just laughed and said, "She'll come around."

Say what? Now that made me mad. "I don't think so," I said defiantly.

Everyone smiled and shrugged. I felt I was being hoodwinked. What did they know that I didn't?

Suddenly a bell rang, startling me. The volunteers seemed to know it was time to stop working and take a seat. Marvin and I followed. The chairs were arranged with an aisle down the middle, just like the church. When everyone was seated, Pastor Turner walked from the back of the room to the podium in the front. An air of anticipation filled the room as silence descended. Even I started to get excited.

"Ladies and gentlemen. We are so fortunate to have Buddy Murray with us tonight. He was in the thick of the riots that broke out the night of September 30, 1962, when Air Force veteran James Meredith was going to enroll as the first African American at Ole Miss. Please welcome him with a round of applause," Pastor Turner said, turning to shake hands with Mr. Murray.

Folks stood up, clapping loudly, welcoming and encouraging the tall, well-dressed black man.

"Thank you for inviting me," Buddy started, inviting the congregation to sit by gesturing with a palm down motion. He waited for total silence, then boomed out, "I am a Mississippi segregationist and I am proud of it.'"

The audience sat back in their seats and audibly gasped at his opening statement.

"Ladies and Gentlemen," Buddy continued, "those were the words of Ross Barnett, governor of this state, when he blocked James Meredith from entering Ole Miss despite a court order to the contrary. At a football game a night later, he said, 'We are getting ready to be invaded, we really want you as Mississippians, as white Mississippians, to respond.'

"The next night, Sunday night, the campus was at war. President Kennedy had called in Federal troops to protect the building where James was supposed to register. But hundreds of students and protestors from the surrounding area merged on the building. When darkness fell protecting those intent on harm, the first rocks and bottles hurled through the night sky. Someone signaled for tear gas and all hell broke out. I was standing by a lamppost. My friend Reverend Larson, here," he looked over at the Reverend, "climbed up the post and called out to the crowd, asking for reason and calm. A rock, probably meant for him, struck my left temple with enough force to draw blood and knock me to the ground. The crowd pushed down on me. I thought I was going to be trampled to death. My duck and cover training was not going to save me from the chaos ruling the mob. If it hadn't been for the Reverend seeing my predicament and jumping down from his perch to pull me up, I'm convinced I would have died. By the time we heard shots ring out, we knew it was time to go."

The vivid picture this man was creating in my head took my breath away. I could feel the crowd pressing in, the fear he must have felt. Where had I been all these years? Living a comfortable life in the morgue? At that moment, I understood I had done nothing to help people of color while other folks risked their lives to improve mine. I thought of Dessie and her future, and I felt ashamed.

God had been good to me. Being a mortician's wife had been a blessing. I had status, a nice home and food on the table every night. I didn't have to walk three miles to work like some of my friends. Marvin and I were always paid for our labor, even if it was in the form of food. My child had never gone hungry. We even drove our own a van and hearse. I had never felt the indignity of sitting in the back of the bus.

"In the words of Wyatt Mordecai Johnson, 'all the colored people, in every section of the United States, believe there is something wrong, and not accidentally wrong, at the very heart of the Government.'" Buddy paused, letting those words sink into the souls of every man, woman and child in the audience. "The only way we can fix this 'wrong' is to have our voices heard through the ballot box. If we were able to sign up fifty percent of our community before June 24th, we could make significant changes to the political views we currently endure. We could elect political officials who represent our voices and strive to heal the void of equality for the races in our great country. Let's make that our goal. Fifty percent this year, one hundred percent next year."

A roar of applause broke out. People were clapping and singing, "We shall overcome," all around me. It was a pivotal moment for me, life changing. I looked at Marvin. He was smiling. He knew I couldn't resist any longer. And when I spotted Dessie and Josey, they were hugging and crying tears of joy. The site of my daughter feeling so inspired by Buddy's speech stirred something ancient and deep within me. I knew I could no longer live my life of comfort while denying my brothers and sisters the support they deserved as they marched to secure freedom for my daughter. That's when it hit me. All along, my job, my real job, had been protecting and guiding my child for the sake of her future. Caught up in the moment, I felt a well of courage build inside my soul so powerful, I thought I was going to burst into tears in front of all those people. Holding back my emotions, I knew what my next step had to be. I had to make a commitment to change the future for my child.

Pastor Turner stepped forward and said, "Brother Murray, thank you for that inspirational call to serve." Then looking out at the crowd, he continued, "Brothers and Sisters, we have work to do. We need your help now more than ever," Pastor Turner said looking directly at me. I felt as though he was talking to me from across my dining room table. "We will gather signatures. We will register voters. We will fill ballot boxes for our freedom. Amen."

As the gathering dispersed, I spied my friend Mayola across the room. Her presence reminded me how much I wanted to question her about the Conrad boy. I quickly crossed the room, grabbed her hand, and whisked her into a corner to bend her ear.

"Mayola, I wish we had time to chat, but I heard some disturbing news last Sunday," I blurted out. "Dessie told me the Conrad boy's been pestering her."

"Lawd, bless me. What is he up to now? That boy has got an evil streak running right through his soul. You're right to worry about him. He is a mean-spirited child," she said, starting to get agitated. "He's always been a sneaky little devil. Used to come into my kitchen to snatch cookies or sandwiches off the trays I had prepared for his mama when she was havin' a bridge party. By the time I'd found out what he'd done, it was usually too late, and I'd catch you know what from the missus. One day I caught the thief in the act. He had six cookies in one hand and four watercress sandwiches in the other. I snatched them back, right out of his hands and threw them in the garbage. He was as mad as a snake. You know what he did? He ran screamin' to his mama goin' on about how I'd slapped him across the face. He musta rubbed his face good and hard because he did have a red mark on his cheek. Mrs. Conrad took one look at her son's face then turned and slapped me across mine. She said, 'Don't you dare touch my son again.' All the while, young Stevie stood in the corner, rubbin' his tear-stained cheeks, but he had a smile on his face. He was proud of what he done. Lookin' back on it, I wish I had slapped him from here to Saturday. His mama's covered for him all his life. She's either lied for him or paid for his sins. You know what they bought him on his sixteenth birthday?"

"No, what?" I asked.

"A brand-new Chev-ro-let C-10 truck. White, of course," she sneered. "Now he thinks his shit don't stink," Mayola said, making me laugh. "You tell Dessie if she sees him coming, she should run the other way."

That sobered me up. "I'll be sure to tell her. Would you do me a favor and keep your ears open. If you hear anything, let me know."

"Honey, you know I will," Mayola said.

"I don't know why you stay with them," I wondered out loud.

"Used to have to, to feed my children. Now they're grown and gone, I guess I stay outta habit," she explained.

By the end of the evening, I was inspired and mad. What a confusing mixture of emotions. I'd never felt this way before. As we were walking out the door, we bumped into Reverend Larson.

"Change your mind tonight?" he asked with a knowing grin on his face. I guessed he wasn't one to beat around the bush. But his question stopped Marvin and Dessie, even Josey. They looked at me expectantly.

"Yes, I did," I said. I felt a smile spread across my face. "I'll help you with your school." When I accepted, Marvin, Dessie and Josey hugged me in excitement.

"I thought you might. Why don't you come to a meeting tomorrow at St. Bartholomew's to meet the board and discuss what comes next," Reverend Larson said. And without waiting for an answer, he added, "Ten o'clock. See you then."

He didn't give me a chance to change my mind. He simply disappeared into the night, expecting to see me in the morning.

Wednesday, May 17

"You look very professional," Marvin said to me as I was putting the finishing touches on my make-up with my new frosty coral lipstick by Tangee.

"Cost me a fortune, forty-nine cents," I said, holding the lipstick up. "Can you believe how expensive things are getting?" I wanted to look nice. I figured as long as I looked good, nobody would notice how unsure of myself I was.

"I hope you're not having second thoughts about doing this," Marvin said. "In case you're worried, I talked to Dessie."

"You did? When?"

"Just now while you were getting dressed. She says if you get involved, she'll take care of the house. She's old enough. Go hear what Reverend Larson has in mind for you. You can always back out if it looks like it's going to be too much," Marvin said.

He was always so reassuring. Tried his best to take care of everything. I was surprised when he told me Dessie offered her time. Not that I would have declined her help or anything. But honestly, maybe I was a little jealous of the bond Dessie and her papa seemed to be forming.

"All right. I'll go see what they say, but I'm not making any promises to them or to you," I said with a firmness I didn't really feel.

I walked into the kitchen where Dessie was eating a bowl of cereal. I started to thank her for offering to help when she said, "Mama, I'm so proud of you" and stood up to wrap her arms around me. The warmth of her hug when she laid her head on my shoulder filled me with the same strength I felt after the meeting yesterday. I knew my life was going to change.

I turned the van into the parking lot of St. Bartholomew's church. Turning off the engine, I looked up at the imposing fort-like brick structure adorned with stained glass windows and felt my stomach do flip-flops. Living and working in the confines of the black community, I often forgot I lived in a fairly big town with a bunch of people who supported grand churches. Made me nervous. Good thing I hadn't eaten breakfast, or I might have lost it right there on the pavement. Now wouldn't that have been mortifying?

"You must be Mrs. Howard," said a tall white woman standing next to my car door as I got out. "I'm Virginia McIntire, parish secretary. Reverend Larson asked me to watch for you. I'm so glad to meet you."

I shook her outstretched hand. "Glad to meet you too, Ma'am," I said pleasantly, hoping she couldn't detect my growing panic.

"Oh, please, call me Virginia," she said, not understanding I would never dare to call a white woman by her first name. We either said Ma'am or Miss Virginia. Her invitation at familiarity presented a dilemma. Now I had to figure out a way not to call her anything. But she didn't know any better. How could she? She was white.

I followed her through the side door of the church into a hallway. The carpeted floors and low ceilings were welcoming and comfortable. They reminded me of the mortuary. I started to relax in the surprisingly familiar surroundings. But then she knocked on a door and opened it. My heart jumped in my throat and my eyes blurred. Sitting around a table were four imposing men. I recognized Pastor Turner, but the rest of the men all looked the same to me. *Get a hold of yourself, Millie. You can do this,* I told myself. I was going to have to concentrate. I kind of recognized Reverend Larson because he was bald like my Marvin. Plus, I had met him at the meeting.

"Mrs. Howard," Reverend Larson said warmly, standing up and coming towards me. He took my arm, guiding me into the room. All the men stood up. "You know Pastor Turner, of course, and this is Rabbi Silberman from Beth Immanuel and Father Bob from St. Michael's Catholic parish."

As the men stood, I could actually see some differences. The Rabbi was about my height, with short black hair, and a full mustache and beard covering the lower part of his face. But he had a twinkle in his warm, dark eyes that invited trust. Father Bob couldn't have been more different if he tried. Tall with a ruddy complexion and greying red hair, he was an imposing presence. I stopped myself from making judgments when I remembered I needed to be careful of first impressions.

I nodded to each one of them, but I no more remembered their names than I could recite the Gettysburg Address. It was as if my ability to think had been erased. I must have looked petrified because Pastor Turner came over to hug me, whispering in my ear, "Relax, Millie. You look like a terrified deer, but we're not hunters. We're here to help."

I don't know why, but me looking like a deer struck me funny, and I began to relax. My eyes started to focus again.

Turned out, I had gotten all worked up for nothing. They were kind men of God who knew I was nervous. When they talked about their plans for me and the school, I could feel the tension in my shoulders start to release.

First, Reverend Larson explained about the Head Start program. Mississippi was supposed to get money for educating and tending to the health of the poor two years ago, but Senator Stennis refused the money earmarked to fund the program. Only recently, the Reverend, who had been working with an aide to someone named Sargent Shriver from the Office of Economic Opportunity, learned Mississippi was going to get their money plus back pay.

My head was spinning. Every black person knew who Senator Stennis was. He was a privileged white power broker intent on keeping the black man down. But I didn't know who Sargent Shriver was. Why was an army guy involved in the economic affairs of the poor? All I'd ever heard about the army was troops being sent in to guard integration efforts, like at Ole Miss. But I wasn't going to open my mouth. Uh-uh. I realized I hadn't been listening. When I tuned back in, the men were laying out their plans.

Rabbi Silberman offered two classrooms in the education wing of his temple. Truth be told, I didn't realize there were enough Jewish people in town to support an education wing at their temple. I wondered if that meant they didn't send their children to public schools. I thought only the Baptists fled the schools when the Brown decision came down from the Supreme Court. As Rabbi Silberman continued, I found out there were a couple of thousand Jews in town. They'd been here since the early 1900s. Started selling goods southerners had never seen before and settled in as their businesses thrived. I was surprised because I'd heard the Klan hated them almost as much as they hated us.

Pastor Turner explained he had hired three ladies who had been running a similar program on a tight budget for the past two years. He was sure they were more than capable of running a school with federal funds. I was beginning to wonder why I was sitting in the room when Father Bob told me my job would be to keep up with the paperwork the government wanted in order to distribute the funds. He told me I could work at home most of the time, but the committee did want me to check on the program at least two days a week.

Turned out, I'd be like the secretary/treasurer of the program. They figured since I had worked with the state government filling out death certificates and all, I'd learn the federal forms in no time. They thought I was the most qualified person in town. That's why they wanted me so badly. Now they may have been overstating the case, but they sure made me feel good about the range of skills they thought I had. I felt my confidence rising.

They asked me if I'd be willing to go out into the countryside to register children. They explained most people trusted Marvin and me. They had me there. It was true. We'd handled so many departed loved ones over the years, we'd met almost every black family in town. I agreed, but I asked, "How will I know who to visit?"

Pastor Turner said, "We're collecting names now. Teachers, parishioners, anyone we can think of has been giving us names and addresses of families who could benefit from the services we'll be offering. We're splitting the list up among you and the three sisters who'll be teaching in the classrooms. You'll meet them soon enough. They're from our family at First Primitive. We'll get the list to you by the end of the week or beginning of next week."

By the time the committee finished, my head was in a tizzy. We had talked about fixing up the rooms to look nice and welcoming. We chewed over ways to socialize and teach basics, what to feed children who often went hungry, how to find doctors and dentists willing to give time to check the ravages of poverty. And we had to do all of this in three months before school opened in September. It was a lot to do, but I was getting excited about it. I thought about Dr. Starke explaining how poor the Brown family was. Maybe we could help families like them. Hallelujah.

To close the meeting, Pastor Turner asked us to stand, form a circle, and each say what was in our hearts. He looked to me to start. Me? Why me? My brain almost shut down again, but out of my mouth came, "I praise the Lord and thank you gentlemen for having the confidence in me to ask me to be a part of this great adventure. I promise you, I will do my best. I feel blessed and honored by your faith." I was so stunned I said anything, I didn't hear the rest of the thoughts until the end when Rabbi Silberman said, "Go in peace and be safe."

As I drove home, the word "safe" stuck in my brain. In all my excitement, I had plumb forgot there were a whole bunch of people in town who hated anything to do with the government unless it benefited them. And they were none too happy about black folks getting something special. Maybe that realization was why the idea of doing something right was growing on me.

I arrived home well after two O'clock. I was so hungry I could have eaten a horse. I fully expected to find Dessie home from school, draped on the divan watching *Love of Life* on the TV. She was hooked on soaps. I didn't complain because I used to be hooked the same way when I was her age. Difference was, we didn't have TV, so I listened to them on the black radio station WQIC.

I looked around, but she wasn't there. Nobody was there. First, I looked in her room. Not there. I knew she wasn't in the kitchen. I called her name. Nothing. I could feel the muscles in my shoulders tightening up again. Where was she? I ran out back to the mortuary, panic setting in. I checked the chapel, office and viewing room. When I burst into the preparation room, I saw Dessie and Marvin, dressed in full gear of gloves and masks, scrubbing the tables and sinks. I screamed out, "What are you doing?"

"Millie," Marvin said through his mask, "Calm down. What's the matter?"

"Are you all right, Mama?" Dessie asked, alarmed.

"I'm sorry," I said. "When I came home, and nobody was there, I guess I overreacted. I think I'm a little hungry, too. Why don't I go back and make us a good early super? How about some ham and collards? I'll even whip up a little cornbread."

"Sounds great," Dessie said, a smile returning to her voice.

"By the time we finish up here, that cornbread should be crisp on the outside and soft as butter on the inside. I can taste it now," Marvin said.

I went back to our home, breathed a sigh of relief, kicked off my shoes by the door—I liked carpet for shoes, but I liked wood floors for bare feet, kept me nice and cool. I walked into the kitchen to start lunch. The only thing I really had to do was make the cornbread. The rest was heating up leftovers. As I stirred the corn meal, eggs, buttermilk and sorghum, I had a brilliant idea. I could make this for the children on the days I went to the school. Bring it in piping hot. I'd cooked for big church groups, I could do it for the program. That got me to thinking, they'd probably love my gingerbread cake, too. Ooh wee, I was getting energized.

The phone ringing broke my spell. I put down my favorite wood mixing spoon and walked to the front hall to answer it.

"Howard's Mortuary."

Silence.

What I heard made me drop the phone.

Marvin and Dessie came into the house chatting and laughing, expecting to find lunch on the table. When they saw me standing by the phone table, the receiver laying on the floor hanging from its long, twisted chord, they stopped in their tracks.

"Millie?" Marvin said cautiously. He walked over to the receiver, picked it up and put it back on the cradle.

I couldn't move. I couldn't talk. I heard his words, but I couldn't make sense of them. It felt like his voice was coming from a radio and someone was fooling with the volume. I wanted to speak, but I couldn't. Words wouldn't come out of my mouth.

"Millie? Can you hear me?" Marvin pursued. He took my hand and pulled me into his warmth and protection. "Why was the phone off the hook? Honey, you can tell me."

"Oh, Marvin," I cried. "Such hatred. Such venom."

"From now on, I'm the only one who answers the phone," Marvin ordered, still not knowing exactly what had happened, but highly suspicious we were under threat.

"But Papa," Dessie protested, not understanding what was going on.

"No 'But Papa.' Millie. Tell her what happened," Marvin said.

I looked at him like he was crazy. I couldn't say the words I heard over the phone to my little girl.

"Tell her. If she wants to be a part of this, she needs to know what we're facing." Turning to her, he added, "Dessie, being part of the movement is not just hugging and singing *We Shall Overcome* at the church with your friends. It can be very dangerous, and if we're going to do this as a family, you need to know all of it." Looking back at me, he insisted, "Tell her."

"I answered the phone like I always do. Howard's Mortuary," I stuttered. "At first, there was silence. I didn't think much about it. Lots of times people are too upset to talk. So, I waited..." I couldn't go on. The words stuck in my throat.

"Say it," Marvin whispered.

"A voice said..." I started to cry.

"Go on. What did the voice say?"

"It said, 'A nigger and a Kike. Two for one in my gun sight.'" Marvin gathered me in his arms and let me cry.

Dessie's hands flew to her mouth, her eyes wide with disbelief. She shook her head 'no' as tears filled her eyes.

"Yes, Dessie. That's the way the Klan operates. They have spies everywhere. We haven't been in this more than 24 hours, and they already know. You still want to be a part of it?" Marvin asked.

"I do. In fact, I want to go to the meeting tomorrow night," Dessie said, letting her hands drop. She took on that same chin up, straight back posture she claimed the other night when Pastor Turner asked her about history.

"Okay, we'll go," Marvin said with a finality not to be challenged.

For the next few hours, we carried on as normal as possible. No one was really hungry anymore. We ate anyway. Ham sandwiches were fine. After we finished eating, I gave the cornbread I had baked to Marvin to give to the Brown family. I insisted they have a little something special for after the interment. Since Marvin and Dr. Starke had wrapped Ida Brown good and tight, he felt safe allowing Dessie to help place her in a body bag. Once safely secured in the hearse, he drove out to the burial site. When he came back, he told me the family really appreciated the treat. He also said Dr. Warren had done what he promised. He showed the family where to dig the grave so as not to contaminate their water supply. Between all the precautions everyone had taken, Marvin reassured me he thought the threat of typhoid had been handled. Then he added, "Remember, no charge."

⚜Chapter Four⚜

THURSDAY, MAY 19

The next day, large boiling thunder clouds built up in the oppressive heat. Nothing like a good storm to cool things down. But there was more than just a weather storm brewing, and I had put myself right in the eye of the tempest.

Once Marvin came in from the mortuary, we ate collards and black-eyed peas then took off for the registration meeting. The first big drops splattered on the cement as we ran up the steps of the parish hall. It was going to be a gully washer. None too soon either. My garden was thirsty. We stood, huddled together, inside the doorway, not sure what to do. Sister Helen spied us from across the room and came rushing over.

"I'm so glad you're here," she said, taking turns giving each of us a cheek kiss. "Dessie, all the kids are in the room over there," she said, pointing in the direction of a room that served as a nursery during church service. "The kids are making posters." Turning to Marvin, she said, "All the men are gathered in Pastor Turner's office. I have no idea what they're talking about, but I do know that's where you'll want to be."

Then she took my hand and led me to a table where a production line of some sort seemed to be working. "What would you like to do? Fold? Stuff? Lick? Or write?"

"I wouldn't lick if I was you. I cut my tongue on one of those envelopes," Mayola called out. Everyone laughed. I winked at her and smiled.

"I think I'll write," I said, noticing Ella May, a waitress at the First Street Café, was the only person addressing the envelopes and a stack was building up next to her.

"Thank you, Lord," she said, crossing off a name from a list, picking up another envelope and checking to see what name came next. "Come sit by me. I've fallen way behind and need all the help I can get."

Taking off my raincoat, draping it over the back of a chair, I sat down and waited for instructions. Ella May put the list in between us, pointed to a name, and handed me a pen.

"Mayola?" Ella May called out suddenly, "How come your name is here? Aren't you registered to vote?"

"Lawd, I've been discovered," Mayola said dramatically as if to make a joke of the revelation.

But Ella May didn't let go. "Whatcha mean, you been discovered? If you aren't registered, that means you never voted. That right?"

"Ella May, you know if the Conrads even knew I was here, they'd fire me on the spot. Mr. Conrad told me 'Negras shouldn't vote because they don't know anything about politics.' I just nod my head and say 'yessah.' I've been tempted to add 'Massah,' but I don't want to push my luck. No way I could have passed those literacy tests anyway. I heard white folks made them deliberately confusing and only gave you ten minutes to take them," Mayola explained.

"She's right. It's even worse than that," Rhoda Roberts, who was stuffing envelopes, piped in. "I studied for that test for months. You know what one of the questions was?"

A chorus of "uh-uh's" rang out from the ladies.

"Does enumeration affect the income tax levied on citizens in various states?"

"What's enumeration mean?" Ella May asked.

"I doubt many white folks could answer that," Mayola said to another chorus of "mm-hmms."

"Doesn't make any difference. When I went to take the test, the registrar—she was one mean woman, never called me anything but 'girl'—she put me in a room and locked the door. There was a policeman with a vicious German Shepherd dog stationed outside the room. I could hear that dog sniffing under the door and growling as I took the test. I was terrified. When they finally released me, the officer had to hold that dog tight, so he wouldn't tear me into shreds. I didn't find out I'd passed the test until two years later when the Voting Rights Act was passed and records had to be released," Rhoda hissed. Then she sat back in her chair with a faraway look in her eye and a furrow in her brow.

We were stunned by what she had said. After a moment, Mayola asked, "You mean all that time you weren't able to vote?"

"That's right," Rhoda said, nodding slowly. "And that's why I'm here. Now that we don't have to take that test no more, we've got to get everyone registered to vote."

"Don't kid yourselves," Mayola said. "If they don't fire us for registering, they'll figure out some other way to keep us from casting our votes."

With that, we all grew quiet, disappearing into our worlds of memories filled with the injustices we had suffered.

I remembered studying for that test. Of course, I knew the easy questions like my name, residency and job title. Problem was, I had to be prepared to read and interpret any article from the Mississippi constitution the registrar felt inspired to designate. They thought they were being so clever giving us long, complicated sections. But they didn't know about the network of support we had, including information pamphlets on how to answer the questions. I read all those pamphlets until I memorized every word. And Marvin worked with me for days, helping me figure out the meaning of the most complex sections of the constitution. I was ready.

The day before I was supposed to register to vote, one of the more sympathetic newspapers reported a brief story about a young black woman who had been attacked and left for dead next to an eight-foot cross burning on her lawn. The final line in the story said the woman had just completed her voter application and literacy test. After reading that, I was so scared, I didn't want to go. But Marvin insisted.

The next morning, I put on my Sunday best and got to the registrar's office at nine o'clock sharp. I signed up, provided the proper identification, then took a seat in the black section and anxiously waited for them to call my name. But they didn't. Not until twenty minutes before closing time. I had to rush through the twenty-one questions on the test faster than I thought possible. I was sure I'd flunked it, but six months later, I got a letter saying I'd passed. Of course, that was long after the election. Doesn't matter, I've been voting ever since.

"Miz Howard," a small voice next to me said, pulling me back into the present. I had been so taken with Rhoda's story and my own musings, I hadn't noticed Lester Ball, a cleaning maid at the Dixie Inn, sit down next to me. Lester was a young, slightly overweight girl who limped from having survived polio as youngster. She still had on her uniform with the motel logo embroidered on the pocket over her left breast. Ever since Marvin and I used some of the special funds to give her mama a proper send off, she treated me like a queen.

"Lester, how nice to see you," I said, giving her a warm hug. "Are you a volunteer too?"

"Uh-huh. But I got somethin' for you I think you should see," she whispered. "Some not so nice people left a mess in one of the rooms I clean at the motel. I was emptying the wastepaper basket and saw these. Don't look at 'em here."

I felt a tap on my leg. I put my hand down under the table and felt her press a wad of papers into my hand. Luckily, I had kept my purse on my lap. I opened the clasp, stuffed the papers in and went on as though nothing had happened.

By the time the meeting was over and we were ready to go home, the rain had stopped. It must have been quite a cloudburst. Little streams connected in the low spots of the parking lot. I felt like I was playing hopscotch just to get to the van and not ruin my shoes.

"What'd you kids do tonight?" I asked Dessie as we piled into the right side of the van while Marvin ran around to the driver's side.

"Made posters announcing June 24th as the last day to register to vote. I volunteered to hang one in the lobby of the mortuary," she said proudly as she dried her hands on a towel we kept in the van for when we picked up bodies. I looked over at Marvin who winced slightly but didn't say anything. I knew what he was thinking. He never let anyone post ads anywhere in the mortuary. He didn't think it was appropriate. I felt the same way, but what could I say? I couldn't say no to Dessie if she'd already promised.

"How many kids were there?" Marvin asked, turning on the engine and headlights. Seeing the windshield was spotted with drops, he gave the wipers a couple of swipes to clear his view.

"About fifteen. I wish Josey had been able to come. There's this guy she likes, and she's gonna be mad when she finds out he was there," Dessie said with a slight edge of smugness to her tone.

I was about to tell her not to go bragging that she spent the evening with him, when Marvin asked, "What're you gonna' say to her?"

"Oh, I don't know yet," Dessie answered. "Maybe I'll make sure she comes the next time."

"What about you? Anyone you're interested in?" Marvin asked.

"Daa-aad," Dessie reacted. Marvin looked over at me and winked.

See what I mean? Marvin was doing a better job of working with Dessie than I was. He was willing to listen where I wanted to lecture. Humph.

"How about you, honey. What'd you boys do?" I asked, changing the subject. Truth be known, I was none too happy Dessie talked decent to him and sassed me.

"One really important thing happened. I told Pastor Turner about the phone call. He told me to listen. The Klan always likes to scare you with a little pause. If that happens, he said to say in the most official way, 'Sheriff's Office. How may I help you?' He said that'll spook 'em. They'll hang up right away."

He made me laugh.

He pulled his head back, dipped his chin and said, "Sheriff's Office," he put on this false deep voice.

"Do that again, Papa," Dessie said, laughing.

He knew he was being funny as he practiced different voices, repeating, "How may I help you?" By the time we pulled up to our driveway, my sides hurt from laughing so much.

"Wait, stop," I said, wiping tears away. "I want to check the mailbox. Reverend Larson said he'd leave something for me by the end of the week."

I stepped down out of the van being careful of the puddles. Our mailbox was in the middle of what looked like a mini lake.

"Careful," Marvin called out. "Maybe you should wait until morning. Whatever it is, it'll still be there in the morning."

"I'm already soaked. Might as well…" I pulled down the door of the box and reached in. Pain. I mean a stabbing pain assaulted my hand like hot pokers burning my flesh. I screamed, yanking my hand back. I leaned over to look into the box and in the rear corner, wound up in its own fear, was Mississippi's most poisonous creature—a copperhead snake.

"I just got bitten by a snake," I wailed. *Oh Lord, save me.*

As I screamed, Marvin and Dessie jumped out of the van. I felt Marvin swoop me up and race into the house, yelling to Dessie to phone Dr. Starke. He almost dropped me on the bed, not realizing how bad my hand was throbbing. I shrieked out in pain, scaring him.

"Millie, honey, I'm calling the doctor," he insisted.

"You can do what you want, but I want Dessie to run next door and get Granny Simms. She'll know what to do better than anyone," I said, starting to cry. Dessie, seeing me cry, shot out of the room. I heard her run down the hall and out the front door. Marvin didn't waste any time either. He left the room. I knew he was phoning the doctor. I couldn't hear anything anymore because I was fighting the pain. The throbbing was intensifying, and I felt the swelling moving up my arm. I broke out in a sweat, beginning to feel sick to my stomach. I tried to ignore the growing fear I was going to die. When Marvin came back in the room, I had no idea what he said because I was praying. *Dear Lord, if I die, please watch over my family and keep them safe.* I kept saying it over and over.

Dessie came running in, placing a large, hand-made carpetbag on our dresser. "She's on her way, Mama. She's right behind me," she said, trying to catch her breath. I couldn't say a word I was in such agony.

A minute later, Granny walked in. An uncommon little woman, she was no bigger than a peanut, grey hair frizzed out as wild as some of her sacred herbs and dressed in the oddest assortment of gingham flour and sugar bags she had collected and layered into clothes designed for maximum comfort. Lots of people were scared of her, but I wasn't. I liked her. She had the wisdom of a thousand years. Her mama, her granny, her great granny…on and on, back through the centuries…passed down their special recipes for their magic potions. Healers, that's what they were. Through the ages, they learned what plants worked for what diseases. I felt my heart slow down as soon as I saw her.

In my fog of pain, I heard her issuing orders. "Dessie," she called out, "bring me four bowls of water. Not hot. Not cold; as many towels as you can find and a couple of pillows. Marvin, get a dining room chair and set it by the bed." She walked over to the bed and gently picked up my arm. I winced in pain, trying not to cry out, but tears streamed down my face.

"I bet you never again stick your hand in no mailbox without lookin'," she said with a chuckle. She turned my hand toward the light, leaning over to get a good look. "Hmm. Looks like you were bit by medium-sized snake. I'd say about two-foot long. See these two fang marks? How far apart they are? Tells me how big the snake was. The good news is he gave you what we call a 'warning bite.' If he meant business, he'd have bit down and chewed on you for a while, makin' sure the poison got into you good."

Dessie came into the room carrying a tray with four bowls filled with water. She had on her concentrating face—pursed lips with her tongue stuck out the side. Marvin was right behind her, holding a chair like you do the first day of school. Stacked on the seat of the chair were a mountain of towels and a pillow from the guest bedroom. I remember thinking, why'd he bring one of my good pillows? I could only see the top of his head over the back of the chair, so I couldn't shoot him one of my 'what were you thinking' looks. Come to think of it, I wasn't in any shape to do anything but gasp in pain.

"She's gonna live. In fact, she'll be good in no time at all," Granny pronounced, picking up her hand-made carpetbag and rummaging through it until she found what she wanted. She pulled out a large canning jar filled with something black.

Opening it, she poured granules into one of the bowls and stirred until the water was jet black and thick. She came over to the chair, placing a towel over the seat and the bowl on the towel. Finally, she took the pillow and built a bridge from the bed to the bowl for my arm to rest on while my hand soaked in the black goo.

"In case you're wonderin', I want her arm below her heart. The mixture is simple ground charcoal. It'll suck the venom right out. We'll change it every 15 minutes."

I couldn't stand it any longer and cried out, "Can't you do anything for the pain?"

"I was gettin' to that," she said, returning to her bag and pulling out two vials holding tiny little pills. Holding up the one with red pills in it, she instructed, "This one's for pain. Put it under your tongue. Don't chew it. Just let it melt under your tongue." She opened the vial, shook one pill into her palm and said, "Open up." She slipped it in my mouth under my tongue. Within minutes, I felt sleep creeping up on me.

Last thing I heard was her giving orders not to give the medicine to me more than every four hours. When I woke, I had no idea what time it was. My arm was beginning to throb again, but not nearly what it had been before. My hand was no longer in a bowl but wrapped with gauze. Dessie was asleep, draped across the foot of the bed. Marvin, still in his clothes, was lying on the covers next to me.

"Is she still here?" I asked.

"No, she left about an hour ago," Marvin yawned, stretching his arms to wake up. "She changed the bowls four times, then put something she called plantain tincture on the area and wrapped you up. She also gave me a vial of pills. She told me it was Echinacea. It'll build your strength up. And some herbal chewy things she cooked up for nausea."

"What about Dr. Starke? Did you ever get in touch with him?"

"By the time I got him, Granny had done her magic. I told him what she'd done, and you had finally dozed off. He said he couldn't add to Granny's medicine, but he'd stop by tomorrow." Noticing it was past midnight, he said, "I guess I should say he'll stop by today, to see how you're doing."

"And the snake?"

Chapter Five

Friday, May 19

Marvin told me to go to sleep. He said he'd worry about the snake in the morning. He gave me another one of those little red pills. They were delightfully strong. I was out like a light. I didn't wake up until the sun was shining bright through my window. My arm was wrapped, but I wanted to see what that snake had done to me, so I undid the bandage.

"Marvin?" I called out. He came running with Dessie right behind him. Maybe I should have been bit by a snake a long time ago if they were going to react like this.

"How you doin', sweetheart?" Marvin asked, really serious.

"I can't believe I slept so late," I said. "My hand doesn't hurt hardly at all." I was exaggerating a tad. When I lifted my arm to take a look, I felt a stab all the way to my jaw, probably because it was swollen. "Look here," I said, using my good hand to point to two small punctures on the top of my thumb. "Look at these two fang marks. Huh! That's where it struck at me. It really was a copperhead, wasn't it?" I wanted to make sure I hadn't made up what I saw.

Marvin had such a strange look of concern on his face. Dessie didn't look any better.

"What?" I asked. "Was it still in that mailbox this morning?"

"No, it was gone," he said. "When I went out, the mailbox was still open. I had our barbeque tongs in hand, ready to grab that sucker and toss it clear from here into next Tuesday. But it wasn't there. I have no idea how it got out. But it did. Praise the Lord."

"Amen," I said.

"Unfortunately, Millie, something just as bad was in that box," Marvin said, his mood turning dark. He had something he didn't want to tell me. I knew him all too well.

"Tell me," I insisted with growing alarm.

Reluctantly, he handed me a nasty, wet piece of paper. I could tell I wasn't going to like this. As I unfolded the soggy edges, I had to be careful not to tear the fragile message. I laid it out flat, smoothing out the wrinkles. There, in a childish handwriting, was the reason for my bite. That snake hadn't crawled up the mailbox pole. We knew someone had put it there.

If you and yur family don't stop,

Yur gonna get more 'n a Snake.

You been warned.

I was so stunned, I had to read it twice before I could comprehend such meanness.

"Who'd do such a thing?" I asked, but I knew the answer.

"You know who," Marvin said. "The real question is, what do we do about it?"

I wasn't so sure this was the right time to be making such a decision, what with my hand and all—and I told him so.

"You might be right," Marvin said. "But we do have a choice. We continue as we are, knowing we can quit if we think things are too dangerous, or commit. We plow through no matter what happens."

"Know what I think?" Dessie asked. I wasn't sure I wanted to hear her either. I wasn't sure about anything right then. I looked at Marvin and shrugged.

"Go ahead. Tell us," he said.

"Mama, when I thought I might lose you, I was terrified. I know I've had attitude lately. But you have to admit, so have you."

Was I going to admit to it? Not in a week of Sundays. However, I did what mothers do everywhere when it comes to their daughters, I surprised myself. I looked at Dessie and tilted my head in agreement. Huh! Where'd that come from?

"Mama, say it," she said sternly.

Ooh wee, who'd she learn that tone from? "Maybe," I said, reluctantly, then I added, "I'll tell you what I freely admit. You've been full of surprises lately. Good ones. For certain, you're not a little girl anymore."

"Thank you, Mama. Point is…" and she started sounding just like her papa… "the meetings we've been going to have opened my eyes. Kids talk. We're not the only family being threatened. Anthony Harrison…"

"Oh yes, I know his Papa. They call him 'Big Tony,'"
I interrupted. Dessie looked at me, irritated by my intrusion
into her story. Even Marvin didn't look happy. I needed to
start listening better.

"As I was saying," she continued, "Anthony told us
something last night. Apparently, his papa is a busboy at the
Golden Ring Restaurant. His papa described a big meetin'
there on Wednesday with all the big white mucky-mucks
talkin' about what to do about the 'niggers trying to get the
vote.' His dad can't believe how freely they talk in front of
him and Brother Clark as if they didn't have ears. Anthony
says that's because they think we're animals. Anyway, they
were talking in code. His dad heard them say Rabbi Silberman
was a code four. Anthony's dad didn't know what a code four
was, but he knew from the way they said it, it wasn't good."

I suddenly remembered the papers Lester had given
me. I interrupted Dessie again, "Get my purse, will you please
honey." She looked really peeved at my second interruption,
crossing her arms across her chest, shaking her head in
disgust.

"Wait a minute," Marvin said, looking around the
room. "Your purse fell on the ground when you were bitten. I
found it and put it around here somewhere." His eyes lit up
when he saw it on the dresser. He picked it up and handed it to
me. Reaching into the purse with my good hand, I pulled out a
wad of papers. Holding them out to him I said, "Lester Ball,
you remember her? We helped her out one time when her
Mama died. She said she found these at the motel in a room
occupied by some not so nice lookin' people. I haven't read
them yet."

He took the papers and read through them one at a time. "I can't make heads nor tails of this," he said putting two of the papers on the bed. "Uh, oh. This one here says 'Millie Howard, Marvin Howard, code three.'"

We looked at each other, then at Dessie, not saying a word. We didn't have to know what a code three meant to have the words shoot fear through us.

"Wait a minute," I said, fumbling around in the bed covers. As I picked up the limp paper and handed it to Marvin, I said, "Here...Look. Does the paper from the note in the box match the paper from Lester?"

He compared the papers. Holding them up and turning over each sheet, comparing each to our threat—trying to see if there was anything similar, a watermark, something. He shook his head, squinting, "Hard to tell. I don't know Millie."

Dessie came over, dropping her attitude. She picked up the papers and did the same as her papa. "I think they might be the same. They're the same size, but Papa's right. It's hard to tell anything beyond that."

The sudden brrring of the phone startled us.

"I'll get it," Marvin commanded, holding his hand out, blocking us from moving to answer the phone. As if we would. Not me. Unh-unh. Dread invaded my body. I felt my heart beat faster. I saw my chest heaving and felt my throat tighten.

Luckily, Marvin didn't waste any time getting down the hall. It was like he wanted to stop the ringing so he could stop our growing fears.

"Sheriff's Office. How may I help you?" Marvin said in a deep voice, just as he practiced on the way home last night.

I looked at Dessie. We locked eyes as we listened to his rehearsed speech.

Then Marvin laughed and said, "Yes, sir. I'm a fast learner. We'd be honored. See you soon," and hung up.

"Who was that?" Dessie and I said at the same time.

"Reverend Larson. Said he heard about the snake incident and wanted to come visit. Wanted to see how you were doing. I couldn't say no."

"What was the 'fast learner' all about?" I asked.

"When I answered, 'Sheriff's Office,' he said I'd been hanging around Pastor Turner too long," Marvin said, smiling.

"He's a nice man," I chuckled. Suddenly, I realized I must look like a wreck. I hopped out of bed only to feel my head spin. I reeled a little, grabbing the bedpost to steady myself. My arm started throbbing. I moaned.

"Whoa, honey. Not so fast. You better stay in bed," Marvin cautioned, coming over to help me.

"At least let me brush my teeth and wash my face," I said. "Just help me to the bathroom."

Marvin took my arm, steadying me. As I regained my balance, I looked around, seeing nothing but mess. I couldn't have a preacher see that. "Dessie, would you mind straightenin' up while I get myself decent?"

Despite the earlier pride with being grown-up, Dessie reverted to the overworked, put upon teenager, slumping her shoulders and emitting an almost imperceptible whine, "Why do I have to do all the work?"

As pouty as Dessie had been, she really made the room look nice. She straightened up the bed placing the guest room pillow where I could lay my arm, took away all the accumulated bowls, glasses, and towels, and positioned two chairs for her papa and the preacher. I didn't know what to make of her. One minute she was pouting like a preteen, the next she was behaving like an adult.

"Here she is," Marvin said, escorting Reverend Larson into the room. "Look what he brought us. A lasagna."

"Oh, you shouldn't have. But thank you so much," I said. I really meant it. I couldn't remember ever getting something so thoughtful from a white person before. Imagine. A whole lasagna.

"Don't thank me. Mrs. Larson. Jill...made it," he said, standing awkwardly by the chair.

"Please, sit down," I said.

"How's your hand?" he asked.

I showed him where the fang marks were. Then I blurted out, "The Klan put that snake in there, Reverend Larson."

"I thought maybe that was the case," Reverend Larson said. "Did they leave a note?"

"How'd you know?" I asked, surprised he felt so free to talk about it. "It's right here somewhere," I said looking around. "Dessie, honey. Come in here please."

When Dessie came to the doorway, I asked where she put the note and papers. She looked at me quizzically but opened a drawer and brought them to me. I, in turn, handed them to the Reverend.

"Those other notes are from someone I know who found them in some trash. We think the two might be from the same people," I wasn't going to reveal my source, but I wanted him to know what was going on. "We're baffled by the codes on some of those papers."

A crease folded on his forehead as he looked at the notes. He did the same thing Marvin had done. He turned them over, held them up to the light, rubbing his fingers over both the note and papers.

"Millie, I think I should give these to Chief Carter," Reverend Larson said.

"Chief of Police Carter?" I asked in disbelief. I wanted to scream no policeman would help a black person. What are you thinking? Instead I said, "You think a policeman would help me? With all due respect, sir, I don't think so."

Reverend Larson held up his hand and nodded sympathetically. "I understand your skepticism. If I were you, I'd feel the same way. Chief Carter may not agree with all the laws being passed, but he believes in the law. He's a fair man and will do everything in his power to protect you from this kind of terror. Let me tell you a story."

Seems to me Pastors always have stories, so I listened.

"When I got called to minister at St Bartholomew's, after the James Meredith incident, my family and I were settling into our new home. The Klan was not happy about a civil rights activist moving into their territory. One night they marched to our house to burn a cross on our front lawn and hang me in effigy. Mind you, they were in full Klan garb, torches and all. My family and I were terrified. I really didn't know what to do. At that moment, Chief Carter phoned me up and said, "Grab your family, a change of clothes and any important papers you can gather. I've got an unmarked car coming to your back alley." Then he drove to the front of the house in his squad car, lights flashing, and sirens blaring and stopped the mob from carrying out their plans. I've trusted him ever since. But he's got to have something to work with. These papers and this note will help him. The more information he has, the better your chances are at stopping the Klan. I guarantee you he's not a Jim Clark kind of guy."

I shook with terror when I thought of the freedom marches in Selma, Alabama where a Sheriff named Jim Clark, outfitted in his paramilitary uniform festooned with the button "Never," carried a cattle prod and zapped every marcher he could. He represented everything Blacks feared and distrusted about the police. Wouldn't that bigot be surprised to know that every time he said, "I can't tell them people apart. As far as I'm concerned, they're all bad," we were saying the same thing about him and his posse. They all wore the same uniform, the same helmets and all swung the same clubs. And they all had the same look of hatred in their eyes as they beat those marchers, young and old alike.

I was getting a little miffed with Marvin. He'd been sitting next to Reverend Larson and hadn't said a word. I looked over at him for help.

He finally saw my look and said, "If we give you these papers, what guarantee can you give us we will be safe?"

"None," Reverend Larson said, honestly. "Quite frankly. We're all in danger. We just heard that there's a code four out on Rabbi Silberman. That means the Klan plans to kill him."

I gasped. Marvin and I looked at each other in disbelief.

We gave the papers to Reverend Larson before he left. He said he'd keep in touch. Later in the afternoon, Dr. Starke came by. After looking me over, he said I was doing really well. But he told me I was to stay in bed for the next week. He warned there still might be poison in my system. Moving around too much would move the poison to places I didn't want it to go. Only way to keep that from happening was to rest easy. He said he'd come back soon.

One week later, Dr. Starke gave me permission to go to the mortuary if I promised to just sit and do paperwork—no cleaning, no heavy lifting and no going out in public for the next two weeks. I sure didn't mind the no cleaning, but Dessie was none too happy about it. Bless her heart, she actually kept the house cleaner than I did. Huh. Seemed life was settling back to normal. I should have known better.

TUESDAY, JUNE 6

After three weeks, I finally felt strong enough to go to an evening meeting. The swelling in my arm had completely disappeared, and I was about to lose my patience just sitting around. I had too much to do. I wanted to find out how many people had signed up. Once the committee knew the numbers, we could start planning how to educate the folks to fill out ballots, how to act at the polls if there was any trouble or disruption from agitators and the hardest part, how to get to the polls. I was sitting at the desk in the mortuary around one o'clock when Marvin came in to tell me he needed gas for the van and was headed out. He asked if I wanted him to get me anything. I couldn't think of a thing, so he took off. I fully expected him to gas up and come right back. When he wasn't home in an hour, I started to become concerned. When he wasn't home in two hours, I was beyond concerned and slipped into panicky. I jogged back to the house to check if perhaps he'd gone there first. Maybe Dessie had asked him to pick up some groceries.

"Dessie," I called out, walking in the back door. Finding her in the kitchen dicing vegetables, I said, "Oh good. You're here. Did you ask Dad to bring you anything? He said he was getting gas over two hours ago, and he's not back."

"No, Mama," she said, setting down her knife and walking over to the window, looking out to make sure the van wasn't in the driveway. A worried look spread across her face. "Maybe we should call someone."

"Who?" I asked. I felt the muscles in my shoulders tightening up and a tension headache building. "I wouldn't know where to start," I added impatiently.

"What about Mr. Giddings down at the gas station. We could phone him to find out if Papa was there," Dessie suggested.

"You think he'd know who we were?" I asked.

"It's worth a try," she said. She rushed down the hall to get the phone book. Bringing it back and laying it on the table, she started singing the children's alphabet song *A, B, C, D, E, F, G* as she thumbed through the pages. She stopped at G for Giddings, then ran her finger down the page. "I found it. Giddings Esso station," she said. She picked up the book and started back down the hall when we heard the crunch of tires on the gravel in the drive. She whirled around and ran to the window. "It's Papa."

When Marvin walked in that door, Dessie and I ran to him. We were so relieved, we were almost crying. The minute he saw the looks on our face, he knew we had been worrying about him.

Gathering us in his arms, he said, "I'm safe." He kissed the tops of our heads. "You need to sit down because you're not going to believe what happened."

We sat. He got a glass of water and took deep swallows before he started in.

"I left here, like I told you, to go get gas. What time was that? Noon?" he asked.

"No." I said, "It was more like one."

"No matter. I drove over to the Esso station and was just pulling up to the pump when a white Ford truck pulled right around me and backed into the van. I knew I was in trouble when this little, bandy rooster in jeans and a racist T-shirt jumped out of the cab and came struttin' back to where I was sitting. Unfortunately, my window was rolled down, it being so hot and all. He started yelling at me that I hit his truck, and he was gonna' string up my black nigger ass."

Fear rose in his eyes as he remembered the encounter. It was contagious. I felt his terror, shivering as if a cold draft wind had blown over my body.

"Luckily, Mr. Giddings came running out." Marvin continued. "He was holding a rifle by his side. He musta seen the whole thing. He looked the guy straight in the eye and said, 'I don't want no trouble, and you look like trouble. Get back in your truck. I'll get you gas, and then I want you outta' here.' The guy looked back at him and sneered, 'I don't want none of your gas, nigger lover.' He got back in his truck and peeled off leaving a track of rubber and smoke in his wake. Mr. Giddings said, 'Sorry about that, Marvin. I saw the whole thing through the window.' I said, 'Thank you, Mr. Giddings. You may have saved my life. I hope I didn't get you in trouble too.' And I meant it. Mr. Giddings musta known what I was thinkin' because he said, 'Don't worry about the Klan. Too many of them buy their gas from me. I got the best prices in town.' Then he waved me forward and filled up my tank. The whole thing musta taken twenty minutes at the most. I paid him and started home."

Marvin took another long drink of cool water then continued. "I'm not two minutes down the highway when I heard a siren blasting and seen yellow lights flashing in my rearview. I pulled over to let the police go by, but instead, the officer pulled up right behind me. I knew I wasn't speeding. I was completely baffled and scared. But I knew the routine. I kept my hands in plain view on the steering wheel and didn't say anything. The officer walked to the front of the car, took a look, shook his head and came strolling back to me. He says, 'I just got a call from a guy who says you hit and run his truck. I can see the dent. I'm gonna' issue you a ticket, and you better get down to the station to explain yourself. I mean, right now.' I couldn't believe it. How'd that guy get a call in so fast? I didn't argue though. I took the ticket and headed to the station."

"That's so wrong," Dessie growled, slamming her open hands down on the table.

"I thought so too, honey," Marvin continued, placing his hands over hers with pats of understanding and reassurance. "When I went into the police station, I walked up to the window to pay my ticket. I had no plans to explain myself. Standing next to the Sergeant who was at the window was none other than Chief Carter. He picked up the ticket, looked at it and said, 'Hit and run? Hunh! I've had it with this kind of blatant disrespect for the law. I'll handle this. Buzz him in.' I can tell you, I was thinking bad thoughts about Reverend Larson and all his bragging about the Chief. I mean, I was really scared. Once in the squad room, the Chief led me into his office and pulled the blinds shut. I was thinkin' I was a dead man." I saw the glint of fear in Marvin's eyes change to anger. He paused to get control of his emotions before he went on.

"Chief Carter leaned towards me real close. I could feel the heat of his breath on my ear. I closed my eyes, thinkin he was going to wallop me upside the back of my head. Then, he said in a real quiet voice, 'I'm going to yell at you, but I'm going to whisper too. When I whisper, I'm telling you the truth. Got it?' I nodded my head—maybe I was shaking so bad, it nodded on its own."

Marvin stopped and ran his hand across his head and down the back of his neck. He gave his tense muscles a squeeze before he went on.

"The Chief yelled something about a hit and run, then whispered, 'The officer who gave you the ticket is one of my trusted men. He saw the whole incident and used it as an excuse to give you a ticket to get you in here.' He yelled something else. I can't remember what. 'The papers you gave us were helpful. If you get any more information, will you let me know?' I nodded yes. Then he pounded the table with his palm of his hand so hard the sound made me jump. He told me they had some good cops and some bad cops, and he was doing all this so the bad ones wouldn't know what he was up to. 'I'm working hard to stop the Klan's White Knights here in town from doing some of the things we know they're planning. Know you can trust the four men your wife is working with at Head Start. You can use them as a go-between to get information to me.' With that, he banged on the table again, then opened the top drawer of his desk. Still afraid, I thought he might pull out a gun and shoot me right there. Instead he pulled out a twenty-dollar bill and handed it to me. He got up, put his finger up to his lips, and escorted me to the door. As he let me out, he said, 'Go on over there and pay your fine. I don't want to see you in here again. Hear me, boy.' He stood with his arms folded across his chest, watching me cross the room. I could feel every officer's eyes on me. It was the most confusing, humiliating, enlightening experience I ever hope to have. And here I am. A little worse for wear, I must admit, but alive."

Dessie and I sat dumbfounded—stunned. I looked down at my hands, saw I had torn up a tissue and made a mess. I started sweeping the pieces into my other hand, grateful to be doing something other than crying hysterically.

Chapter Six

O nce I recovered from my shock of Marvin's...what should I call it...brush with the law, I found my voice.

"Oh, Marvin, I'm so sorry you had to go through that humiliation," I said, getting up to hug him.

Dessie joined me. The three of us stood, our arms wrapped around each other, silent in our love for one another plus a healthy dose of relief.

Dessie broke the spell. She pulled away, and asked, "Will we still go to the meeting tonight?"

"If that's what you want," Marvin said. "I'd like to wash up first. I'm feeling a little out of sorts with everything that's happened today."

Marvin disappeared into the back of the house while I fixed a dinner of black-eyed peas, collards, and deep-fried fish with homemade hot sauce. Ol' Mister Jones had come around in his truck in the early afternoon just after Marvin left. He was tooting his horn and calling out, "Freshwater fish... turnips, tops and bottoms...peas..." I couldn't resist. I bought a mess of peas and five fish. I sure wished they'd already been cleaned. I made a mess. Scales flew all over the kitchen, but, mmm-mmm, they were good.

Fried fish and black-eyed peas made up one of Marvin's favorite meals. After he took his last bite, he pushed away from the table and said, "That was a good meal, Millie. Thank you. If you ladies don't mind, I think I'd like to watch a little TV tonight. I'm not up to socializing."

I didn't mind, but Dessie's whole body slumped. Picking up on her obvious but surprising disappointment, I said, "Would you mind if Dessie and I went? I haven't been out for weeks. I was looking forward to catching up on everyone."

Dessie sat up, looked directly at her papa, and said, "Please, Papa."

"I don't mind. You go ahead. Just be careful." As if we needed a reminder.

Dessie jumped up, collected the dirty plates to scrape, squirted soap into the dishpan and started washing the dishes. Was this my Dessie? Something was definitely going on with that girl. Suddenly, it dawned on me. She must have been more interested in that Anthony boy than she was letting on. I figured it was time to start paying more attention to that boy than I had been. I looked at Marvin to give him a knowing wink, but he was lost deep in his thoughts.

As soon as we walked into the parish hall, Dessie took off to the young people's room. I watched her slow down as she neared Anthony, say something to him, then sit down beside him. She was all bouncy and smiley. Yep, she was smitten alright. I could see it from across the room.

Walking over to my usual place, I could hear everyone was talking about James Meredith.

"Did you hear, Millie?" Mayola asked.

"Course I heard," I said, not wanting to admit I had no idea what everybody was going on about. I hadn't listened to the radio or TV, what with all the happenings with Marvin.

"Can you imagine being shot, then getting up and marching again? The man must be made of steel," Mayola said.

"He was marchin' again? Oh, I didn't hear that part," I said. At least I wasn't fibbing about that.

"You're wrong, Mayola. Tomorrow, Dr. King and Stokely Carmichael are going to continue the March against Fear, not James Meredith," Ella May said.

"Still. He's a brave man," Mayola said with a "harrumph," added because she didn't like being corrected.

"I wonder if Buddy Murray is going to be a part of the march?" Ella May asked, ignoring Mayola. "We should get him back here to talk to us again."

"That's a good idea," Mayola piped in, wanting to redeem herself. "He sure is some kind of speaker. Inspired me."

I laughed, but suddenly I felt very tired. What was this world coming to? So much hatred was boiling up and spilling out.

"Mrs. Howard," the familiar voice of Lester caught my attention. Turning, I saw I was right. I wondered what new information she might have for me.

"Hi, Lester. How are you?' I asked, standing up to give her a hug.

"They're back," she whispered.

"You mean the ones who left the paper?" I asked. When she nodded yes, I quickly directed her to the Ladies room. Pushing the door open and looking in each stall, I checked to make sure no one else was in there. I had to laugh at myself. I'd been watching too many episodes of *I Spy* on TV. I even turned on the water in case the room was bugged. "Can you describe them?" I asked, once I felt we were safe from curious ears.

"Not really. I know it's two men and a woman. They are big drinkers. I emptied two wastebaskets full of crushed Budweiser cans. And that was for one night," she said. "It was more than twenty cans of beer."

"That's four six-packs. That is a lot of beer for three people," I said.

"I know. Maybe that's why the place is such a mess. Stained sheets and pee all over the bathroom. It's so nasty. The big thing is, I got license plate numbers. One guy drives a white Ford truck. I get to the motel at six each morning, and I saw him driving off in it. I wrote down his number. It was not a Mississippi plate. The other two, a man and a woman, drive a rusted Ford coupe. I wrote down the license number from their plate too. It's from Mississippi. I sure hope they're not as bad as the mess they leave," she said.

"Lester, you are an angel from Heaven above," I said, taking the paper with the license numbers.

When she said *white Ford truck,* I froze. I would have bet a hundred dollars the guy driving that truck was the same guy who backed into Marvin this morning. For a moment, I wasn't able to move. But I couldn't afford to be paralyzed by fear, I needed to get this to Chief Carter as soon as possible.

We turned off the water and returned to the hall. I was looking for Pastor Turner to give him the information for the Chief when we heard an explosion somewhere so close the parish hall shuddered in response. Everyone stopped working. Silence filled the room as people looked at each other, straining to hear, almost wishing the explosion would happen again so they could be sure they heard right the first time.

"What was that?" asked one of the ladies standing by the tables, breaking the silence.

"Maybe it was thunder," someone suggested hopefully.

"If you think that was thunder, I got a new Cadillac I can sell you," another voice chimed in, provoking nervous laughter.

The reality was, everyone knew something bad had happened. Alarm triggered folks to start picking up their belongings and head for the door. I realized now, more than ever, I needed to get this piece of paper in my pocket to the Chief. He had told me Pastor Turner was one of his trusted messengers. I looked over and saw him ushering his flock outside to the parking lot, murmuring comforting words as he helped keep order.

First, I needed to collect Dessie. Sitting under a table with the rest of the teens, she was huddled in a threesome of Anthony and another girl. I was proud of their instinct to duck and cover like they had been taught in school. They were beginning to crawl out from their huddle as I rushed over.

"Anyone need a ride home?" I asked, reaching down to help Dessie to her feet.

A smattering of, "No, thank you," mixed with "I've got my own car," and "My parents are here," answered my question. The kids seemed calmer than the adults. Certainly, Dessie was more under control than I was.

"Quick, Dessie. Your papa's gonna be frantic if we don't get home right away," I said, grabbing her hand and pulling her behind me. She half turned to Anthony and mouthed, "Call me." Oh my, shared fright bonds people like nothing else. For sure, Dessie and Anthony would be a couple after this night. But that was a worry for another day.

As we neared Pastor Turner, I felt for the treasured paper in my pocket. I pulled it out and slipped it into his hand. I leaned forward, whispering in his ear, "Make sure you get this to Chief Carter as soon as possible. Tonight, if you can. I think it might have something to do with the explosion we just heard."

For a second, he seemed confused. Then, with a jolt of understanding, he knew he had an important task ahead of him. A slight nod of his head assured me he would do as I asked. He resumed his duty of calming and reassuring the volunteers. I could hear him say, "Go in peace," but there was an urgency to his voice that hadn't been there before.

Fire engines and police cars raced by the Church preventing any of us from leaving the parking lot right away.

"It is going to take forever to get outta here," I said out loud, tapping the steering wheel, annoyed. Adding to my irritation, I watched cars ease out of their spots and start lining up behind each other. I wanted to do the same, but by the time I saw what was happening, someone was behind me, blocking me in. It took at least thirty minutes to get out of that cotton pickin' lot. By the time I pulled out and was on my way home, I could hardly see, I was so mad.

Once back in our driveway, I was in such a temper, I wasn't looking as I grabbed my purse and dropped it, spilling lipsticks, keys, loose change and heaven knows what else all over the driveway. I could hear coins roll, and then jingle as they did their settling dance on the pavement. Dessie tried to help me pick things up, but I was having such a hissy fit over my clumsiness, she backed off.

"Leave it be," I barked. "I'll get it later."

I stormed up the stairs, pushed open the door and rushed into the living room, knowing Marvin must have been frantic with worry. I stopped cold in my tracks. Lord have mercy, Marvin was sound asleep on his chair, snoring even. His recliner was stretched full out like a bed. Roger Moore was running across the screen of the TV in an adventure of *The Saint*. I was getting ready to shake him awake when I heard Dessie giggling. She put her hand over her mouth trying to squelch laughter, but her nose snorted. Hearing my two loved ones snoring and snorting tickled me. Suddenly the tension of the evening released itself. Dessie and I burst into gales of laughter.

We had almost laughed ourselves out when Marvin snorted twice. We burst out again, finally waking him up good.

"Huh? What?" Marvin said, bringing his recliner to an upright position. "What's so funny?"

"Oh, honey. Nothing's funny. You don't have any idea what's been happening, do you?"

"No, I've been watching TV. I must have dozed off. What happened?" he asked.

I told him about the explosion and the traffic jam when everyone tried to leave the church at the same time. I didn't tell him about Lester, the white Ford or giving the license numbers to Pastor Turner. I didn't think Dessie should be burdened with having to keep such important secrets. I figured I'd tell him later.

Looking at his watch, he said, "The news should be on at ten." He got up and changed the channel to ABC. "You sure it was an explosion?"

The staccato drumbeat of the late news theme song filled the room as ABC's local anchorman opened the program with, "Breaking news. A bomb exploded at Beth Immanuel this evening at approximately 8:45 P.M. Few details are available at this time, but our reporters will be on the scene momentarily." The program broke away to an ad for Pall Mall's new, longer, filter-tipped cigarette.

"Oh, no. Not Beth Immanuel. What are we going to do? That's where the school was going to be. We'd started fixing up the rooms already. I need to get over there to see what I can do," I said.

"You'll do no such thing. You'd be in the way. That's a crime scene, Millie. Folks in the Klan are just waitin' for you to show your face, especially at night with all sorts of distractions going on." Marvin said. "No sir, you're staying right here."

"But..."

"No buts, you are not going out. Period," Marvin said. The phone rang. We looked at each other. Marvin waved Dessie and me off, and then motioned not to move while he answered. Listening, his faced relaxed. "Yes, she arrived home safely. Thank you for checking. Anthony, is it? I'll tell her you called, Anthony."

Dessie raced down the hall, stopped short of her father, hands clutched in a begging clasp and mouthed, *let me talk to him, pleeeeasee*. But Marvin held his hand out like a traffic officer and shook his head *no*. When he put the receiver back on its cradle and started back to the living room, Dessie turned away, mumbling, "Y'all been 'round dead folks too much."

"Who is Anthony?" Marvin asked.

"Anthony is the reason Dessie wants to go to the meetings with me. He's Big Tony's son. You met him the last time you were there," I explained.

Marvin shrugged and said, "She'll have to learn I'm not having boys call after nine at night. You tell her that."

Just as I was getting ready to protest being appointed phone monitor, it rang again. I was beginning to like Marvin's new rule of no calls after nine. He answered. Again, he listened. This time, his face told a different story—eyes wide, teeth clenched, lips pursed. He looked so mad, I was afraid he was going to have a heart attack. After an eternal minute of intense concentration, he said, "Thanks, Mayola" and hung up the phone.

"Mayola? She never calls here." I was getting scared.

"Yeah, she was cryin' too. She said, 'They're over here celebrating the success of the bombing.' She was whispering so quiet I'm not sure I got it all, but I think she said the Conrads weren't expectin' her home because it was her church night. But she'd come back early because of the explosion. When Mr. Conrad came into the kitchen to get more liquor and saw her, he told her to keep her mouth shut if she knew what was good for her," Marvin growled. "Can you believe it?"

I closed my eyes, bowed my head in silent prayer and asked the Lord to protect my good friend, Mayola. Then I told Marvin about Lester spotting the white Ford truck and getting the license plate number.

"I bet it was the same guy as hit you over at Giddings place," I said.

"Sure sounds like it. Millie, I need to talk to the Chief again," Marvin said.

"I took care of it," I assured him. "Lester gave me a slip of paper with the two plates."

"Two?" Marvin asked, eyes wide.

"There were other people at the motel with him. A man and a woman. Lester said she wrote down their plates too. I gave the note to Pastor Turner, just like the Chief told you to do," I said.

Marvin gathered me in his arms, whispering, "These are dangerous times, Millie. You did right."

WEDNESDAY, JUNE 7

The next morning, I couldn't get to the driveway fast enough to pick up the morning paper. I didn't care if anyone saw me in my robe and slippers, hair standing out like Angela Davis's new Afro look. The headline said it all—TEMPLE BOMBED. I scanned the lead article as I walked back into the house, horrified.

"What's it say?" Marvin asked, grabbing at the paper.

"Oh no you don't," I warned, pulling it to my chest, turning my body away from him so he couldn't snatch it from me. "I'll read it to you."

"Last night at 8:43 p.m., a bomb exploded knocking down several walls of the education wing of Beth Immanuel Temple. The explosion was so strong, it left a two-foot wide hole in the concrete floor. Rabbi Silberman, head of the Temple, said the building had just been completed two years ago and was going to be used by the newly formed Head Start program meant for the poor children of the community. He estimated the damage at $50,000."

I slumped down in a chair at the kitchen table, utterly devastated.

"You can read the rest," I said, handing the paper to Marvin. "I don't want to read it anymore."

Instead of taking it, Marvin turned on the TV to see if local morning news had anything new. It did.

Standing in front of a podium covered with microphones, Chief Carter was asking for people to remain calm. He said the police department was offering a reward of $10,000 enriched with an additional $15,000 raised by the Jewish community for information leading to the arrest and conviction of the perpetrators of the crime. He promised the department would do everything possible to find out who was responsible. Reporters shot questions at him, but most were impossible to answer. "Do you think the Klan was behind this?" "Have you any leads?" "Why was Head Start using a Temple?" On and on. He did answer "How big was the bomb?" with an estimate of 15 sticks of dynamite. I looked at Marvin and saw the pain I felt mirrored in his face as he shook his head in disbelief. When the station cut away to interview citizens of our fine community, once again, I was so appalled by what I heard, I could hardly speak. Although some were horrified by the violence, some said, "Good riddance."

"You see them interview any black folks?" I asked, rhetorically.

Then, the worst came from the Mayor, "Violence like this is never acceptable. I will never condone it. I guarantee you we will bring peace back to our town. But I suggest if the Jewish community tempered their involvement with Blacks, incidents like this wouldn't happen."

FRIDAY, JUNE 9

When Pastor Turner called to ask if I would come to an emergency meeting of the Head Start committee at ten, I couldn't get dressed fast enough. Normally, I felt guilty leaving Marvin when he had two funerals coming up. Streeter Curry had died last week, cancer having its way with his body, eating deep inside until his six-foot frame weighed no more than 98 pounds. His poor wife Erma had done her best taking care of him, but she was plumb worn out by the time he died. Safe to say, sometimes death was a blessing. His funeral was going to be at one o'clock on Saturday. The other was Granny Hawkins who simply hadn't woken up in the morning. Although she wouldn't be buried until the next week, Marvin had to go to pick her up. Luckily, with Dessie in training, I felt free to go. She was proving to be good at mortician work, and Marvin seemed to love having her as an assistant. Bless his heart, he was such a patient teacher and loving father. When he told her to be ready to help him when he brought Granny's body back to the mortuary, she was dressed and ready.

"I should be home by noon to get you lunch," I called to her, collecting the keys hanging on a hook on the hat rack in the front hall. She usually responded but not this morning. She was giving me the silent treatment. I wasn't the one who told her she couldn't talk to her boyfriend, but I'm the one she blamed. Hunh! If that didn't beat all.

I had to drive the hearse since Marvin took the van to pick up Granny. I always felt like Moses parting the Red Sea when I was driving it. One thing about Southerners, they respected the dead. So, when they saw a big old hearse coming up behind in their rearview mirror, they pulled over to show respect.

I finally pulled into the St. Bartholomew's parking lot. Rabbi Silberman was right behind me. We got out of our cars at the same time.

"That's some limo you got there," he said, trying to be funny, but I could tell he was in a world of pain.

He looked like he slept, if he slept at all, in his clothes. His shirt was wrinkled with a food stain just above his rather generous stomach. His sagging pants were held up by straining suspenders. But his face showed the real damage– red, dull eyes, worried brow, forced voice—all screamed, *Why us?*

I ignored his attempt at normal conversation and said, "Rabbi, I'm so sorry for you and your congregation. It's not right."

He looked at me with soulful eyes and gratitude in his voice, "Thank you."

We walked in silence down the hallway to the meeting room. Pastor Turner stood up and hugged the Rabbi. Father Bob grasped his hand and patted him on the back. Then, as Reverend Larson neared, the Rabbi began to sob. The Reverend pulled him in and held him until he collected himself. No one said a word. We took our seats not knowing how to begin. Pastor Turner finally started to pray, asking for strength to carry on. He said exactly what we needed to hear to move forward.

"Well, I guess the Temple is out," Rabbi Silberman said, breaking the tension. He added, "Sorry, I can't stay today to help plan, but I have so much to do. The only reason I came was to tell you the bomb demolished all our hard work. There's nothing left. Whatever you decide, you'll be starting from scratch." He lowered his head, shaking it back and forth, still in the shock of disbelief.

"We appreciate you coming, Rabbi," Pastor Turner said. "We'll take care of everything and let you know what we've decided."

The Rabbi stood up, thanked us again, and closed the door behind him as he left. I felt sorry for him. I really did. A snakebite had fired me up, but I was beginning to understand how sinister the Klan was. Seemed like they'd bonded with the Devil. A deep emotion I couldn't identify was welling up inside me. The Jews and the Blacks had a lot in common.

"A place to run the school is the question we have to settle today," Father Bob said once we settled back down. "I'm going to be frank here. Our church has been very slow in its support of integration. While the bishops preach the ideals of equality and racial justice, they have done very little to implement their beliefs."

I started to tune him out. First, he talked kind of uppity about things, and second, he was making excuses for white folks not changing their ways. I almost missed hearing him say, "Luckily, the congregants of my parish are embracing the Vatican II mandate to embrace social justice, so I'd like to offer two of our rooms in the parish hall to Head Start."

I wasn't up on all that Vatican talk, but I sure liked his offer of two rooms.

"Funny, you should offer," Reverend Larson said. "The senior warden of our vestry called me early this morning to say St. Bartholomew's should fix up two rooms for the program."

I couldn't believe what I heard. Two offers from white folks. I looked over at Pastor Turner. I could tell he was thinking the same thing I was. This was getting very interesting until they looked at me. Really? I wasn't inclined to get in the middle of two preachers. I looked down so quick they didn't have time to corner me with their eye power.

"Actually Bob, it would be easier on us if you held the program at St. Michael's since you have two available rooms," Reverend Larson said. "I've been trying to figure out where we'd put the classrooms ever since my warden called. It would have been tough. I'm not even sure the new parish hall will be ready by September. More I think about it, the better I appreciate your offer. Also, given the low profile of the Catholic church, St. Michael's is less likely to get bombed, though the Klan doesn't like Catholics any more than Blacks or Jews. Or Protestants for that matter. Heaven knows, I've had a fair share of Klan hatred come my way."

"St. Michael's it is," Pastor Turner said, smiling at the quick resolution. "I didn't offer because I knew we'd be a sittin' duck. And we all know, it appears to be huntin' season all year 'round in the south these days. I have been cajolin' members to give volunteer time, and I've spoken with our children about donating toys and books they no longer use to those less fortunate. The best part is the ladies of the quiltin' bee surprised us with two beautiful, colorful rag rugs for the children to gather on and share stories."

On and on they talked. Planning how to get ready by September when school started. I didn't say anything until the end when I finally asked if they had prepared the lists of names of children we needed for the school.

"I've got your list here, Millie," Pastor Turner said. "I think you know all of the families. I've given the rest of the names to the other teachers."

I took the list and looked over the names. I did know everyone, even the Browns.

"Are these the Browns who just lost their little girl?" I asked.

"They are. I'm sure Marvin told you how poor they are. Millie, why don't you take one of your famous gingerbread cakes out to them when you go," Pastor Turner suggested. Then announced to the others. "Millie makes the best gingerbread in the county. Melts in your mouth good, mmm-mmm. My mouth is watering just thinking about it. Maybe you should make one for me too," he said with a wink.

Good thing I'm so dark-skinned, otherwise I'd be scarlet pink I was so embarrassed. But deep down, I was more than pleased by the Pastor's compliment.

⟡Chapter Seven⟡

SATURDAY, JUNE 10

The Curry funeral was on Saturday. I was glad for a one o'clock service. It gave me a little more time to collect myself. Dessie was learning, but there were a thousand details that needed tending to on funeral day—vacuuming, dusting, arranging chairs, putting out the guest book, just to mention a few. Streeter Curry was a popular man so lots of people would be coming to pay their respects. Then too, I was worried the florist wouldn't arrive before eleven. Made it so much easier when I knew how many stands I had to put out for the wreaths. I threw on an old wash dress to run over to the mortuary to get all this done.

When I opened the side door and walked into the entry, I could not believe my eyes. Everything was ready.

"Dessie," I called out, standing dumbstruck in the vestibule.

"Yes, ma'am," Dessie said, coming out of the chapel with a dust rag in her hand.

"Did you do all this?" I asked, sweeping my arm in a broad wave around the room.

"Yes, ma'am," Dessie said with a broad grin.

"You vacuumed?"

"Yes."

"You set up the pedestal with the guest book?"

"Yes."

"With a pen?" I was trying to find something she hadn't done.

"Yes."

"Put out extra chairs and straighten them in rows?"

"Mmm-hmm."

"Easel stands for flowers?"

"Ready. I phoned the florist to ask how many and what time they'd be here. They said there would be six wreaths and four vases. And Mr. Giannini, Streeter Curry's boss at the hardware store, phoned to say everyone at the store chipped in to buy a casket spray. It came about 15 minutes ago. Wait until you see it, Mama. I've never seen anything so beautiful," Dessie said. "Oh, and Mrs. Curry said her sister is going to sing some of Mr. Curry's favorite songs, so I got the music stand out in case she wants it."

Now I was looking for something to say. Dessie had thought of details I admit had never crossed my mind.

"What about programs?" I was certain this important detail had been overlooked. I glanced around not seeing any.

"I haven't finished folding them, but they're in your office. I didn't know who was officiating until two days ago, so I had to wait to finish the program," Dessie explained.

"Who's doing it?"

"An assistant pastor from the Tabernacle Baptist Church, Pastor Worthy," Dessie said.

"Come here and give me some sugar," I said, my awe in her abilities overriding my slightly injured pride. Reaching to give her a big hug, I added, "You have made me so proud. I can't believe you've done everything and then some."

"Well, Mama," giving me a quick hug, "between the snake bite, the voter registration meetings and the school meetings, you've had lots on your plate. I actually enjoy working with Papa and learning how to do all this. Now I got to go wash up." And off she went.

I realized I had to get ready too, but with everything being done, it seemed more a leisurely process. Glowing with satisfaction, I went back to the house. My black suit was hanging on the door of my closet, waiting for me as always.

One o'clock came. I stood by the guest book pedestal, greeting the mourners and handing out programs. Suddenly, Dessie stepped right in front of me, nudging me to step back. With a glowing smile and a voice tuned to perfection with sympathy, she started handing programs to the guests. Didn't take but two minutes to see why. Anthony Harrison, accompanied by his father Big Tony, was standing in line. I must say, that young man did look mighty handsome, all dressed up in his Sunday best. I heard the tone of Dessie's voice change when he stepped forward. It sounded sweeter, more inviting. And the smile that spread across his face and look of adoration in his eyes said it all.

I realized Dessie knew all along Anthony was going to be here because Big Tony was Streeter's youngest son which, of course, meant Anthony was his grandson. Now I understood all the hard work and attention to detail. I had to stifle a laugh at how naïve and manipulated I'd been. My baby girl was no baby anymore. She was a beautiful young woman, and I wasn't the only who noticed.

The service was a fitting tribute to a man who had served in the Great War and worked for the same family business for forty-four years until he was struck down by cancer. Even a few white folks came to pay their respects. They told me Streeter was their "go-to" guy at the hardware store. If he didn't know where something was in the store, it wasn't there.

At the end of the service, Pastor Worthy invited everyone to the repast at the Curry home following the interment at the black cemetery. Finally, watching Big Tony and his brother help Streeter's wife Cilla follow the casket to the hearse waiting out in front, I realized Anthony was one of the pallbearers and Dessie was the assistant at the end of the procession. Her papa must have appointed her to that position. She'd be helping him at the cemetery. I was none too happy about that. I needed her to help me. I had to get all the flowers and wreaths into the van and over to the Curry home before the repast started. No matter, I had done it alone before, I could do it alone again.

Once the last person left, I loaded up the van and headed over to the Curry's. Luckily, a group of ladies from the Tabernacle were at the house getting everything ready for the reception. Lord, the spread they'd set out was amazing. Hams, fried chickens, sweet potato pies, bowls set out for greens and peas heating in the kitchen, a rainbow of jello dishes, and biscuits, jams and cakes. Separate tables held large pitchers of sweet tea, water, and punch. I hoped Cilla had a big freezer because she was going to have enough food for a couple of months. I placed the flowers so that each table was decorated, and each room had a tribute. No sooner had I finished than the Curry car pulled up in front.

Normally, I would disappear before the mourners came, but not today. I knew Dessie was going to attend, keen on being with Anthony. I needed to keep an eye on her. She would never believe me if I told her I knew what she was feeling. I knew what first love was like—heart pitter-patting, warm feelings surging, good sense out the window. I needed to remind her papa, too. Seventeen-years-old boys were no different.

About the time the reception was slowing down, Dessie came up to me. "Mama, Anthony wants to take me for some ice cream," she said in the sweetest voice you ever heard.

"Isn't there enough to eat here?" I interrupted, thinking I was being funny. Dessie looked at me with such disappointment, I realized my mistake so quickly added, "Of course. Go ahead. But don't be too long. Anthony has obligations today. And remember, behave like a lady."

"I will, Mama," she said, then floated off to Anthony.

With all that had happened over the past few weeks, I figured Dessie starting to date Anthony was part of the natural order of life. I didn't like it, but at least it was expected.

An hour later, Anthony dropped Dessie off in front of our home. As she walked in, I hounded her like mothers everywhere in the world. I wanted to know everything.

"Dessie," I called from the kitchen. "Come on in here and tell me all about it."

I was putting some food together. We'd had so much at the repast, we didn't need much dinner. In fact, I really wasn't hungry but felt I needed to fix some cornbread and collards for

Marvin. Men needed three meals a day or they didn't think they'd eaten.

"What do you want, Mama?" Dessie asked, walking in. As if she didn't know.

"For starters. Was that his car or his papa's?" I asked.

"His papa's. But he said he was saving up to buy his own." I liked that answer. Shows Anthony's got ambition.

"Where'd you go?" I asked.

"Over to the Esso."

"And?"

"And what? We got some ice cream," she mumbled.

"Did you eat it there? Or go to a park or somewhere else?" I asked. I was getting frustrated. I was expecting her to be bubbling excitement. Instead this was like pulling teeth.

"Yeah."

"Yeah, what?"

"Yeah, we ate it there." She said.

"Dessie, this isn't like you. I thought you'd be floatin' on air. What's goin' on?" I asked, truly baffled by her lack of enthusiasm. When I saw her eyes brimming with tears, I knew something was very wrong.

"Oh, Mama, Steve Conrad and his buddies drove up. When he saw me sitting with Anthony all happy and smiling, he and his friends came over and started jumping on the fender making it bounce something fierce. They were laughing, making nasty remarks as they rocked the car. If it hadn't been for Mr. Giddings, I don't know what we'd a done. It was so humiliating. Not only that," she said breaking into tears, "as he was getting into his truck, he looked back, pointed at me then

97

pulled back to make a slitting motion across his neck." Sobbing she said, "I was so scared."

"Marvin, come in here, if you please," I called out.

Thinking dinner was ready, Marvin appeared at the door. His face changed from a smile to furrowed brow and pursed lips when he saw Dessie slumped in a dining chair, head buried in her arms folded on the table.

"What's goin' on?" he asked.

"We need a family meeting."

"I can see that," he said, pulling up a chair next to Dessie and putting his hand on her back. "What's the matter, Des? Tell me."

She sat up, wiping her face with the back of her hand. Marvin reached in his pocket to pull out his hankie and gave it to her. She took it, wiped her face, blew her nose and told her story to her papa. As Dessie calmed down, I saw Marvin anger up. I matched his fury, finally owning the deeply hidden awareness of injustice I had always tried to deny. At that moment though, I wanted to rebury my resolutions and protect my child.

When she finished, I piped in, "My question is, how should we continue?" I looked directly at Marvin. "First, you're assaulted by some mad bomber..." Hearing about Marvin's ordeal for the first time, Dessie sat up straight, turning her head quickly to stare directly at her papa. I realized my mistake, but it was too late, so I started talking loud and fast. "Yes, your papa was almost attacked at the same gas station day before you were. And then all those phone calls. We can't answer the phone in our own home without our hearts racin'. Oh, and don't forget me gettin' bit by a snake. I was off work for three weeks. Is workin' for other people's betterment worth sacrificing ours? That's what we have to decide. I'm ready to tell Pastor Turner we are through. No more. It's too much to ask of us." When I finished my tirade, I crossed my arms and waited for my family to agree with me. The silence that followed did not please me.

"Mama," Dessie started, "How can you say that? What about Mayola and Lester? They're risking their jobs and their lives to help. Or how about all the children who are going to be helped by Head Start? How can we quit now? I was scared, but the Steve Conrads of this world need to know their bullying isn't right."

"Dessie's right," Marvin said. "The Klan wants you to quit. That's why they do what they do. If they get enough people to quit, they don't have to change. They win."

"I can't say I like it, but I know you're right," I said, taking a deep breath for renewal. "I guess this means we're in."

SUNDAY, JUNE 11

After going to church and praying for strength, I spent the afternoon making gingerbread cakes. Four in all. I made each one special, thinking of the person it was for while I stirred. I planned to deliver three of them personally, the fourth was for our dinner. Placing each cake on a piece of cardboard I'd made from cutting up a box, I dusted them with powdered sugar and covered them with Saran wrap. They looked right pretty, even if I did say so myself.

"Marvin," I said, interrupting his nap as he "watched" a ball game on TV, "I'm heading out for a little while. I'll be back in about an hour."

"Okay. Did I smell a cake baking?" he asked.

"You did, but don't you go eating it now. It's for dessert tonight," I ordered. Marvin laughed and waved as I walked out.

Afternoon build-ups lay across the sky. June was already so hot, I hated to think what July and August were going to be like. In the five minutes it had taken me to secure the cakes in the back of the van and jump in the front, I'd broken into a sweat. My mama used to correct me, saying, "Millie, men sweat, girls glow." If that was true, I was glowing like a thousand June bugs on a hot summer's night.

The drive across town took a while. Mississippi roads outside of downtown were not very good—two lanes with steep culverts on either side. I took my time, careful to avoid potholes in the road. Potholes were like weeds. The more rain there was, the bigger they got.

The Esso sign at the service station loomed overhead as I pulled around the driveway to the back where Mr. Giddings' house sat. There was a time when Mr. Giddings had a reputation of having the cleanest, friendliest station in the county. At the Giddings' Esso, customers could get their automobile lubricated and washed while waiting in the make-shift lounge Mrs. Giddings had created. For a nickel, a person could buy an ice-cold Coca-Cola to sip on while savoring one of Mrs. Giddings' delicious homemade lemon bars. Poor Mrs. Giddings. She was never able to have children. She always said the Lord blessed her with the love of her life and the opportunity to be of service to weary travelers who passed through their station.

But in the difficult years leading up to her death, she watched Mr. Giddings slowly lose his will to maintain the house or the station. The white washed cladding on the exterior of the house was weathered and cracked, nails popped out reflecting sunlight like abandoned Jacks spread across the floor forgotten by some careless child. The rickety railing leading up the steps towards the front door leaned to the left and was missing some balusters. Moss had overgrown the roof towards the back of the house where an ancient hackberry tree had been growing since the early 1800s.

Mr. Giddings had hired high school boys to work the station in the late afternoons and on Sundays, so I hoped he was home. I felt reassured when I saw someone pass behind the curtain drawn across the front window. Same time as I stepped out of the van, Mr. Giddings stepped out on his porch, the boards squeaking under the strain. He held his hand up to his forehead shading his eyes so he could see who was visiting.

"Well, as I live and breathe, if it ain't Millie Howard," he said, watching me open the back of the van.

Mr. Giddings was a short man with balding hair and a thinning frame. Looked like he hardly ate anymore. Before settling down with Mrs. Giddings at the Esso, he'd made a reputation as an amateur boxer. I remember Marvin once called him a light welterweight. For the longest time, I thought he was referring to the color of Mr. Giddings' skin. Oh Lord, I was mighty embarrassed when I learned that was a category used to define a boxer's weight. Seemed to me his apparent frailty led Steve Conrad and his like to underestimate him, but they misinterpreted his indifference for a lack of ability.

"Whatcha got there?" Mr. Giddings asked peering through glasses thick as coke bottles.

I picked up the cake, holding it for him to see.

"Is that what I think it is?" he asked, smiling. "One of your famous gingerbread cakes I've heard about all my life?"

"It is, Mr. Giddings. It is," I said, pleased as punch with his compliments.

"To what do I attribute this honor?" he asked, then added, "Where are my manners? Come inside out of the heat." When I hesitated, he said, "I won't bite. Come on in."

Cautiously, I handed the cake to him and climbed the three squeaky steps to his front porch. He opened the door and motioned with his hand for me to come inside.

The house was cooler than the outside but not by much. I remembered how awful summers were in a house without air conditioning and tried not to show my discomfort. Secretly, I blessed Marvin for his investments in our window units. Mr. Giddings must have seen my look because he raced over to a window, pulled back a curtain and turned on a hidden unit.

"Ever since my wife died, I've not cared about the weather. She was the one who was more sensitive to the heat, fanning herself all the time," he said. "In fact, you have a similar look. Would you like a Coke or water?"

"Water'd be fine," I said and blurted out, "I made the cake for you to thank you for being so brave and saving my husband and child this past week."

He shook his head. "There's some bad people in our town and some from outside who want nothing more than to harm others. Ever since I fought in the war in Europe, I said, no more. Not if I can do anything about it. I saw what that devil Hitler did to the Jewish people. But enough on me, I'm rambling. How is Marvin? Not sure I remember your daughter unless she was the girl with Big Tony's boy."

"That's her. Her name is Dessie. She was mighty scared. Said she didn't know what woulda happened if you hadn't helped 'em out," I said. I was about to say more when a knock at the door startled us.

"Hunh," he said, "I go for months with nobody visitin', and now I have two in one afternoon."

I felt a slight cooling coming from the window unit as it revved up to full power. I hadn't planned on staying this long, but I didn't know how to excuse myself. Mr. Giddings seemed so hungry for company.

I heard him say when he opened the door, "Afternoon, Chief. This is a surprise. Come on in. You're just in time. Millie Howard is here and brought me a 'thank you' cake."

"I've heard of her cakes. Gingerbread is it?" the Chief asked.

Oh my, I didn't know my cake had such a reputation. I remember thinking maybe I should have gone into business but knew I had enough to do.

"Millie," the Chief said, taking off his hat, hoisting up his belt and adjusting his holster, "I was trying to figure out how to talk to you. Now I don't have to do no more figurin'. It's the fates puttin' you here. Didn't know how to let you know you did the right thing when you gave the note with those license plate numbers to Pastor Turner. He got 'em to me right away. We've been able to identify two of the three people. The guy who drove the truck is a guy named Randy Randall. The other car is registered to a Norman Fielding. We don't know who the woman is yet, but we're working on it."

When he revealed all that information right there in front of Mr. Giddings, I musta looked panicky. Right away he added, "Don't worry. Ted here, I mean, Mr. Giddings is on your side. We've got more people 'n you know working to stop the Klan."

"Speaking of the Klan, that Conrad boy and his gang were up to no good yesterday. They were rocking Big Tom's car fixin' to tangle with Anthony and Dessie," Mr. Giddings interrupted, looking at me for confirmation. "That's why Millie's here with the thank you cake. I ran him off. That and the other day some mean ass, 'scuse my French, some troublemaker in a Ford truck was getting ready to hurt Marvin when I ran him off too. That musta been that Randy feller."

The Chief perked up and looked at me. "Sounds to me like we're talking about the same truck. What'd you think, Millie?"

I shrugged, tilting my head, hands up, "Maybe." Even though I was sure it was.

"I ask because we think these three were in town to bomb the Temple the other night," Chief said.

Hearing the Chief confirm what I'd been suspecting set the hair on the back of my neck straight up. I had to swallow hard.

"Millie, talk to your source. Ask them to keep their eyes open. If any one of those three comes back in town, I need to know right away. Word's out they plan to harm the Rabbi," the Chief said with a grim expression.

I was so tongue-tied, I couldn't answer.

"Can you do that for me, Millie?" he softened his voice.

"Yes, sir. I will," I whispered.

I excused myself saying I had another cake to deliver. I had been planning to take one to Pastor Turner, but it was getting too late. I needed to get home to make dinner and to tell Marvin what I had learned. Turning onto the highway, I glanced over as I passed the Dixie Inn. I thought of what I needed to tell Lester when I saw it—a white Ford truck.

Chapter Eight

MONDAY, JUNE 12

I got up this morning full of hope. Excited even. I had been able to get back to the Chief last night to tell him what I saw. He thanked me and told me I may have saved lives with the information I passed on to him. Time would tell. Either way, I felt I had done something important.

Today, I planned to visit at least four families on the list Pastor Turner gave me. I decided to bring along the two other gingerbread cakes I had baked yesterday in case I needed them. When going out to the poor folk's country, you just never knew what might come in handy.

My first visit was to the Browns' house. I knew lots of colored folks who are poor, but not like them. They lived far down a bumpy old road if you could even call it that. It sure wasn't on any map I had. Seemed more like a path made by hitching up a team of mules to a wagon and hauling it around after a heavy downpour of rain.

Truth be told, I was surprised I found it. All the address said was "last house off Wildflower path." I had no idea where that was. I had asked Marvin for directions on account of he'd been around to the Browns' place to pick up their little girl two months back.

"Remember, their grief is still fresh," Marvin cautioned me.

"I will. Says here, they have five children," I said looking at the list Pastor had given me. "Did you see any of them when you took little Ida back?"

"Yeah. I met one," Marvin said. I could see he was trying to search his memory. "Linda. I think that was her name. She seemed to be carin' for the other children what with her mama so paralyzed by pain. I remember being surprised because she couldn't have been more than six years old, but she was in total control. Talked like a real grown-up. Told me she'd make sure her daddy buried little Ida like Dr. Warren had suggested."

"Six?" I asked. "Sounds like she's just the kind of child we're hopin' to sign up."

"Tiny little thing. Wait till you see her," Marvin said. "By the way, you better wear boots and coveralls. It's pretty rugged out there."

"I can't wear coveralls. That'd be unprofessional."

"Millie," he said, "they'll think you're uppity if you go struttin' up there in your Sunday best." He started to laugh, adding, "And if you wear your Sunday best, it won't be your best for long. You'll see."

"Bless you, Martin," I whispered aloud as I trudged up a narrow path overrun with Kudzu, struggling to keep hold of a gingerbread cake wrapped on cardboard. Praise be, I was glad I'd listened to Marvin. I wore my rubber boots that went high up to my knees and my oldest wash dress. I felt bugs crawling in my boots and under my skirt, and skeeters the size of airplanes circling around my head ready to eat my face off. By the time I broke through to the clear patch of dirt where the Browns' shanty sat, I must have looked all torn up. Sweat poured down my face, my hair frizzed out of control and dead burrs stuck to my dress like flies on roadkill.

I'd seen a lot of shanties in my day, but Lord, the Browns' was barely more than a lean-to. Poor Mr. Brown hadn't worked for two years after an accident at a well-digging outfit. A chain snapped, whipping around like an angry snake and slashed his arm into a useless appendage. His boss accused Mr. Brown of causing the accident. "That lazy good for nothin' nigra didn't watch what he was doin'." No one was willing to hire him after that. His broken spirit, not to mention his never tended to mangled arm, and lack of a job left the family living on what they could raise in the garden or poach from surrounding streams and fields.

Four children of various sizes and ages, all suffering from the ravages of malnutrition, all with runny noses and scabs dotting their bodies like polka dots, scattered as I approached. One ran through the front opening of the shanty, crying "Mama, Mama, they's a witch comin'."

"Hush, baby. That ain't no witch," Mrs. Brown cooed at she stepped out into the light, crossing her arms over her middle to hide her crudely made dress. I recognized the burlap she must have used from a 100-pound sack of feed I saw on the shelves two years ago at the Farmer's Supply store. Her dress reminded me of a story my grandma told about buying a gingham bag of flour during the depression. She planned to make some panties for me from the bag. When Grampa saw her cutting up the fabric, he asked what she was doing. She told him she was making some panties for me. He said, "Oh no you don't. No baby of mine is gonna advertise flour for Pillsbury on her butt." I tried not to smile at the memory.

"Wha' can I do ya fo?" Mrs. Brown asked, unaware of the memory her dress triggered for me.

"I'm Sister Howard. My husband, Mr. Howard, is the town's mortician. He took care of your little Ida. I'm so sorry for your loss," I said.

"I remember," she said. Mrs. Brown didn't move when her little girl, who issued the warning about me, sidled up to her, wrapped her arms around her mother's legs, and started to suck her fingers.

"Mrs. Brown, I'm here to help," I said, trying to sound more confident than I felt. I brushed a few burrs off the wrapped cake and held out it out as an offering of goodwill. She seemed to recoil as if insulted.

Just when I thought I had made a mistake coming so soon after the loss of Ida, a little girl appeared out of nowhere and took the cake.

"Thank you, ma'am," she said. She looked up at her mama and added, "Mama, this lady brought us a nice cake. She wants to help us."

Confused, I said, "Are you Linda?"

"I am."

Quickly, I reminded myself I was offering an opportunity. I started to explain our program. Focusing on how the children would get medical and dental help, how they'd get two meals a day, I only touched on how they'd see a different way of living. Mrs. Brown listened, never changing her expression.

After what seemed an eternity, she said, "An' jes how'r these babies gonna git to this paradise o' yurn? Y'all see a car 'round here? Y'all see I got any help 'round here? Y'all may got hope, sister, but me? I ain't got none."

"But Mama," Linda pleaded, "I want to go to that school."

A person without hope is as good as dead. *Dear Lord, let me find the right words*. I talked as fast as I could. I didn't want to give her time to say no. I told her we would come get her children, we would ease her burden, we would send someone to fix the road, we would give her free time to tend her garden. And finally, I assured her this was not charity but a program for all children. It was my last sentence that changed her mind. She didn't want anyone to think she took charity. She needed to keep her dignity.

"Ya shore this ain't no char'ty? Mr. Brown won't 'cept no char'ty," she said.

"Mrs. Brown, I promise you, this isn't charity," I said. I held my breath, hoping I'd earned her trust. I looked over to see Linda clutching her hands together in prayer, squeezing her eyes shut, waiting for her mother's answer.

Mrs. Brown took the longest time then nodded yes. Linda's eyes popped open. She started dancing around, her little head bobbing left and right. "Thank you, Mama. Thank you, thank you, thank you."

"That's enough," Mrs. Brown said, but I could see a slight smile break through her sadness.

With a promise to keep her informed and the completion of enrollment papers, I quietly walked away saying to myself, *"Praise the Lord."* I had signed up our first three children—Linda, Grace and Jerimiah into the program. Hallelujah.

When I got back to my car, I was so full of burrs 'n bugs, I knew I'd have to get home to change before I could make any more calls. I drove down the alley in the back of our place and slipped into the house. Didn't want any grieving family who might be planning a burial for their deceased loved one to see me. Once in the bathroom, I caught a look of myself. Dear Lord, no wonder that poor child thought I was a witch. My hair was a two-foot-wide halo around my dripping wet face. I stepped in the tub to shed my clothes. So many bugs were crawling in and out of my dress, they could have carried me home on their own. Looking down, I saw my worst nightmare, disease-carrying, blood-sucking, disgusting ticks. They were crawling up my legs getting ready to bury their tiny little heads into my flesh and dine on my blood.

"Ewwww," I shuddered and yelled for Dessie, "Come in here, quick!" Luckily, she was close by and came running.

"What's the matter Mama? Are you ok?" She took one look at me and gasped. "You look a mess. Where've you been? Oh, yuck. Did you step into a bed of ticks or something? Eww."

"Could be. All I know is if we don't get 'em off me right away, I won't have any blood left," I said.

An hour later, thanking my daughter but suffering from the indignities of debugging, I rinsed out the tub, taking pleasure in seeing those repulsive parasites whirlpool down the drain. I enjoyed a hot bath and finally felt refreshed enough to restart my day.

After four visits and seven more sign-ups, I was feeling pretty proud of myself. The last stop of the day was a shotgun house that looked like the last three I'd visited. They were all small rectangular houses built about a foot off the ground, fronted by covered porches cluttered with buckets, broken chairs, various sized canning jars, corrugated tin roofs, and slat walls unevenly sewn with wood cut from the surrounding trees. It looked like someone had drilled holes in the walls to allow the summer air to circulate. I imagined they plugged those same holes with newspapers in the winter to try to stay warm. In the open spaces in front of the houses, fires burned under large pots filled with water, soaking out the worst stains from soiled clothes. I saw two women lift the clothes out with a pole and scrub them by hand on washboards. About twenty yards behind the houses were privies as crudely built as the houses.

I cautiously approached the last house on my list. Earlier in the day, two skeletal hound dogs had appeared suddenly from underneath the porch of one of the houses I was visiting, half baying, half barking. I feared I was going to be their one and only meal in a year, but their owner staggered from around the side of his house and called them off.

There were no dogs at this last house, so I climbed the two stairs of the stoop and tapped on the door. I heard someone's steps moving towards the door interrupted by what sounded like someone falling on the floor, followed by a child's whimper. I heard, "You stay right there. Don't you git up," before the door opened.

Standing before me was a rod thin, mean-looking man with a wispy grey beard draped down the front of his coveralls. Red spider veins stood out on his transparent white skin making his face read like a road map. He smelled as if he hadn't changed clothes for months and soap was his personal enemy. He stood in the doorframe purposely blocking me from seeing inside even though it was so dark I wouldn't have been able to anyway. Silently, he looked me up and down, turned his head, spit on the porch just past me. Wiping the back of his hand across his face, he growled, "I don't talk to no niggers. Get off my property." He spit again and slammed the door in my face.

For a moment, I was too stunned to move. Then, dread took over, and I high-tailed it out of there. Once back in the van, I counted my blessings. Between the dogs, the ticks, and mean folk, I was truly surprised I had survived the day. On the bright side, I signed up ten children—all of them black. Only people who turned me down were the white folks. Humph. If somebody had told me way back in May this was what I'd be doing, I'd have told them they were plumb crazy.

When I arrived home, I was eager to share my day with Dessie and Marvin. As I entered the house, I heard Marvin on the phone saying, "I'll be right there." Funny how a month ago, someone's death was routine, now it broke my routine. I was disappointed. I wanted to share my day's successes and failures with Marvin, but I understood. For the next few days, we were extremely busy handling the shattering consequences of an automobile accident. In fact, we were so tired and busy, we decided not to go to the voter meeting on Tuesday evening. Dessie grumbled, but since she had become part of the business, she understood what tired meant. Difference between her and me was she had energy to spare and wanted to be with Anthony. Even so, when I said no, she didn't argue much.

WEDNESDAY, JUNE 14

I asked Dessie if she'd take over while I went to the Head Start meeting at St. Bartholomew's. She didn't seem to mind. In fact, she was quick to say, "I've got it, Mama." I was beginning to wonder if I was getting in her way. Imagine.

Excited to share how many children I signed up, I pulled the van into the parking lot, hopped out and hurried to the office. As I entered, I was surprised to see so many new faces sitting around the table. Two white ladies were sitting together on one side and three black women I recognized on the other. Father Bob and Rabbi Silberman at one end and Pastor Turner and Reverend Larson at the other. The only seat open was the one between the Reverend and one of the white ladies. Oh my, I wanted to evaporate. Instead, I nodded to the ladies and sat down.

"Millie, I can tell from your expression, you're wondering what's going on," Pastor Turner said, adding embarrassment to my already natural shyness around white folks.

"Um-huh," I mumbled.

"Let me explain," Reverend Larson broke in. "We got a phone call last night. Senator Stennis got wind of what we were doing. He said he'd been told the program was being filled with black children only. Because it wasn't integrated, like the law dictates, he was canceling all funds." He let that sink in, and for a moment I felt deflated. Then, with a smile he said, "Millie, meet my wife Jill and a new parishioner from California, Vickie Scott. They have agreed to teach at the schools. They satisfy our need for integration, so the Senator will have to release the money."

I was so surprised, all I could do was grin and nod my head. I liked it. I really did. Almost made me chuckle out loud to think a small group in a small community could outsmart the powerful Senator. I looked at each woman and said, "Thank you, ma'am." Deep down though, I wondered if the lady from California had any idea of the trouble she might be signing up for. Mrs. Larson knew, but did Mrs. Scott? Not a second passed when out of her mouth came the answer to the question I was thinking.

"I have to say, I was reluctant to answer the Reverend Larson's request until I picked my daughter up from Bible school here at St. Bart's, and she asked, 'What's nigger lover mean?' I almost ran into a tree out there in the parking lot," Mrs. Scott said. "Sure as shooting, I didn't expect that from anyone in the Episcopal church. Just goes to show how wrong I am. Jill told me there are bigots everywhere. Even California. Which is true. Maybe they're more subtle about it where I come from. Or maybe I've had my head in the sand."

I've never heard anyone talk like she does. I wanted to say, "You are anything but subtle, but welcome to Mississippi." Like always, I held my tongue. Poor thing. She had a lot to learn.

Not to be ignored, Pastor Turner said, "Millie, you know the three ladies I brought to the meeting, but no one else does. I'd like to introduce our three paid teachers." As he introduced Sister Doris, Sister Lydia and Sister Leona, I thought Pastor Turner had a nice way with words. Without offending, he made it clear the three black ladies were the real teachers. I was impressed.

"I'm certified to teach high school, but I put my dreams of being a teacher on hold when I had children of my own. When they were old enough, I started teaching at a preschool in the Episcopal Church I went to in California," Vickie said, clueless. "I have some terrific lesson plans. One was an art project where we taped butcher paper on a wall then projected a famous painting on the paper. For Head Start children we could use a picture of a quilt done by one of the famous Gee's Bend Quiltmakers of Alabama."

Miss Vickie was full of surprises. I wondered how she knew about them. I only heard about them recently when one of the ladies at church started a quilting group. But I started listening again, almost out of pity as she babbled on, "After talking about the picture, the children use crayons to color on the butcher paper, copying the image of what they see. It teaches them colors and shapes. I bet we could find a book about quilts, or better yet, children might have quilts at home they could share. It would be an awesome lesson."

I saw the sisters look down at their hands, glancing at each other, trying not to roll their eyes or break out in laughter. Miss Vickie was as green as grass when it came to our children, but none of us dared to say anything.

"That sounds wonderfully exciting," Reverend Larson interrupted, "but right now we need to get some logistics taken care of. Harvey, have you found anyone willing to check the children for health issues?"

"I have," Rabbi Silberman answered. "Dr. Rothman said he'd dedicate every Wednesday morning to the program. Said he was giving up his golf game for us. When I pointed out he didn't play golf, he shrugged and said that's why he was able to give us every Wednesday." Rabbi Silberman cracked me up. He was always so cheerful despite everything that's happened to his Temple. He was an inspiration to me. "Big question is," he went on, "where will he check out the children? Bob, have you got any ideas?"

"At St. Michael's we have what we call a crying room. It's where mothers sit with their crying babies to observe the service. It's small but might work. Do you think that would that do?" Father Bob asked.

"Does it come with a mother? Might be comforting for the children," Rabbi Silberman said. Father Bob smiled but shook his head at the same time.

"One of my parishioners is a dentist, Dr. Rice," Pastor Turner said, getting back on task. "He said he would help, but he wasn't sure what he'd do if the children had cavities or needed work."

"Mmmm. We need to write other Head Start Programs to find out how they handle some of these problems," Reverend Larson said. "Jill, would you draft a letter along those lines. Check out where to send it."

The meeting continued with discussions about progress on decorating the rooms, collecting supplies, and organizing donations. I half listened, half remembered my promise to help Mrs. Brown. I sat there, rehearsing in my head what I wanted to say. Ratcheting up my courage, I finally said, "I have a problem." Having been so quiet, when I finally said something, all heads turned my way.

"What is it?" Pastor Turner asked with an encouraging smile.

"How are we going to get these children to school? I signed up ten who live way out in the country. They don't have any way to get into town. No buses, no cars, and they're too young to walk," I stopped talking, letting the problem linger like mist on the bayou.

Sister Doris spoke up, echoing my concern. "We've had a problem with that for years. Most of our families don't have cars. The folks either walk to work or take a bus. Their children do the same to get to school. Some walk as far as three miles into town and three miles home every day because buses don't come out to where they live. Even though this is a big town, the bus routes are mainly in the white parts of town for the white folks."

"I have a big station wagon," Vickie piped up. "I could pile in at least ten children, more if they squeezed in the back. If I made two or three trips, I could get them all there. But I could only do it on Tuesday and Thursday."

The fog was lifting. "I could do it the days you wanted me to come in. Part of my duties would be transportation. I could use the van or the hearse," I said.

"You have a hearse?" Vickie blurted out in excitement. "What a kick. My father had a 1948 Woody we'd take to the beach on weekends. We decked out the windows with these really funky curtains. We could do the same thing for the hearse. Only, we could make the curtains bright and cheery, something children would like. You could put them in on the days you drive. It would be excellent. You know, like the Beach Boys?"

Oh my, this woman had so much to learn. I'll admit, I liked her enthusiasm, but I did wonder if it was a California thing.

"Our driving might work. But that would be a big responsibility. We need to check liability insurance for driving children around," Reverend Larson said. "Jill, add that to the list of questions we have. We need to think this through. Luckily, we have time."

"What date did you have in mind for opening?" Pastor Turner asked.

"Probably the same time schools start in the fall. Labor Day is September fourth. Doesn't school usually start the day after?" Reverend Larson answered. "But, and that's a big but, everything depends on whether Jill and Vickie are white enough to get the funding released."

ᴄᔕᔰ Chapter Nine ᔦᔕᓲ

TUESDAY, JUNE 20

F
unerals at Howard's Mortuary finally settled down enough for the whole family to go to the final voter registration meeting before the June 24th deadline. Dessie's best friend Josey came over for dinner and planned to drive to the meeting with us. After we ate, the two disappeared into the bathroom to "freshen up," only to reappear sporting the new Afro look that I have worked so hard all my life to control with straighteners.

"We haven't seen you for a while," I said to Josey, trying not to let my eyes pop out of my head looking at two heads coifed in a frizzy mess. I chose my battles carefully these days, and hair was not on the list.

"It's been a busy summer, Mrs. Howard. Crops are not too good, what with the drought and all, so we have to work really hard to harvest as much as we can," Josey said, touching her hair gently. I wanted to tell her she needed some kind of product to control her uneven tangle, but I didn't. They were going to have to be a lot older before they'd think I've got any sense or might know something about hair.

"Let's go," Marvin called out, picking up the keys off the hat rack. When the girls appeared, he rolled his eyes and said, "Nice hair."

Dessie looked at Josey and rolled her eyes too, but only after her papa turned to walk out the door. She shrugged dismissively with the tiniest scowl on her face when she saw me looking at her, grabbing Josey's arm in solidarity.

The parish hall was jammed with volunteers and newly registered voters. I was surprised to see the room arranged differently than it had been in previous meetings. Rows of folding chairs commanded the middle of the room, while the long tables we normally sat at lined the perimeter. I didn't know what was going on. I guessed that's what happened when you missed a meeting. Marvin and I stood back, waiting to find out what was going to happen. I spied Mayola across the room and waved. She waved back, making gestures indicating she wanted to talk to me. I was ready to walk over when Pastor Turner stepped up to the lectern and, in a booming voice, asked everyone to take a seat.

"We have a lot to do tonight, so the quicker you sit down, the sooner we'll complete our work," Pastor Turner said. He stood, glaring at us like a strict parent. In no time, the gathering settled in.

"First, on the agenda." Pastor Turner started, "We are very excited and extremely proud of the results of our efforts. We have achieved our goal of over fifty percent signed up. We know many of you have never voted before so we want to make it as easy as possible for you. That's why we've set up homes throughout the county where we will meet in small groups to provide sample ballots to practice with. We've also printed instructions on how to deal with any obstructions people at the polls might present. The folks volunteering to run these educational sessions have also agreed to provide transportation on voting day."

I looked at Howard and grimaced. Why didn't we know about this development? I whispered, "We should have offered our house. Do you think we still can?"

I was so busy thinking I'd missed out, I almost didn't hear Pastor Turner say, "tonight, after a question and answer session, there will be an opportunity for additional volunteers to sign up at the tables under the clock to provide their homes for educational sessions and driving services. For those of you seeking education on the voting process or who are in need of a ride, write your name, address and telephone number, if you have one, on the forms on the tables under the cross. We'll try to match you with your closest brother or sister's host house." Pastor Turner waited a moment, checking his notes and asked, "Any questions?"

Hands shot up all over the room. The first person Pastor Turner acknowledged almost ruined the whole night.

A tall, dark-skinned man stood up. Holding his cap, revealing close-cut gray hair, his long arthritic fingers nervously turned the rim like prayer beads. He said, "Sir, when I went to that registrar's office to sign up, he did everythin' he could to befuddle me. Claimed he couldn't read my writin,' made me fill out the form three different times, each time makin' me wait an hour in between. He finally had to accept it. I never have voted so I was proud to think I could. Two days later, my boss calls me in 'n says, 'I heard you registered to vote. You do, you don't work here no more.' I can't vote if I'm gonna' lose my job."

As he stood there, confessing his distress, a smattering of "same thing happened to me," and "Oh Lawd, they got my address." And "They know where I work."

Big Tony stood up, not waiting to be called on. I thought the old man's story was ominous until Tony looked around at the crowd and said, "Y'all know where I work. Today there was a private luncheon. I don't have to tell you who was there. Yep, the same registrar and his cronies. They figured out a way to stop us from votin'. Gonna close seven polls on the black side of town. The two they leave open will be open from 11 to 2. No way we can get everyone there and finished in that time." Big Tony didn't get to finish what he knew.

"Can they do that?" "What are we gonna do?" "Pastor, it ain't right." "Pastor, it ain't fair." A roar of complaints filled the room.

Pastor Turner put his arms up, palms facing down, pulsing for quiet. It took a few minutes to restore order. Small groups still grousing gave Pastor Turner more time to think of what to say. I looked around watching the group settle in and was surprised to see Reverend Larson stride down the middle aisle and sidled up to Pastor Turner, whispering in his ear. The sight of a white man standing next to Pastor Turner silenced the crowd immediately.

Looking up at the questioning faces, Reverend Larson said, "Some of you know me. Those of you who don't, I'm Reverend Larson from St. Bartholomew's Episcopal Church. I came here tonight to tell your Pastor exactly what this gentleman just told you. It is true. I heard the same scheme today. I hoped Pastor Turner and I could work out what to do before your meeting tonight, but obviously I didn't make it in time."

Pastor Turner, having collected his thoughts, said, "Clearly, this news changes everything. I suggest we say a prayer of thanks we learned this plot before election day. We will not continue the question and answer part of the meeting.

Unlike most meetings, we found out in two statements what we needed to know." A nervous chuckle rose from the gathering. He continued, "Before you go, please take the time to sign up to either teach folks about the election process or, if you're a first-time voter, to find out how and where to vote. I know for some of you it's going to be a hardship, but I'd like to regroup here on Thursday evening, same time. By then we will have the matchups of names and places and a plan for solving our newly discovered roadblocks. And that's it for tonight, my friends." He did not waste any time on further discussion. He bowed his head, raised his arms to the heavens and said, "Let us pray."

Marvin and I signed up to be one of the places for education. Before we left, I wanted to catch Mayola. I spotted her with a cluster of ladies deep in conversation.

"Whatcha talkin' about?" I asked, insinuating myself into their whispered discussion.

Looking up and seeing me, Mayola pressed her index finger to her lips. I looked around but didn't see anyone I thought was a threat.

"We're not sure about that minister," Mayola hissed. "Can't trust white people anymore."

My heart sank. The Klan was responsible for all this. They've put the fear of God into us. What could I say? I didn't...I couldn't go down that road. Not when I knew different.

"No, Reverend Larson is one of the good men. Pastor Turner trusts him completely. I know that for a fact," I said. "Don't you remember how fondly Buddy Murray talked about him?"

"Oh yeah. Come to think of it I do," Ella May said, brightening up with the mention of Buddy. "He even said James Meredith took to him."

A chorus of "Uh-huhs" lightened the growing, and probably justified, paranoia.

"Mmm, I guess you're right," Mayola said, reluctantly. "The Conrads have me mistrusting everyone."

I could understand that. I said, "That's what I wanted to tell you. That Conrad boy hassled Dessie the other day."

Alarm registered on Mayola's face. She warned, "Lawd, he's meaner 'n a 'gator when he's sober. But he's been drinking a lot lately, and he's the devil when he's liquored up. If he doesn't get his way, watch out."

"No wonder you don't trust whites, Mayola. I don't know if I could if I were you," I said. She glanced at me, her eyes filled with tears.

"Thank you for understanding," she said. "Working around them is hard."

WEDNESDAY, JUNE 21

I didn't sleep a wink last night. Worry after worry swirled around my brain. First, I stewed about Dessie. I needed to have a talk with her. I didn't want her having sex with Anthony, but how could I stop all those raging hormones, especially since she knew her Granny was fourteen when she had me? I meant no disrespect to my mama, but I needed to point out how difficult life had been for her. I didn't want that for Dessie. I knew she didn't want it either. Babies raising babies was challenging. And grandparents raising grandbabies was exhausting. I wanted to spoil my grandbabies, not discipline them. Although I wished I could have asked Marvin to talk to Dessie, I knew he wouldn't. He'd be too embarrassed. Then again, it never hurt to ask.

I no sooner put one worry to rest and the next one popped into my head. The Conrad problem. If that snake hurt Dessie, I didn't know what I'd do. Mayola's warning felt like a dagger being held to my throat. I had to fight hating that boy. I didn't want to hate anyone. But I had to think of some way to keep him away from my cherished child. Circling 'round to the beginning, I thought about the sex talk. I had to tell myself, *"STOP, you're not going to do anything about any of it in the middle of the night."* And for a moment, I'd relaxed. Then I thought about the registrar threatening to shut polling places. I was so tired of injustices. I'd like to take his vote away. No, not enough. I'd like to have sicced Steven Conrad on him or had him fired. See how he liked it. I kept getting darker thoughts. What was it about the middle of the night that did that to me?

Finally, I got up at midnight, hoping to break my growing agitation and negativity. I wandered into the kitchen and attacked straightening out a junk drawer. By one o'clock, I thought I was tired enough to fall asleep and went back to bed. Instead, I started stewing all over again. I must have slept a little, but it sure didn't feel like it. By first light, I got up for good. If I couldn't sleep, I could make a mouth-watering breakfast.

By 8:30, we were ready to start the day when the doorbell rang. Who'd be calling on us at this hour? We didn't have any funerals planned. More than ever, I wished Marvin had put that peephole in the door like I asked him. With everything that'd been going on, I was becoming super spooked.

"Reverend... Pastor... What brings you here so early? Come on in," I heard Marvin say. Hearing who it was helped some, but why were they here so early? Wiping my hands on my apron, I stepped into the hall and waited.

"Morning, Millie," Pastor Turner said, echoed by Reverend Larson. "I bet you're wondering why we're here."

"Mmm," I mumbled as they neared the kitchen.

"Come on in and have a cup of coffee and some of Millie's amazing morning cake," Marvin said, stepping back, guiding the men in.

I stepped aside as they walked past me and said, "Please," indicating the chairs for them to sit down.

Once we gathered at the table, breakfast cake and coffee ready, Marvin and I looked at each other as if to say, *What's going on?*

"Pastor Turner and I have been talking for hours trying to figure out what to do about the whole voting situation," Reverend Larson started. "Neither of us could sleep last night so we've been talking since five this morning."

Nice to know I wasn't alone.

"What we've decided is we need a delegation to go to Washington to petition the Justice Department to order election officials to supervise our elections. Polls must be open, and hours must be such that workers and domestics can have a reasonable opportunity to vote," Pastor Turner said.

Reverend Larson added, "We need the Federal government to enforce voter's rights as guaranteed in the Voting Rights Act. We wondered if you would be willing to go to Washington with me. For most people, it's very difficult to take time off, but you are your own boss. You won't fire yourself for missing work or voting." The Reverend smiled and kind of giggled. It occurred to me he tickled himself. Sobering up, he said, "Of course it's dangerous. Despite changes in laws, we all know Blacks' traveling in the south has its risks."

Marvin and I looked at each other. We had never thought of going to Washington, but I liked the idea. We hadn't taken a vacation in all of our married life. Maybe fighting for the right to vote was the only reason we'd ever leave our business.

I almost fainted when Marvin said, "I'm honored you're asking us. If we can choose the time we go, we'll do it."

"We'll have to go before August because Congress adjourns for the summer then," Reverend Larson said.

Suddenly Marvin's face brightened. "I've got a great idea. I think we'd be safe if we drove the hearse."

"The hearse from the mortuary? Hallelujah. What a brilliant idea." Pastor Turner exclaimed, almost laughing out loud. "Southerners do respect the dead. In fact, seems to me, they honor the dead over the living. It's one of the few moral truths in this land of selective Christianity."

"Mind you, we share it with the hospital when we're not using it. Bought it back in '59 from Miller-Meteor company who made a combination hearse-ambulance. It's got a jump seat in the back Dessie can use, and cabinets we could use for food and clothes," Marvin explained.

Let me tell you, I was excited and terrified by the idea. I looked at Marvin, making sure I heard him right. "You're sure, Marvin? It's a long trip, and we'd be gone for...," I paused unsure of how long they intended.

"Nearly a week," Pastor Turner added.

"I'm sure, Millie. Time we put our money where our mouth is. We need to go. It's a long trip, but we could share the driving," Marvin said. I was shocked but pleased by his resolve.

"You want Dessie to go, too?" I asked.

"Yes. It'd be a great education for her," Marvin said.

"I could follow you. Not close, mind you, maybe ten minutes behind you," Reverend Larson said, getting caught up in the idea.

"That'd be good. In case anything bad happened, he might be able to help," Pastor Turner said.

"Anyone got a map?" Marvin asked.

"We're way ahead of you," Reverend Larson said, pulling a map out of his briefcase and unfolding it on the kitchen table. "I drew a red line along the various potential routes. Looks like there are about three ways to go."

"Wait a minute," Marvin said and disappeared. He came back holding a book. "This here is *The Negro Travelers Green Book—The Guide to Travel and Vacations*," he said. "I don't think they publish it anymore, but it may come in handy."

"I never knew Blacks had their own travel guide," Reverend Larson said.

"Sir, there's places it's not safe for us to stay or buy gas. There may be laws passed to say we have equal rights, but there are a whole bunch of people who don't believe those laws shoulda been passed in the first place, so they don't abide by them," Marvin explained.

Reverend Larson didn't try to deny Marvin's words. He looked back at the map and said, "I think we should go this way up," pointing out the route with his finger, "and this way back. Don't want to draw too much attention, especially if you're driving a hearse. Since you don't have a body, if you get stopped on the way up, you could say you're on the way to get it. And if you get stopped on the way back, you could say you dropped a body off."

"Sounds right," Marvin said. "Millie and I need some time to think this through. Not sure how we'll handle not being here if someone dies, but I'm sure I can pay someone to stay in the mortuary to at least take calls. For now, let's just say we're committed."

"That's great. We will work out the details over the next couple of days," Reverend said. Then, he and Pastor shook our hands, thanked us for being open to their plans and took their leave.

"Des, come in here," Marvin called absently, sitting at the kitchen table studying the map. When she didn't answer, he looked at me. "Where is she?"

"I don't know," I said. "But I'll go find her." I walked down the hall to her room. "Why are you still in bed?" I said, surprised to see her balled up under her sheet. "Aren't you feeling well?"

She perched up on her elbow, looked at the clock on her bedside table and flopped back down on her pillow. "Do we have a funeral today?" she asked.

"No, but your papa wants to talk to you. Get yourself up and come into the kitchen. Now," I said firmly, a little disgusted she had slept half the day away. I doubted I'd ever slept past seven in my whole life, and even that was late for me.

When she appeared in the doorway, she clearly hadn't put any effort into getting ready for the day. Marvin didn't seem to notice.

"Come sit here," he said pulling a chair next to him and patting the seat. "I want you to see this."

She walked over, sat down, looked at the map and then at her papa. "Umm," she sighed, laying her head down on the arm she had stretched across the table.

"Sit up, I want to show you somethin'," Marvin cautioned, finally noticing her attitude. "We're goin' to Washington, D.C. I'm surprised you didn't hear Pastor Turner this mornin'. He and Reverend Larson were here and asked us to go to the capitol to petition the government to keep the polls open. All we've been workin' for, all you and your friends have been workin' for," Marvin said, emphasizing her role in the task, "could be lost if we don't go."

Not seeing any enthusiasm from Dessie, Marvin scolded, "This is a great honor and opportunity for our family. For safety, we'll take the hearse. Probably drive straight through the first day. Look here on the map," Marvin pointed out the route Reverend Larson had highlighted, "spend two or three days in the city," tapping his finger on D.C., "then come home. Might take two days gettin' back because we'll take a longer route," running his finger on a different route.

Dessie sat up, but her shoulders slumped. She started to say something, then stopped short. I could tell she wasn't overjoyed. Marvin looked at her expectantly. When she didn't react as expected, he said, "What's the matter with you? This is the trip of a lifetime."

"Mmm," was all she replied, showing little interest. At first, I was baffled by her reaction but gradually realized she was more concerned about not seeing Anthony than interested in a trip that would take her away from him.

"I don't understand your attitude," Marvin said. "I thought you'd be happy."

"It's Anthony, isn't it?" I said. When she looked down at her hands, I knew I was right.

"Anthony? Well, I'll be," Marvin said, letting the sound of the "e" linger in the air before he continued. "Let me settle this for you, Dessie. You are not stayin' here so you can be with some boy. You are goin' with us. And that is final."

c╱╲Chapter Ten╲╱

THURSDAY, JULY 6

5:30 a.m.–I dialed Reverend Larson's house, let it ring twice and hung up. That was our signal we were on our way. We agreed he would take off about fifteen minutes after us, following our route.

The last three weeks had been a flurry of activity getting ready for this moment. We had two funerals to attend to, but that was routine for us. Preparations for the trip took the extra effort. Marvin told the hospital the hearse needed work, and he'd do it. Said it would take at least a month. He did work on it, making sure the engine was in good working order with good tires and even a new spare. He'd spent hours memorizing the roads we planned to take. Reverend Larson provided us with really good maps from a place called Triple A.

Marvin also had to hire someone to take calls in case someone died. I suggested Mr. Brown. I wasn't sure why, but I trusted him. He didn't have a job and given where he lived, I didn't think he'd mind sleeping on a makeshift bed of blankets on the rug in my office. Turned out he was grateful for the work and needed only a few lessons on what to say when he answered the phone.

My part was to pack sandwiches, snacks and drinks. I made sure to bake two cakes—one for the family in a home Pastor Turner arranged for us to stay in Washington and one for the family in Spartanburg, South Carolina on our trip home. Deciding on what clothes to take was easy. Dress for hot and hotter.

Sitting on the front seat with Marvin, I was the map reader. Marvin called me his "Navigator." He thought he was the only one who'd poured over the maps. Huh! I studied those maps as much as he had. I also studied the *Traveler's Guide* for gas stations and rest stops where Blacks could go. At one of our Head Start meetings, I'd given Reverend Larson a list of the places we planned to stop to fill up so we'd be sure we never ran out of gas. I explained most Esso stations allowed Blacks to use their facilities. He'd understood our anxiety. You'd have thought we were planning a March on Washington so much thought went into the trip.

Dessie dragged herself into the back, pillow in hand. She spread a blanket in between the rails where the coffin usually sat, punched her pillow two or three times, and plopped down. Looked like she fell asleep right away, but she might have been playing possum so as to keep us from bothering her. Her attitude had not improved much over the weeks. When I finally threatened to put her at her granny's place 40 miles away, she improved, realizing she wouldn't be able to see Anthony there either.

The first hour of the trip was fun. Only negative was the weather. Ooh wee, it was hot and humid. I knew I was going to miss my air-conditioned house. We drove with the windows down. We tried chatting about how much fun the trip was going to be but soon gave up. The road noise was too much. Every once in a while, I commented on the landscape we were seeing which, to be honest, wasn't much different from Mississippi's. When I looked and saw the first sign announcing Birmingham in 30 miles, my heart started pounding.

"Did you see that sign?" I asked, raising my voice over the wind blowing in.

"Sure did. I'm being extra careful. I'll keep to the speed limit—no slower, no faster," Marvin said.

"Marvin, I think I have to go to the bathroom," I said.

"Millie. If you mean it, we better stop right now," Marvin said.

I quickly pulled out the traveler's book.

"Book says there's a station about two miles ahead on the right. Let's stop there. I'll go really fast so Reverend Larson won't pass us," I said. "Des, you got to go to the rest room?"

"No ma'am. I'm fine," Dessie said.

"I see the sign. Slow down," I said to Marvin, pointing ahead to the right. As he started to slow down, I could tell the place was closed. Looked like it had been abandoned years ago. Two old fashioned red pumps with clock faces stood like sentinels to the past. "It's not open. Just go on," I said, signaling Marvin by pushing my hand forward, in case he couldn't hear me.

"Probably was new when this version of *The Green Book* was written," Marvin said, apologetically. "I think we can trust Esso stations. I'll stop at the next one I see."

"No, let's get through Birmingham first. I can wait. I think it's nerves," I said.

The highway system was far more complicated in real life than it looked on the map. I almost had us going to Decatur which would have been way off. "We're in the wrong lane," I yelled as we approached the off-ramp to the highway going due north. "Move over. We want to go straight."

Marvin pulled over a little too hastily for the car behind us whose driver blasted us with a horn.

"So much for respect for the dead," Dessie laughed.

Once through town, we relaxed a little.

"Let's hope the station I originally planned to stop at is open," I said, referring to my notes. "It should be within the next two...oh, I see it." I said. "Praise the Lord. It's open." Marvin pulled up to one of the pumps. I couldn't get out of the hearse fast enough, Dessie right behind me.

A man came out to fill our tank, nodded his head to the side of the station and said, "Keys in there."

"It was super clean, and we left it that way. Thank you, sir," I said to the attendant as I handed back the key.

"Mighty nice vehicle you got here. You morticians?" he asked.

"Yeah. We're on our way to pick up a relative who died," I lied. I didn't want him to have to lie to the police if they were following us and hassle him about serving out-of-towners.

"Any tips?" Marvin asked.

"Just stay in the speed limit, especially in small towns. Got a few sheriffs would love to brag about ticketing a mortician. They'd call it a ticket to heaven," he chuckled to himself. Looking up at the sky, he added, "Those clouds up there are beginning to look mean. You keep your eyes open. You see rain on the horizon, you think of pulling off for a spell. The gully washers we get around here turn into twisting devils."

Removing the hose, he capped the tank. "That'll be five dollars and sixty-one cents."

Soon as Marvin paid, he asked for the record book in the glove compartment. We kept detailed records since we shared the car with the hospital. After doing some calculations, he wrote:

Date	Mileage	Gal	$/gal	MPG
7/6/67	56,315	17	$0.33	11

"Price of gas is skyrocketing. Ever since the gas wars in April, those Arabs have been jacking up the price," Marvin complained, slipping the pencil in the slot, closing the book and handing it to me. I wanted to say everything was getting expensive, but I let it go.

"Before we get going, I'd like a sandwich and some tea. I'll pull forward so as not to take up space," Marvin said.

I turned around to motion to Dessie to get out some food, but she was already pouring tea into cups. It was like a picnic without the bees. I really kind of enjoyed it. I would have liked it more if it hadn't been so hot. Just as we were finishing, we saw Reverend Larson pull into the station. Another man I'd never seen was in the car with him.

"Oh, there's Reverend Larson. Who's that in the car with him?" I asked, gathering the napkins and paper and stuffing them into a trash bag.

"Don't know. But if he's supposed to stay fifteen minutes behind us, we'd best be on our way," Marvin said, turning on the engine and, with a slight nod of his head at the Reverend, took off toward the highway ramp.

For the next hour and a half, I watched the sky grow darker as it slowly sank to the ground. I could feel the temperature drop while the humidity rose. Any worse and it might have rained inside the car. When I saw broken branches whip across the road as the wind picked up, I sensed impending danger.

Dessie must have felt it too because she said what I was thinking. "Papa, do you think we ought to find a place to stop for a while? Didn't that gas station man say a storm was brewing?"

Too late. With unexpected ferocity, the heavens opened up. Suddenly, we were driving in blinding rain. Marvin slowed down immediately, turned on his headlights and the windshield wipers to full speed. It was as if someone was throwing buckets of water at us. Something slammed against the side of the car, jolting any sense of security we falsely held. I tried not to show the fear I felt, but I wondered if we were in the middle of a tornado.

"I don't want to close the windows, but if we don't, I'm afraid debris is going to hit me in the head," Marvin said as he rolled up the window to shut out the storm.

"Oh Lord, I see flashing lights ahead," I said. "Dessie, hide. If there's trouble, don't say a word."

I watched Marvin struggle to keep the car from blowing off the road as gusts buffeted first one side then the other of our once comfortable cocoon. All he could do was concentrate on the taillights of the car ahead of us and hope the driver behind us was doing the same. For ten minutes, I felt hopeful we were going to be safe as we inched along. Then I saw him.

Sweeping a flashlight back and forth, an Alabama Highway Patrol officer directed traffic forward to an off-ramp. Rivers of rain poured off the transparent shower cap covering his campaign hat, a broad-rimmed felt Stetson, its high crown pinched symmetrically in four corners. A yellow slicker covered a uniform I knew harbored a gun and nightstick so often used to crush dark-skinned men and women into submission. Every black person feared Alabama's police force. No getting around it, the rabidly segregationist Governor George Wallace and his wife Lurleen gave permission to law enforcement agencies to ignore the law. And the rain-soaked officer was about ready to fulfill their directive.

The minute I saw the flashlight stop swinging side to side and start moving up and down, I knew we were in danger.

"Uh-oh," I murmured.

"Just keep your hands in plain sight on your lap and don't move," Marvin instructed, trying not to move his lips. "Dessie, you pretend you're asleep if he shines his light in on us."

"Okay," Dessie whispered. I could tell she was fighting back tears. I felt so guilty about insisting she come on the trip. If we ended up hurt or in jail, I'd never forgive myself. Then again, if we ended up hurt or in jail, she'd probably never forgive me either.

I watched the officer straighten up, patting his side where the outline of his gun holster bulged. He sauntered over, slapping the side of his raincoat with his flashlight, clearly indicating he was in charge. He walked to the front of the hearse to check out the license number. Ignoring the line of cars backing up behind us, he took his time striding to Marvin's side and rapping his flashlight on the window. A gust of wind sprayed water into Marvin's face as he lowered the window, but he didn't move. He returned his hand slowly to the steering wheel.

The officer aimed his flashlight directly into Marvin's eyes, letting it linger for a blinding minute. Then, leaning down, did the same to me. I could hardly see when he flashed it into the back of hearse.

"What's a hearse with Mississippi plates and no coffin doin' on the border of Alabama and Georgia. You negras wouldn't be hiding something, now would you? Dealin' in drugs? Hunh?" he hissed.

"No sah, we's goin to Va-gin-ee-ah to pick up a relative who died," Marvin said, mimicking stereotypical slave talk. I almost cried hearing Marvin degrade himself.

"You got paperwork?"

"Yes'sa."

"Well, git it. Don't just sit there," the officer barked.

"It's in the glove compartment. I gots to move to git it," Marvin said.

"Then do it, ya dumb ass nigger."

Right then and there, I had to bite my tongue. If Dessie had ever talked like that to anyone, black or white, I'd have washed her mouth out. But I dared not say a word.

A second officer stepped forward, appearing eerily from a curtain of rain. I thought I was afraid before, but the officer's clenched jaw and curled fists set terror in my whole body. I began to shake.

"Charlie, what the Hell's going on here?" he yelled. "You're holding up traffic. Why?"

"These niggers are from Mississippi and..." our tormentor started to say.

"Who cares? We got an eighteen-wheeler overturned up ahead and a line of cars a mile long behind. Don't we have enough on our hands without you hassling some mortician?" our savior said. Dismissing Charlie, he motioned us forward with his flashlight, saying, "Move along. At the bottom of the ramp, go straight 'bout ten blocks 'til you get to the next ramp. That'll lead you back on the highway, and you'll be past the wreck."

Marvin rolled up the window and slowly inched toward the ramp. As we left, we heard, "Charlie, sometimes I think you're a card short of a full deck."

"Dessie? You okay?" Marvin asked, glancing in his rearview mirror.

"Yeah. I guess," she said. "I've never been so scared in my whole life. I didn't move. I couldn't move, I was so terrified."

"You weren't alone," I said, adding, "I'm still seeing black spots from his flashlight shining in my eyes."

"Me, too," Marvin said, blinking his eyes. Between black spots and heavy rain, I was amazed Marvin was able to find the on-ramp, but he did.

"How come you were talking so funny, Papa?" Dessie interrupted.

"Des, that's a man who likes to think he's smarter than any black person could ever be. If I spoke better English than he did, he'd think I was uppity. We were in enough danger without provoking him," Marvin explained.

A blast of rain pelted the car, jarring Marvin back to the task at hand. He sped up ever so slightly. All he wanted to do was get out of Alabama. We drove in silence for another hour, out of Alabama, through a corner of Georgia and into Tennessee.

"Well, I'll be," Marvin said, breaking the silence and smiling.

"What?" I asked, surprised at his sudden change in tone.

"I think Reverend Larson is right behind us," Marvin said, looking in the rearview. "Yep, it's him. Huh. He's speeding up. I think he wants to pass us."

And there he was, right beside us. The man we didn't know was driving. Reverend Larson, sitting in the passenger seat, was making all sorts of hand gestures. At first, I didn't understand what in the world he was doing, so I simply waved at him. He frowned, shaking his head "no," pointing to himself, then to the front of the hearse. Ahhh. I got it. He wanted us to follow him. I made an 'ok' sign with my hand, indicating I understood. He smiled and turned to say something to his friend who proceeded to pull in front of us. I leaned back, smiling for the first time in hours. Something about a familiar face, a white one to boot, comforted me. Knowing support and understanding were a car-length away eased my tension.

Chapter Eleven

THURSDAY, JULY 6

Two hours later than expected, we arrived in Washington. Making our last stop at a Phillips station to finalize our plans with Reverend Larson, we pulled up right behind his car. Reverend Larson had suggested the new self-service station because the men could talk without an attendant hanging around. At first Marvin was a little confused what to do, but he copied what Reverend Larson's friend did. Turned out to be easy and two cents cheaper per gallon.

As the tanks filled up, Marvin and Reverend Larson quietly made arrangements to meet at 10:30 in the Capitol Rotunda the next morning. No other sign of recognition passed between the two men. The Reverend went one way, we had no idea where, while we drove to the house Pastor Turner had arranged for us. Following Pastor Turner's instructions, we drove to an area called Hobart Place N.W. Driving slowly, we found the row house address he had written down.

When we found what we were looking for, Marvin parked the hearse, turned off the engine and pulled on the brake. We stepped out, stretching our backs. Dessie was slow to push open the back and jump out. Frowning as she took in the surroundings, she mumbled, "Oh brother. Told you so."

Looking up at the slightly dilapidated house badly in need of paint, I said, "Mmm. I'm not very impressed with the neighborhood. When Pastor Turner said we'd be a ten-minute walk from Howard University, I imagined it would be in a better district. Apparently, I was mistaken." My second mistake was thinking our nation's capital would be the model of equality and integration for the rest of the country to follow.

"Now, Millie," Marvin cautioned. But before he could say anything more, a small, grey-haired lady came charging out of the house and down the steps.

"You must be the Howards. Welcome to Washington. Pastor Turner told me I'd know you right away because of the hearse. I'm Agnes Green." Turning around to look up at two men descending the stairs, she added, "And this is my husband Cecil and my son Joseph."

Looking at the approaching family, I broke into a smile so wide, my face almost cracked. I was sure Agnes thought I was either very happy to finally be in Washington or some kind of country bumpkin. She didn't know my smile had to do with Joseph. I knew the minute I saw him, life in D.C. was going to be highly successful. I had looked over at Dessie and, oh my, what a moment. When Dessie saw the handsome son skipping down the steps, she about melted like ice cream on hot day. I'd never seen her attitude change so fast. She went from sour to sweet, from slumped to standing tall, from pouty to all smiles. *Thank you, Lord.*

"We'll help you collect your things and carry them in. Probably best you clear everything out. We've found you a garage a couple of blocks away because this isn't the best neighborhood in the world," Agnes said matter-of-factly, no hint of apology.

"Oh dear," I said, blushing, "I'm so embarrassed. I hadn't planned on having to take everything out. I didn't pack suitcases. I used the cabinets in the back of the hearse like our dressers at home. We'll need some bags to…"

"No problem," Agnes broke in. "You are so lucky to have such a lovely vehicle. Joseph'll get…" She didn't have to say anymore. He was already halfway up the stairs.

Trying to catch Dessie's eye to indicate I was sorry I'd been an embarrassment yet again, I watched her shoulders slump, her gaze shift down. But as soon as Joseph reappeared, handing her an assortment of bags, she brightened up as if nothing had happened. I was beginning to feel like I was on a merry-go-round watching a giraffe rise up and sink down as I circled around.

In no time, we had our clothes, food, and sundries packed. As soon as we'd gathered our possessions, Cecil and Marvin drove the hearse to a waiting garage. Agnes led Dessie and me into the house, escorting us down a hall, pointing out the bathroom on our way to the back of the house.

"We fixed up the screened-in porch for you. It's so much cooler at night out here," she said, leading us into a large room arranged with three mattresses made up with a bottom sheet and a light cotton blanket, a table for our sundries and an empty curtain pole attached on a stand with some hangers for our clothes.

"This is lovely," I said. "And nice and cool. We thank you so much for all your hard work to make us comfortable."

"Soon as you're settled, I've got dinner made. No hurry," Agnes said. She was so cheerful and so welcoming, she made us feel like family.

We sat around a kitchen table enjoying a meal of fried chicken, grits, collards, topped off with my gingerbread cake for dessert. Agnes was such a good cook. I wished I'd made a pie to give them as well as the cake.

"Dessie," Joseph said, "I heard your parents were here for business, so I thought maybe I could take you to see the campus at Howard University tomorrow. I'm headed there as a freshman in six weeks."

I could have kissed that boy's feet for his offer. I'd always dreamed of Dessie going to Howard. I wanted the best for her, and, as far as I was concerned, Howard was the best. What a joy to be with nothing but young, intelligent black people. No whites to take over a classroom or unknowingly push their carelessly assumed entitlement on her. Even if she said yes for the wrong reason—infatuation, I hoped seeing the campus might open her eyes to the future.

"You are?" Dessie said with just the right amount of awe and excitement. "I'd love to see it."

"Mrs. Howard, would you like to go too," Joseph asked.

Oh, oh, talk about being in between the devil and a deep blue sea. I didn't know what to do.

I really wanted to see the campus, but I was here to find out about the voting situation. Was I a bad mother if I didn't go with Dessie? Was I a bad mother if I let Dessie go sightseeing with a young man we just met two hours ago? Weren't we here to get an injunction to keep the polls open? I must have looked pained and confused because Marvin jumped in to answer my dilemma.

"I'd like Millie to go with me. She's been workin' hard on both the voting rights and the Head Start program. We only have one day, and we have a lot of people to see. I'm thinkin' we might have to split up to get everything done. I tell you what, Joseph, you take Dessie to see the University. But you take her to see the Lincoln Memorial, too. I want her to see where 25,000 people gathered to hear Dr. King speak. We came here to work on his dream," Marvin said.

"That's a deal, sir," Joseph said, smiling.

I didn't need to look at Dessie. I could feel her excitement clear across the table.

FRIDAY, JULY 7

The next morning, after a surprisingly good night's sleep, we gathered in the kitchen to plan the day. The Greens had written down a schedule of the buses going to Congress and to some of the major sites.

"Since you were so enthusiastic about the Lincoln Memorial, I included the bus you could take from the capitol to the monument," Cecil pointed to the X on the bus map. "I realize you have a busy day, but the memorial is lit up at night. Somethin' to see. It'll give you goosebumps. I can guarantee."

"Don't worry about what time you get home. Cold chicken'll be waitin'," Agnes said.

As they talked about the realities of D.C. where the President of the United States lived and worked, where Dr. King inspired action, where a Supreme Court supported civil rights, I had to catch my breath. I wanted to pinch myself to make sure I wasn't dreaming. Marvin could tell I was a bundle of nerves and excitement. He placed his hand over my tapping fingers, settling me down.

"If you'll get your purse, I'll gather up these maps and schedules," Marvin suggested.

We were almost ready to walk out the door when Dessie floated in, looking as grown-up as she could. She looked so pretty in her red sleeveless cotton dress. The color showed off her dark skin and eyes. I was relieved she didn't do that silly Afro again but smoothed her hair into a lovely pageboy. I could tell Joseph was impressed. Made me relax a little seeing her so happy.

"You two have a great day," I said, and we left.

Waiting for the bus I had a chance to really look at the neighborhood. Didn't look any better in morning light than it had at dusk last night. I could only imagine how beautiful the houses once were. The bits of color from the peeling paint hinted at former glory but sagging gray steps and broken windows screamed of years of neglect.

Boarding the bus, Marvin paid the fare and whispered in my ear, "Don't want trouble. Let's sit in the back." He didn't get an argument from me. The two seats we found were as good as any tourist bus we could have taken. Even though we had no idea of what we were seeing, for forty minutes we enjoyed the beauty of the city. And when the Capitol loomed on the horizon, I could feel my heart start to pound. Postcards didn't do justice to the imposing size of the dome. I started to worry about how we'd ever find the Rotunda or Reverend Larson.

I needn't have worried. Capitol police were most helpful. Took us a few times of asking, but we finally found our way to the Rotunda. I felt humbled by the daunting size and history of the room.

"I feel like a hick," Marvin said as we stood in the middle of the room and looked up to the dome.

"Me too," I said, rubbing my shoulders. "I'm gonna' get a crick in my neck if I look up any longer."

I walked slowly around the room, studying the enormous historical scenes. I had a funny feeling about the paintings. Something was missing. Starting with the Declaration of Independence, they were all about the promise of freedom. I was looking at the Surrender of Cornwallis when a voice behind me said, "The artist painted a small self-portrait of himself. See the face under the American Flag on the right side? That's a picture of John Trumball who painted four of these pictures."

"Am I glad to see you," I said, turning to greet Reverend Larson. Standing beside him was the mystery man we hadn't met yet.

"Where's Marvin?" Reverend Larson asked.

I smiled. "Right here," I said, pulling Marvin from behind the Reverend next to me.

"Marvin and Millie Howard. This is Gil Reasoner. He's the person who set up our appointment with John Willis at the Justice Department. I brought him along because of his connections in D.C.. Speaking of which," Reverend Larson said, looking at his watch, "we better get going. Gil will get his car and bring it around to the front."

In no time at all we were on our way to the Justice Department building. Mr. Reasoner became our tour guide as we drove along the edge of the Mall, pointing out the Department of Labor, the National Gallery of Art, and the Air and Space museum. Stopped at a signal, he drew our attention to the Obelisk way off in the distance.

"Our daughter is going there later today. Maybe, if we have time, we'll get there too," Marvin said, hopefully.

"I'll make sure we do," Mr. Reasoner said.

Like magic, Mr. Reasoner found a parking space right in front of the building. We entered the Justice Department through two huge doors into hallways of marble and mosaic ceilings. Mr. Reasoner said the building had over one million square feet of space. One million! I was stunned. A person could be lost for months inside this place. Must take hundreds of maids and janitors working day and night just to keep it clean. No wonder so many Blacks came to Washington to find work. Probably all of them were hidden somewhere in this building. That wasn't true, but it tickled me to think of it. I wasn't listening closely, but I did hear Mr. Reasoner say he was off to meet an assistant to Sargent Shriver to talk about the money for Head Start. I blinked, confused.

"We thought it best if Gil talked to the Head Start people alone. Gil knows the system. We're hoping he can solve some of our problems," Reverend Larson explained. "Our job will be to make sure the people who signed up to vote are protected." With that explanation, we followed the Reverend to an elevator.

"Here we are," Reverend Larson said as the doors opened on the fifth floor. "I hope the dear Lord gives us the right words to get the injunction we need." Walking down the hall, counting off the door numbers, he stopped in front of 524. "This is it."

The room we entered was unimposing. A secretary sat at an all-steel desk, typing away. She looked up and said, "You must be the contingent from Mississippi. Mr. Willis is expecting you. You may go in." She reached over to an intercom to announce our arrival.

Mr. Willis was halfway across the room to greet us as we walked in. As simple as the outer office was, the inner office astounded me. A thick carpet bordered by highly polished hardwood floors, a round inlayed mahogany meeting table, comfortable leather executive chairs, an impressive executive desk, quite frankly, the fanciest furniture I'd ever seen. I thought our mortuary was beautiful, but this room made me feel old and out of date. Marvin glanced over at me and smiled, knowing I would want to redecorate the minute I got home. His almost imperceptible negative nod told me to "forget it, it's not going to happen."

"Please, sit down," Mr. Willis said, breaking my fantasy. As we sat down, he went back to his desk, picked up a thick folder and took a seat across from us, leaving an empty chair on either side of him. Although I wasn't savvy in the world of powerful of men, I recognized a man used to power.

"I'm glad you alerted the Justice Department. If your registrar closed polls and reduced hours, that would be in direct violation of the Voting Rights Act," Mr. Willis said. "We depend on constituents like you to let us know when potential disruptions are about to occur." Opening the folder and lifting a stack of stapled packets, he handed three to Reverend Larson who, in turn, handed one to Marvin and one to me. I observed the official Justice Department seal at the top of the first page and knew we had achieved what we came for.

"I understand you've had multiple incidents in your area with the Klan. Am I right?" Willis asked.

"Yes, we have. We're pretty sure Millie, here, was a victim of the Klan placing a cottonmouth in her mailbox when they heard she was willing to work for Head Start and voter registration," Reverend Larson said.

"Whoa," Mr. Willis's eyes widened as he looked directly at me. "You were bitten?"

"Yes, sir," I said, hiding my hand in my lap, not sure why I felt embarrassed.

"And you survived to tell the tale. Well, congratulations Mrs. Howard. You're a brave woman," Mr. Willis said, "That makes this injunction even more meaningful to me." He picked up his packet and continued. "This is a copy of what we're sending to every registrar in the state so each one is not only clear about what the rules are, but each knows the Federal government will take action if the rules are not enforced."

He proceeded to go through the pages, point by point. I knew it was important information but halfway through, I tuned him out. I was busy recounting the snakebite and worrying about the Klan's reaction to the injunction. What more would they do? Maybe my reaction to Mr. Willis's praise was not embarrassment but fear re-emerging from deep within for what lay ahead.

✑Chapter Twelve✑

"**I**'m so hungry I could eat a horse," Reverend Larson said as we exited the elevator on the first floor. "Gil said he'd meet us at a little café a couple of blocks away around one. Doesn't want to have to look for another parking space. It's twelve-thirty now. His treat."

"Sir, we might stroll around to see the sights," Marvin said, trying to beg off. We weren't accustomed to eating out or being paid for by a white person we didn't know.

"Oh no you don't," Reverend Larson commanded. "We'll have lunch first then we will all go sightseeing together." He softened, "Don't you want to find out how Gil fared with his Head Start assignment?"

Marvin looked at me. I surely didn't know what to say. I wanted to hear what Mr. Reasoner had accomplished, but I would never counter Marvin, so I shrugged. Luckily, Marvin correctly interpreted my shrug as a sign I wanted to hear what had happened.

"You sure it's okay for Millie and me to go into a restaurant with you?" Marvin asked.

A glimmer of understanding crossed Reverend Larson's face. He reached out, patting Marvin on the back, and said, "We aren't in Mississippi, Marvin."

We found the Café and sure enough, Mr. Reasoner was waiting. When he saw us, he broke out in a smile that would've made the angels happy.

"Have I got good news for you," he said. He nodded to the waitress holding menus who led us to a booth overlooked by a picture of a gondola heading toward a covered bridge. I felt like I was in Italy what with tables covered with red and white checked oilcloth, waiters in black outfits adorned at the waist with tasseled sashes, and the aroma of Italian spices drifting from patron's dishes. Marvin and I slid in one side of the table, and the two men sat across from us. Looking at the menu, I wanted everything even though I didn't know what some of the selections were.

"Have you ever had cannelloni? It's a big round noodle filled with ricotta and spinach covered with delicious cheese sauce and tomato sauce. I highly recommend it," Mr. Reasoner said.

"Sounds good. I'll try it," I said.

"I'm going to have a glass of Chianti too. Join me?"

"Oh, no, I'll have iced tea," I said. I never drank. Liquor caused too much trouble in this world for me to ever want any.

Marvin and Reverend Larson ordered pizzas and cokes.

Before the food came, Mr. Reasoner told us his good news. "We've got transportation. Not sure you know," he said looking at Marvin and me, "but I have an automobile dealership in town. I have access to all sorts of vehicles. I made what we call a fleet deal for Head Start. The government will buy five VW buses and distribute them to centers in need of transportation for the children. Naturally, our center qualifies because so many of our clients live so far out of town. It's one thing for adults to walk miles to get to work. But little ones? No way. I happen to have a beautiful lime green and white bus on my lot. It will be perfect for children."

I must admit I was delighted. Those children would have been so scared if I drove up in the hearse, balloons or no balloons. They've seen folks taken away in the hearse, never to be seen again. I also had my doubts about Vickie piling too many children into her station wagon. Maybe once they knew her, she could drive. But they'd have been terrified if on the first day some white woman came to pick them up. I didn't want to say what I was thinking, but I didn't have to worry. Reverend Larson spoke for me, thanking Mr. Reasoner for what he did.

Our food came. The cannelloni melted in my mouth. I was going to have to find a recipe to make it. I knew I'd use collards instead of spinach though. More flavor. Marvin enjoyed his pizza. He was never one to try new foods, but when I gave him a taste of my cannelloni, I knew he wished he'd ordered it.

After we finished our meal, Mr. Reasoner made good on his promise. He jumped up from the table, told us to wait outside in front of the restaurant while he went to get his car. He picked us up and took us on a tour to what he said are the most important places to see if you only have one day. The Space and Air Museum, the National Museum of American History, the Lincoln Memorial, the Washington Monument, and the White House. By the time we were through, I was plumb tuckered out. Knowing we were tired, he insisted on driving us to the Green's house. I was grateful. I did not think I could've walked another step. We said our thanks and goodbyes right then because, although we were both driving home the next day, we were taking different routes.

Once inside, I found out Dessie and Joseph weren't home yet. I was a little worried, but really, I was so tired all I wanted to do was go to bed. We had a long day ahead of us, and we needed sleep.

Using up what little energy I had left, I packed as much as I could, after which I collapsed on my mattress. I didn't even remember falling asleep. I vaguely remembered Dessie coming in. Did Marvin warn her she best be ready by five in the morning because that's when we were leaving? I had no idea.

SATURDAY, JULY 8

Mr. Green knocked on the door at first light, which turned out to be four-thirty in D.C.. He told us he got up at that time every day in order to get to work by six. When the smell of bacon cooking wafted into the room, we were up and dressed in no time. Bless Agnes.

Marvin disappeared to get the hearse, while Dessie and I folded sheets and blankets and stacked our bags by the front door. A quick bite, a quicker goodbye, and we were on our way.

I was kind of surprised Dessie seemed okay with Joseph not getting up to wish us good-bye. Lord, if curiosity killed the cat, it was about to do me in. I tried to keep my mouth shut, but I couldn't. An hour out of Washington, I blurted, "How was your day with Joseph? I thought he might get up to see us off."

"Oh, no. After he dropped me off, he had to go to work. He cleans classrooms at the university at night. That's how he'll pay part of his tuition next year. That and an athletic scholarship," Dessie said in such a grown-up manner she didn't sound like our daughter.

"I see," I said, though I didn't. "Tell me about Howard."

"Well, I've decided if I take six classes this fall, six in the spring and go to summer school next year, I could graduate early. I could be at Howard in the fall of '68," Dessie announced.

"Whoa...whoa. Slow down," Marvin said. "How do you know you can get in?"

"Don't worry, Papa," Dessie said with assurance. "We went to the registrar's office and talked to them about what I needed. I've got the grades. I only need seventy more credits and I'm in. I filled out the papers to apply. They're going to send us and my school all the forms and information I need."

Was this my little girl? Where did Dessie go? I could not believe my ears. Marvin glanced at me, wiggling his eyebrows. I almost burst out laughing with joy, but I knew Dessie would have misinterpreted the laughter as mocking. Instead I said, as calmly as possible, "What else did you do?"

"We spent most of the day on campus. We ate in the student union where I met some of his friends. Mama, do you know how wonderful it felt to see nothing but the faces of people who respected me? Who asked what I wanted to major in? Who assumed I was smart? Who talked about important subjects? Instead of that police officer lookin' down on us like the one did on our way to Washington," Dessie said with a passion I'd never heard from her. She was almost shaking, she was so worked up. I suddenly saw how humiliated she had been for her papa when he talked slave talk to that officer. She was too inexperienced to know how smart her papa was to mollify that man.

"I'm proud to hear you want to go to Howard. It'll be hard work, but you can do it," Marvin said.

"Your work with voter registration is important too. Colleges like that. Shows dedication and leadership," I added, keeping the conversation off anger and on hope.

"We talked about that. One of Joseph's friends, Frank was at the mall when Dr. King gave his Dream speech. He was fourteen at the time but said it changed his life. He couldn't really hear it all that well, just knew something great was happening. He took us over to the mall. Joseph said I had to see it, and we stood right where Frank had stood, then we climbed the steps to the Lincoln Memorial and looked out just like Dr. King must have. Gave me goosebumps. Look, here," she rummaged in her backpack, pulling out a paper, "Here's the speech. I've almost completely memorized it."

I did not expect a bonus from our trip, but if Dessie ended up at Howard, no matter what else happened, the trip was a success.

We stopped overnight just outside Spartanburg, South Carolina. Pastor Turner had arranged for us to stay with a woman named Jean. She was a widow. She was a dear and gave us her bedroom with a nice double bed. She and Dessie slept in a spare bedroom with twin beds. Dessie told us later it was her children's bedroom, but they were grown and gone and lived in California.

Dessie enjoyed listening to the widow's stories. Turned out she had been a teacher in a one-room schoolhouse back in the 40's. She told Dessie about having students ranging in age from six to twenty-two. Dessie was surprised by the age differences, but Widow Jean explained lots of children had to work in the fields, so it took them longer than normal because they couldn't come to school regularly. They wanted to learn so badly she taught them until they graduated from the eighth grade.

Widow Jean told Dessie the story of a boy named Thomas Hodges. Said he was a big boy, probably six foot two or three. A shy boy but very smart. Apparently, one day the sheriff came to the classroom and tried to arrest Thomas. She didn't like them bursting into her school but wasn't anything she could do about it. Thomas wasn't about to let the sheriff take him away. He stood up, pulled a gun out from under his belt and shot the Sheriff and his deputy then ran off. Widow said she never saw him again although she often wondered what happened to him. When Dessie expressed concern about the children watching the shooting, Widow said they'd seen much worse. Lynching was common. Dessie tried to make her feel better by speculating he might still be alive and well. And if he was so interested in education, maybe he was a professor or something big. Then, Dessie told Widow about our trip and how she had decided to go to Howard. Widow Jean let out a whoop that made Dessie laugh and smile with pride.

Next morning, we ate breakfast, thanked Widow Jean and Dessie promised to write. I gave her my famous gingerbread cake, and we took off for home. As we drove through Georgia, I found myself holding my breath, but Marvin was steady as a rock. He reminded me Sunday was a day of rest and most folks were either in church or enjoying Sunday supper, not out looking for trouble. He must have been right because we didn't see but a few cars out on the road. But I confess I sang out, "Thank you, Jesus," when we drove into our driveway and saw our house.

Monday, July10

I won't lie to you. I thought I was gonna' be happy getting home to my air-conditioned house. Don't get me wrong, I was. But mercy, there was so much to do. You would have thought we'd been gone a month, the amount of cleaning we had to do. Luckily, Mr. Brown informed us no one had died while we were gone so Marvin paid him and drove him back to his home.

Marvin took pride in his hearse looking fine, but after the trip, it didn't. He spent half the next morning washing his travel splattered pride and joy. He said he didn't think there were any bugs left from here to Washington. They were all squished on the grill and windshield. He spent the other half of the morning bringing in all the wrappers, leftover food, and collected pamphlets from the back where Dessie sat. He polished the cabinets and brass fixtures, adding a final touch of air freshener to clear any hint of stale air.

While Marvin worked on the car, I spent the time washing clothes. Once done, I asked Dessie to hang them on the line outside. She mumbled something about they weren't going to dry in the humid air but picked up the basket and marched out. I happened to be looking through the kitchen window when the mailman came by holding something up. He called to Dessie. She tossed whatever laundry she was holding back in the basket and ran over to him. He handed her a large manila envelope. She took a look at it, clutched it to her chest, said something to the mailman. Racing into the house, waving the package in the air. "It's here," she yelled out. "Howard sent the packet for admissions." She was tearing it open with little regard.

"Dessie. Be careful," I warned. "You might tear something important."

She took a few breaths, slowing down. "You're right, Mama. I'm just so excited. They must really want me to mail it here so quickly," she said with pride. She shook the package over the kitchen table. Out dropped a stapled packet of forms and a beautiful book about the University. "Papa, Papa," she called out the window. "Come...see."

Dessie and I watched him back out of the end of the hearse, spray can in hand. He spritzed one last time before he closed the door, and then turned to look up at us. Dessie called her message again through the closed window. He nodded his head, held up his hand, index finger wiggling as if to say, give me a minute and disappeared. By the time he came inside, we were drooling over the book championing the school.

"Look at this," Dessie gushed excitedly, pointing to a picture of the student union. "I was there."

Dessie and I hardly heard the phone ring, we were so delighted by the pamphlet, but Marvin never ignored a call.

Instead of the usual, "I'm so sorry," Marvin said, "Yes, she's here. You need to talk to her?"

I looked up as he stood with the receiver pointed toward me. "It's for you."

I took the receiver. "Yes?"

I recognized Lester's voice. "Tonight's the night" was all she said. And then, silence.

I held the receiver out from my ear, looking at it, willing it to give me more information, but of course, it didn't.

"You all right?" Marvin asked, a frown of concern covering his face. "What's the matter? What's going on, Millie?" Marvin insisted.

"Mama. Come see this," Dessie called from the kitchen, unaware of my growing panic.

"In a minute," I called back. I whispered to Marv, "That was Lester Ball. Remember her. She works at the motel." I was trying to jog Marv's memory. "She found those notes about Head Start and code three, same time I got bitten by the snake…same time you were harassed by that man in the white truck, you remember."

I could see Marvin struggling to put all the pieces together when suddenly the "ah ha" stirred his face.

"There's trouble coming. We have to get in touch with Chief Carter," I said. "We need to go see Pastor Turner right away."

"Oh, yeah, I remember now. She said there were three of them. Didn't she get their names?"

"I think so," I said. "Main thing is they were here the night the Temple got bombed, left the same night. I guess they're back in town. She promised she'd let me know. She must have overheard something. Oh, Marvin, do you think they're after us? They probably know we were in D.C., and they're coming to get us."

"I don't know, but we better get outta here," Marvin said. He turned and went into the kitchen.

"Dessie, I'm sorry but you're going to have to put that down and collect your things. We got a big problem on our hands. Your mama got a call that might mean trouble for us. We need to get over to Pastor Turner's right away."

Dessie looked up, confused.

"Remember the Temple bombing couple of weeks ago?" I said. "Well, the people we suspect might have done it are back in town. They're after someone, and we don't want to be here if it's us."

"Us?" Dessie said, still confused but trying to understand. "Why us?"

"You're going to have to trust your mama, Des. We've got to get word to the police and to do that we have to talk to Pastor Turner," Marvin said.

"Okay." Fear was taking over her need to understand.

I collected my purse, Marvin gathered his keys, and Dessie picked up the Howard University catalogue and forms. Making sure we locked the house uptight, we packed ourselves in the newly cleaned hearse and drove over to the church to find Pastor Turner. He was pulling out of the parking lot as we drove in. *Thank you, Lord, for good timing*, I said silently to myself. I did not like the feeling creeping up my spine. If I was going to die, I didn't want some cracker to be the one who killed me.

Rolling down his window, Marvin stopped opposite Pastor Turner and said, "We got an emergency on our hands. Hope you weren't going anywhere important."

It was Pastor Turner's turn to look confused. He said, "I was on my way to the dedication of a new fountain in the town square. Can you wait until I get back? I'll only be gone about an hour."

Marvin pushed the gearshift into Park, pulled on the brake and got out of the hearse. I watched as he walked over to the Pastor's car, leaned down and explained the situation. Since I knew what he was saying, I was intent on what Pastor Turner's reaction would be. I sure wasn't expecting him to shut off his car, jump out, grab Marvin by the elbow and lead him into the empty parking lot. The two men stood, talking back and forth. After shaking hands, each returned to his car. Pastor Turner took off, and Marvin drove us into the lot and parked by the back of the church.

"What happened?" I asked.

Dessie leaned forward from her jump seat and, in an uncharacteristic show of affection, draped her arms around my shoulders. "Yeah, Papa, what's going on?"

"We're to go inside and wait," Marvin said.

"How do we know we're safe in a black church?" Dessie asked.

⟪Chapter Thirteen⟫

MONDAY, JULY 10

"What are you doing here? I thought you were still in Washington?" Sister Helen asked, surprised to see us. She put down the flowers she was arranging in vases on two large pedestals bordering the sanctuary. Walking toward us, wiping her hands on her apron, she looked confused.

"We got back late last night," I said. I wasn't too sure how much to tell her, so I looked to Marvin for help.

"We wanted to thank you and Pastor Turner for setting us up at the home of the Greens," Marvin said. Oh my, I was so grateful Marvin could think fast. He added, "They were so helpful and kind. Their son took Dessie to see Howard University. Whole experience was life-changing for us. We thought you and Pastor Turner would like to hear about it."

"How nice, but I'm afraid Nathan isn't here. You just missed him. He had a dedication to go to," Helen said.

"If you don't mind, I think we'll wait," Marvin said.

"Of course. After I finish these flowers, I'll make us a bite to eat," Helen said, returning to place the remaining few flowers into the arrangements.

"That'd be lovely," I said. Normally we wouldn't intrude, but we needed to stall for time. Who knew how long Pastor Turner would take?

Five minutes later, after dumping the stems and leaves into a basket and wiping the little pools of water from around the vases, Helen led us to the kitchen in the church auditorium.

"Sure feels different when there aren't any people around," Dessie said as we passed through the room where the voter registration meetings happened. "I like it better when it's filled with friends."

Dessie was right. For me, the empty room mirrored the isolated feeling I had inside. I knew better, but I felt so alone. Like I was the one responsible for putting my family in harm's way. If I hadn't accepted the Head Start job, hadn't gotten involved in the voter registration or hadn't gone to Washington, we might not be in this danger. At that moment, my resolve was fading.

We lingered over some ham sandwiches and sweetened tea Helen made for us, recounting every detail of our trip, including the episodes with the highway patrol, the successes for voters, the new vehicle for Head Start and Dessie's day with Joseph. She listened to our stories, cleared the table, washed the dishes and, after two hours, started taking side glances at the clock on the wall. Helen must have begun to wonder if we'd ever leave. Ordinarily, I'd have taken the hint she had chores to do, but I played dumb. I was looking at the clock too, and my right leg started jiggling in agitation.

Finally, Pastor Turner walked through the kitchen door followed by Chief Carter. Fear welled up in me like the Mississippi River during a flood.

"Millie," the Chief said, wasting no time, "I understand you got a phone call from a trusted source. Your source is the same source who gave you the information before the bombing of the Temple?"

I shook my head, yes.

"Last time, your source identified three people. Right?"

I shook my head, yes.

I was so worked up, I almost didn't hear Chief say, "The three suspects are in town again. Is that what your source meant?"

"I think so," was all I could say, but I remembered telling Lester to call if she ever saw those devils again.

"You think so? Or are you sure?" the Chief insisted.

"Our agreement was she'd call if they ever returned," I said, realizing I had said "she." I could have kicked myself. If I'd put Lester in the crosshairs of the Klan, I'd never forgive myself.

"Mmmm." The Chief didn't seem surprised. Instead he appeared to be thinking how much to say. After what felt like an eternity, he said, "We have information substantiating what you've told me. These yokels are up to no good, but we don't think you and your family are the target. That's all I'm at liberty to say."

I almost started crying with relief, Dessie's eyes filled with tears, and Marvin took in a deep breath and blew it out.

"You're sure," Marvin said.

"Pretty sure. But for safety's sake, I want you to stay with the Turner's for a while. The Pastor said he and Helen would be happy to invite you to dinner tonight. I suggest you accept."

Looking startled, Sister Helen said, "So that's why you been sittin' here for hours. Why didn't you tell me? Of course, you're welcome. You can spend the night if you want. Oh my. This is so distressing. What is this world coming to?"

"We live in dangerous times, all right," Chief said. Looking at me, he added, "I hope I've relieved you some. You've been a big help and if any arrests come from this, I'll see you and your source get some of that reward money. Now, if you'll excuse me, I've got a busy time ahead of me. I'll see myself out."

We sat for a few minutes collecting ourselves. Marvin finally broke the silence, "Pastor? How'd you get to the Chief?"

"Turned out, he was at the dedication. I took him aside and told him what Millie's caller had said," Pastor Turner explained. "No sooner 'n I got the words out of my mouth, he disappeared like a shot. I didn't think too much about it. I was thinking more about the dedication prayer I was scheduled to give. About ten minutes later, when the ceremony was winding down, he came up behind me and asked where you were. Said he needed to talk to you but didn't want to use a phone. The rest you know."

Life changed so fast. Twenty-four hours ago, I was thinking life was good. The trip to Washington had been so successful, only to come home to trouble. Mississippi sure wasn't D.C.

"I guess we better go to the house," Sister Helen said, getting up to lead the way to the parsonage. Like morticians, preachers' homes were often next to their houses of worship. Pastor Turner was no different. We silently entered the kitchen through the back door.

"Make yourselves at home," Pastor Turner said. "Marvin, why don't you rest in the living room and let the ladies do whatever ladies do to get supper ready. I'm going to change my clothes to something more comfortable, if you don't mind."

As kind and generous as Pastor and Sister were, I couldn't stop worrying. Every nerve in my body was like a jackhammer cutting up cement. Two or three times, I was sure I heard sirens. Each time I said so, everyone stopped talking and listened intently. Each time turned out to be a false alarm. After supper, as Dessie and I helped Sister do the dishes, I thought I saw someone looking in the window. I about jumped out of my skin, dropping a dish I was drying in the process. Finally, I was so fidgety, Marvin suggested we go home. Trying to ease my worry, he said if we were going to be bombed, we might as well be where the action was. I didn't think he was funny at all, but I did agree I wanted to go home.

My concern for Dessie's safety was taken care of with one phone call to Josey. We made arrangements for her to spend the night there.

We thanked the Turners, dropped Dessie off, and went home. Right or wrong, I wanted to be in my own home.

TUESDAY, JULY 11

At breakfast the next morning I remembered Pastor Turner said, "See you tomorrow" before we left his house last night. I had no recollection of what he meant so I asked Marvin if I was supposed to be doing something today.

"You and Reverend Larson are supposed to report to the Head Start committee on the Washington trip. Pastor Turner reminded me about it."

"Good thing you reminded me. I had plumb forgot with all this other trouble. Yes, of course I'll be there. That is if I'm not in a thousand little pieces," I said, as if staring danger in the face would make it go away.

"Now, Millie. Don't talk like that." Marvin scolded.

By mid-morning, since I was still in one piece, I dressed and readied myself to go to the meeting. I was relieved we hadn't heard about any trouble during the night. So, before I left, I went over to the mortuary to discuss my plans with Marvin. I wanted him to know exactly where I'd be and when. He offered to pick Dessie up from Josey's then they'd take the hearse to the hospital, and I'd pick them up there.

The meeting was set to start at ten. I drove to St. Bartholomew's and parked, getting there five minutes early. I walked into the rectory and down the hall to our usual place. Uh oh, I knew something was up when I saw Reverend Larson and Pastor Turner deep in conversation outside Reverend Larson's office. They stopped the minute they saw me.

"What's happened?" I asked, feeling my heart start to race and the hair on my neck starting to raise.

"Let's go into my office," Reverend Larson said, guiding me to a chair.

Good thing because my legs had turned to rubber.

"Looks like your source was right," Pastor Turner said. "You weren't the target, but Rabbi Silberman was."

"Lord have mercy, is he alright?" I whispered. I was having trouble breathing.

"Thanks to you and your source," Pastor Turner said.

"What happened?" I asked.

"I talked to Chief Carter this morning. He told me he has an informant who identified Rabbi Silberman as the target. I guess that's how he knew it wasn't you. But, and this is an important point, until you notified Pastor Turner about your source telling you the three suspects were in town again and saying, 'tonight's the night,' he didn't know when or how the Klan planned to murder him. Your quick action allowed him time to activate a plan he'd been working on for months. Last night, after dark, fifteen officers surrounded Rabbi Silberman's house. Apparently around midnight, a car pulled up, and a man got out of the car. The officers could see a box tucked in the crux of his arm. Turned out it was sticks of dynamite, but they only suspected that at the time. They ordered him to stop. Instead of stopping, he dropped the box, ran back to his car and drove off. As the police chased him, he started shooting at them with a submachine gun…"

The door to the Reverend's office burst open unexpectedly, jolting me and the two men to attention. Vickie exploded into the room. I knew I looked tired, but she looked like death warmed over.

"Oh my God…sorry Reverend," Vickie said, breathlessly, almost in tears, "you are not going to believe what happened last night. My husband and I were asleep when a shattering sound woke us up. My husband looked at me and said, 'that was a gunshot.' He was out of bed in a flash, looking out the window. He ducked and yelled at me to get the kids and hide in the middle of the house somewhere. I almost threw up I was so scared. My husband found us and whispered to me, 'there's a dead man in our yard.' Our house was surrounded by police cars, red lights twirling patterns on our walls—I'll never forget those images as long as I live. We must have hidden with the children for half an hour before the doorbell rang. Finally, some officers told us we were safe. Honestly, I don't know how you all stand all this violence."

Suddenly, as if she'd been in a trance, Vickie looked around the room, blinked her eyes, and literally, came to. She looked at me with such compassion, as if she really understood for the first time what it was like to be the victim of forces over which you had no power and no control.

"We were just talking about the situation, Vickie," Reverend Larson said. "And you're right. The man who shot himself in your yard was planning to kill Rabbi Silberman."

"Our Rabbi?" Vickie gasped. "The police wouldn't tell us anything last night. You're sure? Rabbi Silberman? Is he okay?"

"Yes, I'm sure. And yes, he's okay. A little shaken, but he and his wife are extraordinarily brave and resilient," Reverend Larson said. Then he looked at me and added, "They found the car where the bomber abandoned it. Inside it was a dead woman—from a gunshot wound. They assume she was an accomplice, but they don't know for sure. They also don't know if she died in the crossfire during the car chase, or if she killed herself, or if she was shot by someone else."

"My source knows there was a third person. Have you heard about him?" I asked.

"I don't know anything about a third person, but I'll ask if you want me to," Reverend Larson said.

I really did because that third person was the worst of them all. I didn't want to say anything, but until he's caught, no one was safe.

"Who are these people?" Vickie interrupted, outrage slowly replacing fear.

Compassion for Vickie filled my heart. Reverend Larson, Pastor Turner and I looked at her with sympathy. She was Humpty Dumpty and her wall of safety was crumbling.

"These are people who think Blacks and Jews are subhuman and should either be eliminated or kept in slavery," Reverend Larson explained. "In many ways they've been successful, especially with Blacks. They say they're lazy, stupid, irresponsible. They really don't want that to change because if Blacks started to prove them wrong...well, they just might lose their power, and they couldn't handle that. It would upset their idea of order. It's very complicated, and it's very ugly, but ignorance and bigotry are not new."

"I knew about their hatred for Blacks, but why the Jews?" Vickie asked.

I flinched when I heard her say that. Pastor Turner did too. Where's this child been?

"Vickie," Pastor Turner said, displaying greater patience than I could have mustered up, "the Klan hates anyone who isn't white and Christian. You've got to be both, or you're a marked person. Throughout western history, Jews and Blacks, well, they've never had 'both.' Consequently, they've suffered unrelenting persecution."

"I did know that. I guess I'd never put it all together," Vickie confessed. "I feel so...sheltered."

"Perhaps," Reverend Larson said with a smile. "You are experiencing, what we in the church call an epiphany. If you want to talk more, you can stay after, but now I think we need to get to the business of Head Start."

As Reverend Larson told of our experiences in D.C., I realized with a sudden clarity that all I really wanted was what Vickie had taken for granted all her life—a good education for children, equal rights without strings, and the luxury of feeling safe. I guess I was experiencing an epiphany too.

Chapter Fourteen

After the meeting I went shopping for food. By the time I got home I started feeling poorly. At first, I thought perhaps all the worrying over those devils being back in town and the trauma about Rabbi Silberman had worn me down. But as I was putting the groceries away, I swallowed, and I knew immediately, I had a summer cold. Don't know why they felt so much worse than any other time of the year. Maybe it was the combination of heat, headache, sore throat and stuffy nose. Marvin reminded me I said the same thing when it was winter. Well, if so, it was because I hated being sick. Got in my way.

I was grumbling to myself when Dessie walked in and said, "I don't feel too good, Mama."

What could I say? I fixed us some hot water loaded with lemon and honey, and we each took two aspirin.

"I don't think we should go to the voting meeting tonight," I said. "Even if we start feeling better, we wouldn't want to pass whatever we have around. Your papa can go tell people all about our trip."

Dessie was about to say something when she sneezed all over the kitchen table.

"Des, cover yourself when you do that," I said, disgustedly. I reached in the cabinet under the sink and pulled out a bottle of Pine-Sol. Handing her the bottle and a rag, I said, "Here, clean the table."

"I didn't mean to," Dessie grumbled and started cleaning.

"I know you didn't. I'm sorry. You were going to say something?" I felt bad. Sneezes didn't wait for an invitation from a hankie. They had a life of their own.

"I don't remember," Dessie said. Which got me to laughing because that was my line.

"You're too young to forget so quick," I said and then I sneezed as bad as she did.

She smiled and handed me the Pine-Sol and rag.

When Marvin walked in from the back, we must have been a sight because we were giggling and snorting and sneezing to beat the band. He didn't say anything, he just shook his head as he walked on through and headed to the mortuary.

"Wait," I called out. "We both have colds and don't think we should go to the meeting tonight. But we want you to go to find out what's been goin' on. Everyone's gonna want to find out….ahhh, ahhh choo…" I sneezed into the Pine-Sol soaked rag… "about the injunction. And maybe they'll be some talk about the Rabbi and find out if we're goin' to be group leaders and…ahhh choo."

"I'll go," Marvin said, impatiently, and left before I could say anymore.

174

Dessie and I continued our hot lemon and honey cocktail with two aspirin every four hours. We felt pretty good, or at least I did. I knew from experience if I stayed on this regimen, my cold would last a week. If I did nothing, it would last seven days. I simply felt better with my magic potions.

I sent Marvin off to the meeting after dinner and plopped down with Dessie on the sofa to watch TV. The summer fare was pretty weak, mostly reruns, but the Red Skelton Show was always good for a laugh although I think I dozed off. I woke up with a start when I heard Dessie ask, "Was Anthony at the meeting?"

"Yes, he was," Marvin said. "I told him all about your day at Howard University with Joseph."

"Papa! You didn't," Dessie cried out, tears welling up, then whispered, "How could you?"

"I could, but I didn't," Marvin said with a laugh. Dessie pulled a sofa pillow over her face and scrunched down in the sofa before Marvin could toss one at her. "Anthony did ask about you. I told him you were sick."

"Okay, you two, enough," I said. "Tell me what happened."

"At first," Marvin said, "everyone was talkin' about Rabbi's ordeal. There were stories like the Klan, in full dress and carryin' torches, marched on Rabbi's house and burned a cross on his lawn. After Pastor Turner heard that rumor, he stood up and cautioned about spreadin' gossip. But his warning didn't work. Finally, after hearin' Dr. King had saved the day by holdin' off the mob at the front door, Pastor Turner rang the bell to get the volunteers' attention... told the real story of the two men and one woman trying to attach a bomb to the house. He didn't go into any detail, but said he hoped folks would stop spreadin' false rumors. I was standin' next to Mayola while Pastor Turner was talkin'. She whispered Steve Conrad came home drunk, swearin' he'd get those Jew boys yet. She said he'd been out all night, warned me to keep an eye out for him. Said he was lookin' for trouble. She reminded me of the code three the Klan had on us. While I was listenin', I could also see Lester's reaction as Pastor Turner talked. She kept her face expressionless but nodded a few times as if to say, I knew it."

"Did you ever get a chance to talk?" I asked. "Or did…"

"No, I got a chance," Marvin interrupted. "When I told them about the injunction, the whole atmosphere in the room changed. Suddenly, everyone wanted to get back to work. Pastor Turner talked about what should happen now that we had the sign ups. He said he'd posted the matchings of new voters to volunteers who will guide the folks through the voting day process, ballot and all. You'll be happy to know we're one of the chosen homes. I wrote down the new voters' names and how to get in touch with each person. We know most of them pretty well. Shouldn't be any trouble gettin' in touch with them. Some have phones. Some don't, but I can stop by to invite them once we figure out dates."

"Oh, Marvin. I can't believe we've done this," I said. I didn't say it, but he knew how important this whole movement had become to me.

By the next morning, I would have been truly thankful and ready to plan our next step except my throat started to hurt so bad in the middle of the night, I didn't even want to swallow. I felt so terrible, I went into the living room to lie down on the sofa rather than toss and turn all night bothering Marvin. I couldn't sleep. I finally got up at dawn and stumbled into the kitchen to make Marvin's breakfast, but I ached all over. This was no cold.

Marvin took one look at me and said, "Don't you worry about my breakfast. You call Dr. Starke's office and make an appointment." He no sooner got the words out of his mouth than Dessie came in looking as bad as I did.

"Make that appointment for two," Dessie said, leaning against the doorjamb so as not to fall. She looked as bad, if not worse, than me.

Turned out Dr. Starke came to the house. Said a mean form of strep was going around, especially considering it wasn't winter, and he didn't want his office filled with contagious patients. He told us to take it easy for a least a week, then he prescribed penicillin and a decongestant. Thankfully, Marvin picked them up from the pharmacy for us. If that didn't beat all. Two months ago, I was looking for excuses not to get involved. Now I wanted to be involved but got sick. Seemed my timing was bad.

TUESDAY, JULY 25

For ten days, I stayed in the house. I felt bad because Marvin was busy with two funerals. Only way I was able to help was to complete paperwork and make phone calls from the house. But I didn't go over to the mortuary. I didn't want to be around the public or any of the families. They had enough to worry about without getting sick from my germs.

Pastor Turner called to ask if he could drop off the first forms the government sent to register the children we had signed up. I had no problem with doing everything I could as long as I stayed inside my own home. The forms turned out to be typical—more data than necessary and in triplicate, but not difficult to do. Part of my job was making sure Mr. Stennis and his cronies wouldn't find any reason to withhold money.

If I was slightly bored, Dessie was antsy. She about drove me crazy during the day. We talked some about adjusting her plans to graduate early. She said she still wanted to try and asked me to get in touch with the school. I phoned the school, but no one answered. Dessie didn't seem surprised or worried. She said she'd take care of it the first day of school. Then why did she ask me to phone? I didn't understand her mind sometimes. Marvin thought she was doing fine because he didn't have to deal with her. When he did, it was in the evening. By then, she was fine. Her two best friends were home from work, and she spent hours on the phone talking to Josey or Anthony. I wondered if Joseph was simply a happy memory.

After two weeks, I reckoned we were well enough to go to a Tuesday night meeting to help plan voting strategies. Dessie was thrilled. She spent most of the day fixing her hair like the styles she saw on the college girls at Howard. I gave her some old hair straightening products I'd tried to use a couple of times but long ago had given up. It was too much work for someone my age. But she seemed more than happy, and that made me happy. When she came out of her room for dinner, I noticed she had put on cream-colored eye shadow and something called lip gloss.

Marvin took one look, shook his head and said, "Unh-unh." She must have known he'd react like that because she turned around and went back to her room. When she returned, she looked like our girl again. Marvin smiled and said, "That's better."

Walking into the parish hall that night was like slipping into an old robe and slippers, familiar and comfortable. I watched Dessie instantly shed the sophisticated college image as she raced over to Anthony to give him a shy hug. Marvin took off to the men's section, and I resumed my place with the ladies, sitting between Lester and Mayola. I'll admit, I was a little disappointed they didn't seem more interested in my trip to D.C., but it was as if that was last week's news. Instead they wanted to update me on what they'd been doing.

As we worked on folding newsletters about candidates and issues, Mayola said, "The Conrads had another big party last weekend. All's they talked about was the failed bombing of Rabbi's house. Lots of tryin' to make themselves feel important. And lots of meanness."

"Mayola, you got to find yourself someplace else to work," Shirley Lansing, owner of Beads and Braids Hair Salon, said. "I could teach you how to do hair. I need someone to help me. These new cornrow hairdos take so much time. Everyone wants somethin' different. Ole Mrs. Jamison tol' me cornrows date back to three thousand years before Christ. Can you imagine? Said each tribe had its own unique braiding style. That's how people knew where you came from. Seems like ladies here want the same thing. Each one wants somethin' different."

"Naw, I'm too old to learn somethin' new like that. Besides, what would I have to complain about if I changed?" Mayola said, knowing everyone would laugh.

"Not to change the subject, but one of our successes in D.C. was to make sure there are polls in the black community, and they stay open the right hours," I said. I was tooting' my own horn a little. I was about to ask where the polls were on our side of town when Shirley piped up.

"My shop is going to be one of the places," Shirley said proudly. "I figured if Barber shops can do it, so can a beauty parlor. I think black women will feel more comfortable coming to my place. Don't you?"

"Yep. I'm comin'. I'll tell the Conrads I'm goin' to get my hair done. They won't know I voted too. That's pretty good," Mayola said, breaking into a giggle at the thought.

"You gonna' get cornrows?" someone shouted out.

"Now, that would be somethin'," Mayola started laughing out loud. "Mrs. Conrad'd like to pop her girdle she'd be so mad if she saw me in cornrows. Naw, I'll stick to my curls."

We finished stuffing our envelopes right on time. Pastor Turner rang his bell for us to congregate in the chairs to plan next week's meeting and final prayer.

"I'd like to stay, but I better get going. You let me know what's up," Mayola whispered to me and disappeared.

Pastor Turner gathered us together to hand out what he called "homework." He assigned Sister Addie to compile the polling places with addresses and phone numbers, Brother Stanley to collect bus schedules and maps to hand out, and Brother Lucien to enlist volunteers who'd be willing to drive those living in remote areas to the polls. He wanted everything done by the next meeting so we could distribute all the information. He ended with a prayer of peace, strength and thanks for all volunteers, voters and candidates.

As the last amen died down, I collected my purse and said my goodbyes to the ladies. I didn't know why but I felt renewed by the group. We had accomplished so much. Maybe we could override some of the hatred of the Conrads in this world.

"Ready to go," Marvin said, coming up behind me.

"Where's Dessie?" I asked, looking around, not seeing her.

"She asked me if Anthony could drive her home. They're with Josey and her boyfriend. I figured we'd be right behind them, so it'd be okay," Marvin said, leading me to the door.

"Millie, I'm glad I caught you before you left," Sister Helen said, touching my arm to stop me, "I need a big favor. The ladies' auxiliary is having a bake sale next week and I wondered if you could make one of your gingerbread cakes for us. It's a favorite, you know."

"Why, of course, I'd be happy to. I'll make two if that'll help," I said. She thanked me and took off to find another baker.

"Sister sure knew how to manipulate you," Marvin said, laughing.

"She did," I agreed. Even I had to smile. All anyone had to do was compliment my cake, and they got one.

As we were walking out the door of the parish hall, Mayola came rushing towards us. I'd never seen her look so tortured.

"Millie, you got to find Dessie. I just saw Steve Conrad and two of his buddies sitting in his truck by the parking lot. I saw him toss a bottle out his window. He's liquored up. I know him. He's dangerous. He took out after a car, and I think I saw Dessie in it," Mayola said, her whole body shaking with rage.

In no more than two seconds, Marvin and I were in the van and driving out of the parking lot.

"What way do you think they went?" I asked Marvin. My mouth was drying up so fast I could hardly speak. I actually felt a little dizzy I was so scared. I tried to take deep breaths but all that did was make me feel like I was going to faint. I could hear Marvin, but I couldn't make out what he was saying.

"I'm hoping it's the way we came," Marvin said, slowing down a little as he turned onto the back road to our house. Narrow and bordered by culverts on either side, the two-lane road was lit only by our headlights.

"I think I see something ahead," I said, pointing to a dim light in the distance. Marvin sped up to close the gap. "That's a Chevrolet truck. Mayola told me his mama gave him a new one for his birthday this year."

"That's him, all right," Marvin said, starting to close in. "He's all over the road. Drunker than a skunk. I think that's Anthony's car right in front. He drives a '42 Ford coupe, doesn't he?"

"I think so," I said, then shrieked, "Watch out," as we watched the truck ram the back fender of Anthony's car.

"Damn him," Marvin hissed. "He's using his truck as a battering ram. He's trying to run them off the road. Not on my watch," he said speeding up.

Suddenly, the truck pulled out and drove alongside Anthony's car, battering it from the side. Once, twice…I knew Anthony was desperately trying to steer straight after each sideswipe, but his car was no match for the powerful new Chevy Truck.

"Do something," I screamed.

One final hammering assault sent Anthony's car flying off the road, over the culvert and crashing into a tree. It settled precariously on the edge of the culvert. Front hood buckled with steam hissing from the radiator, awkwardly tipped headlights shining eerily up into the limbs above.

As the truck sped away, I could hear cheering and saw an arm rise out of the driver's window, middle finger waving an insulting salute. For the first time in my life, I wanted to hurt someone. But there was no time for that. I braced myself as Marvin slammed on the brakes, ground the gears into reverse and backed up. Marvin parked so the lights shone down on the crash site.

"Oh Lord," Marvin whispered.

He had the presence of mind to retrieve the stretcher he used when picking up bodies. I, on the other hand, flung open the door, jumped out and raced down the culvert to the tangled disaster. The smell of oil and rubber burned my nose as I ran. When the moans of fright and pain pierced my ears, I looked into the car to see who was moving. I recognized Josey's voice. Her cry, "Help me," from the back seat sent shivers of fear up my back. But it was the spider web crack on the windshield casting an eerie shadow over Dessie's blood-streaked face that stopped me cold. My heart raced. I prayed, *Lord, please don't let her be dead. She's such a good girl. She can't die, and that monster live.*

"Move over Millie," Marvin ordered. He tried opening the door, but it didn't budge. He tugged, kicking it, with no luck. Finally, with superhuman strength, he yanked as he yelled out, almost falling back when the door released. He picked up the stretcher and laid it beside the door.

"Help me lift her," he said, gently pulling her to him, then placing his arms under her legs and behind her shoulders. I pulled the door open as far as I could to give him as much room as possible and helped him lay her on the narrow canvass. We carried her to the edge of the road.

"Wait," he said, placing his end on what little shoulder there was, keeping the stretcher level like a bridge between my end and the road. He stepped down to take the handles from me and said, "Now you pick up that side while I lift this. That way she won't slide off." We maneuvered carefully, finally sliding the stretcher into the back of the van.

"I can finish here. You go check the others. I saw a body on the ground about ten feet from the tree. Must have been thrown out of the car," Marvin said as he pushed me aside and secured Dessie with straps. I almost screamed at him to let me be, I'd take care of her, but something inside me knew we had to act fast. I ran over to the young man lying lifeless in the jungle of Kudzu. Tears already flowing, I felt for his pulse. Nothing. I started sobbing. I'd been in the business of dying too long not to know when someone had died.

"Marvin," I cried out, "he's gone."

"We'll have to leave him and come back. We got three here who need to get to the hospital right away," Marvin said with such sadness I almost couldn't move. But I knew he was right, so I said a short prayer over the boy before I went back to helping Marvin. We carefully extracted Anthony who appeared to have a broken arm and maybe ribs, given the position of the pushed in steering wheel.

He kept saying, "I'm so sorry. I tried to keep the car on the road."

"I know you did," Marvin assured him. "Don't you worry. We're going to get you to the hospital." We stood on either side of him, wrapping our arms around his back and guided him to the van. All the while he kept repeating, "I'm so sorry."

"Let's put him in the front. I'll sit in back with Dessie," I said.

"Good idea," Marvin said.

Pulling a blanket from behind the seat, I tucked it around Anthony to keep him warm as he slipped into shock. Then I raced back to help Josey. She was crying in the back seat, holding her shoulder. Although she seemed better than the others, she was in pain.

"That horrible Steve Conrad and his awful friends. I could kill him," Josey cried.

I didn't say anything, just helped her walk to the van. I'm ashamed to admit down in the darkest corner of my being I agreed with her. I pushed the thought aside to settle her, covering her with the last available blanket, then climbed into the back.

"Let's go," I called to Marvin.

Driving to the emergency entrance of the hospital seemed to take forever. As Marvin pulled up to the doors, I shot out of the back before he came to a complete stop. I pushed through the large metal doors and ran smack into an orderly.

"Quick. This way. There's been an accident," I said, turning to lead the way.

He didn't budge. "We don't take no niggers in this hospital."

⊂ℐ∂Chapter Fifteen℘∿つ

"**B**illy Larkin. How dare you," an admitting nurse standing behind a counter scolded, scowling at the orderly. "Get your lazy butt out there and help these people." She reached over to a microphone. "Doctor Starke to emergency. Dr. Starke, emergency."

"Is Dr. Starke here?" I asked hopefully. *Praise the Lord for small blessings.*

"It's your lucky night. He's here," the nurse said. When a light blinked on the phone, she picked up the receiver. "Uh-huh. I will."

Huh, lucky night. If she only knew. I wanted to scream at her, "Lucky? What kind of luck is it when a hateful white boy tries to kill four innocent black kids who've never done anything to hurt anybody? What kind of luck is it when an orderly calls me the 'n' word?" But I didn't.

"Wait," the nurse called. "We'll do the triage in the car." She followed me out and recognized the van immediately.

"Oh," she said, "you must be Mr. Howard's wife if you belong to that van. I'm Vera Kelly. I know your husband when he comes for black patients who have died." She talked, but she didn't stop rushing to the van.

Marvin had opened the doors of the van for easy access. He had a grim look on his face. As soon as he saw the nurse, he beckoned her over and said something I couldn't hear. She looked up at him and rushed to where Dessie lay.

I couldn't look. I started to cry. The shaking of heads and whispered conversation paralyzed me with a grief I never imagined feeling. I'd been in the business of grieving all my working days. I'd said what I thought were words of comfort. But at this moment I understood the horrible pain of sheer terror. I looked up to see Nurse Kelly run back to the counter, push the lever on the microphone and order in the most commanding voice I'd heard in a month of Sundays, "Prepare OR, STAT. Be ready in five. Need all the gurneys and more help here."

"Millie," Marvin whispered in my ear, pulling me back to the moment. "She's a trustworthy person, and she'll make sure Dessie gets the best care. As soon as they get everyone inside, I'm going back to get the boy. You stay here."

Presently, a flurry of nurses, gurneys and orderlies surrounded the car, calling out this and that. I was too busy hovering over what the doctors were doing to Dessie to comprehend much else. I started to cry again. Mercy, I was falling apart. *Lord, give me strength.* I had to get ahold of myself.

"Millie," a deep voice said to me, "why don't we go inside?" Took a second to register that Dr. Starke had arrived and was suggesting I was in the way.

"But I need to be with Dessie," I protested, stuttering through my tears.

"Listen to me, Millie," Dr. Starke said as he gently took my elbow, guiding me into the entry by the nurses' station. "Dr. Abraham is our best surgeon. He's on his way.

He's going to operate on Dessie to relieve the pressure in her brain. They're going to take her into the operating room right now and prep her for surgery. The more you stay out of the way, the quicker the procedure will start."

I nodded yes, but I didn't agree. I reached out when the orderlies rolled her past me. They'd already hooked her up to IVs. When they saw the expression on my face, they stopped for a second giving me the chance to bend down, kiss her and tell her I loved her. I straightened up, said "Thank you," and they disappeared down the corridor.

I hardly cared that the waiting room for Blacks was in the basement next to the ward for black folks. Took Marvin over an hour to retrieve the body of the boy and take him to the morgue. When he finally appeared at the door of the room, I jumped up and clung to him, feeling the warmth of his arms holding me. Not saying a word, we sat together on uncomfortable folding chairs lining the wall in a room no bigger than a closet. Once or twice we walked outside to get some fresh air, but we didn't want to be gone too long in case the doctor came by. We perked up when we heard footsteps coming down the hall. The door opened and there stood Big Tony, Anthony's father.

"Oh, Tony," Marvin said, extending his hand in friendship, "we're so sorry 'bout all of this mess. How's Anthony?"

"He's okay," Big Tony said. "They settin' his arm now. I guess he broke it and two ribs. He's gonna be fine. They say I can take him home as soon as they're finished. Nurse said you brought him in. Can you tell me what happened?"

Marvin started in on the story for Big Tony. I stopped listening as soon as I heard Anthony was going to be okay. Seemed like he was bad off when I saw him at the accident, but I guess in the heat of the moment things look worse than they really are.

I perked up when Tony said, "We got to figure out somethin' to do about that Conrad boy. He's outta control. You know there's no way we can take him to court. No jury'd believe us...I mean you... or the kids. It'd be whole bunch of black folks against one big shot white lawyer defendin' his white boy client. We got to think of somethin' else."

Marvin looked around and held his finger to his lips and whispered, "Better not talk here about it. Wrong person overhears us, we might find ourselves in jail."

Big Tony nodded, but I could tell he was fired up. "I best be going," he said. "Thanks for lookin' after my son. Too bad 'bout Junior, Sam Clay's son."

"That was Junior?" I asked.

"Yeah," Big Tony said, shaking his head, "and Sam just lost his mama. Too much grief."

"Amen," I said, shutting my eyes before I started crying again. "Too much grief."

No sooner had Big Tony left than Josey's mama and papa came in to hear the story for themselves. Turned out Josey had a separated shoulder the doctor popped back into place. They said if we'd been listening, we could have heard her scream. I didn't doubt that. Must have hurt like the dickens. If Josey's parents were as angry as Big Tony, they didn't show it. Maybe they were too scared, figured they had too much to lose.

Alone again, we sat down and waited. I heard the bells of a church chime twelve times. I'd lost track of time and was surprised to realize it was midnight. Why didn't someone come to tell us something?

"You think they've forgotten us down here?" I asked Marvin.

"Sure seems that way," he said. "Want me to go see what I can find out?"

I did, but I didn't. I really didn't want to sit in this depressing room alone. "Couldn't I go with you?"

"Naw, Millie. I don't think that'd be a good idea. They're used to seein' me when I come for someone. They're not used to seein' you," he said.

I guessed he was right. I didn't like it, but I told him to go. He was just fixing to walk out the door when Dr. Starke came in.

"Looks like she's out of the woods," Dr. Starke said. "Dr. Abraham is finishing up now. He said it went better 'n he expected. Dessie is going to need rest and some physical therapy, but she's going to be good as new in a month or so. He said you two should go home and get some rest. He'll make sure she's taken care of. Visiting hours are from one to three tomorrow."

"You mean I can't see her tonight?" I asked, unbelieving. I started to cry. Marvin put his arm around my shoulder.

"Millie," he said. "I can guarantee you, the less fuss we make, the better care she'll get. Let's go home."

"I'm afraid Marvin's right, Millie," Dr. Starke said. "Lotta folks here already think we've overstepped by getting

Dr. Abraham to do the surgery. Best do what he says. He's a good man. No one slacks off when he's in charge."

WEDNESDAY, JULY 26

Next morning seemed like the whole town knew what'd happened. Even though I hadn't slept much, I didn't feel tired. The phone rang constantly with well-wishers giving me all sorts of suggestions for how to take care of Dessie, how to "take care" of Steve Conrad, and how to take care of myself. I appreciated their concern and good wishes, I really did. Didn't feel so alone.

Granny Simms stopped by on her way to work to offer her services once Dessie was home. Said she had some special brain pills that would help healing. Maintained no one had put together in one pill the formula she had. Guaranteed results. Then she gave me some rosemary oil, telling me to put four drops in the wash with Dessie's sheets. Claimed aromatherapy was an important part of improving sleep and focus. Who was I to argue? She surely had saved my life, maybe she could save Dessie's brain. Then about ten, I saw Reverend Larson park his car out front.

"Marvin," I called. "Reverend is coming, and I'm in my robe. Will you let him?"

Marvin came out from the kitchen, took one look at me, and laughed, "You better clean up before we go to the hospital or they'll want to admit you." I swatted him as I left for our bedroom.

I heard Marvin invite the Reverend in. He must have brought some food because Marvin thanked him, and I heard the refrigerator door open and close. The two men were talking, probably about the accident, when the phone rang, and

I heard Marvin say, "Chief Carter here," I froze for a minute. I wasn't in any mood to put up with threats again. I dressed in a flash and came storming out of the bedroom.

Reverend Larson was no fool. He suspected something was up. When he saw me, he was about to ask, but I beat him to it.

"Marvin Howard. Was that a threatening call?" I asked, trying to control my fury. I didn't care if Reverend heard or not. Our daughter was lying in the hospital. Another boy was dead, and someone had the nerve to call trying to intimidate us.

"'Fraid so," Marvin said.

"What'd they say this time?"

"I didn't give 'em much time to say anything," Marvin said.

"Well, they musta said somethin' for you to say Chief Carter. What did they say?" I asked with a firmness I not only felt, but I wanted Marvin to feel, too.

"We'll get you yet."

Reverend Larson looked alarmed but didn't say anything. He simply stood up, said, "I can tell you have much to discuss. I best be going. Give my regards to Dessie," and left. Marvin and I stood looking at one other, confused.

"If that don't beat all," Marvin said. "Wonder why he headed outta here so fast?"

I shrugged and said, "Maybe he was a little rude. No matter. We need to get to the hospital."

I packed some sandwiches and sweet tea in case we had to wait. We were going to be way too early for visiting hours, but I didn't care. I needed to be near my baby.

When we arrived at noon, we were told, "No visitors until one."

When I pointed out we weren't visitors, we were Dessie's mother and father, the day nurse huffed, "To the other patients in the ward, you are visitors," and turned away.

Discouraged, we trudged down to the basement waiting room. My, oh my, was I surprised when I came face to face with Chief Carter, Reverend Larson, Pastor Turner and Rabbi Silberman.

Huh? "What're y'all doin' here?" I blurted out.

Chief Carter spoke first, pulling out a notebook and unfolding it. "Millie…Marvin…" He stopped to look at each of us directly. "This is what I know. You went to a voter registration meeting last night in parish hall at Pastor Turner's church. Four young people" he referred to his notes and recited the names and ages of the four, "left in a '42 Ford coupe. A new 1967 Chevy truck occupied by," once again, referring to notes, he recited Steve Conrad, his age and the same for his friends, "were waiting for the four who got in the '42 Ford. Also, someone threw a bottle of Chivas Regal out the window of the '67 truck onto the street in front of the church, suggesting but not proving, drunk driving. The truck followed the '42 Ford. Marvin, you and Millie followed about three minutes later and caught up. Did you see the accident?"

"Yes," Marvin and I answered together.

"Will you tell me what you saw?" Chief asked. And Marvin did. Everything. Any detail he left out, I filled in, including being turned away by the orderly who called me a nigger.

Chief took notes the whole time we talked.

"Let's back up. Do you think the truck hit the car hard enough to leave marks?" Chief asked, looking at his notes as he flipped back, studying each page.

"Sir, he hit it hard enough to send it flying off the road. That's all I can say," Marvin answered.

The Chief verified a few more details, then asked, "And this morning you received a threatening phone call?"

Marvin and I looked at directly at Reverend Larson who shrugged and said, "I've said it before. This cannot continue. It isn't right."

"Really?" Marvin said. "There's no way we can do anything about it. If we took this to court, we'd never be believed. Last jury hearing a case like this was all white 'n all men. When one of the jurors was asked if he could believe a black person, he said, 'Naw. Negras always lie.' If you think we'd get a fair trial against the Conrads, think again. Sorry, but that's the truth."

The room was silent. Reverend Larson and Chief Carter pursed their lips in a frown and looked down. Pastor Turner and Rabbi Silberman just looked sad. They knew Marvin spoke the truth.

"You're right," Chief said. "But don't sell all white men short. How do you think I got all this information?" He held up his notebook, shaking it for emphasis. "There are other ways for justice that are legal."

"If there are, I'd like to see them," Marvin said with the first edge of bitterness I'd ever heard from him.

Suddenly, the mood changed when Vickie burst into the room, a beautiful bouquet of summer flowers filling her arms.

"Are you kidding me?" She said, furiously. "Four children in an automobile accident and only one is hospitalized? And the one who had brain trauma and surgery is in the basement? What kind of hospital is this? Why isn't she in ICU? I couldn't believe the nurse when she told me where to go."

Rabbi laughed. "You're lucky. There are people who tell me where to go, and its way below the basement and got a lot more heat."

"I'm serious," Vickie insisted. "I never knew hospitals were segregated."

"Vickie," Reverend Larson said. "It's only because of Medicare that Blacks are allowed in hospitals at all."

"What are you talking about?" Vickie insisted, naïve but incensed.

"With Medicare came money. Tied to getting the money was integration. Hospitals that didn't integrate, didn't get money. Sounds simple, but one way to integrate is to put Blacks in closets or basements or in the hospital when federal inspectors come and throw them out as soon as the inspectors leave," Rabbi Silberman said, not able to hide his anger. "I came today to thank Dr. Abraham for bucking the system and operating on a young black woman. Doesn't happen very often in the south. If he hadn't been willing to operate, Dessie might have been left in a hallway to die."

Vickie slumped into one of the folding chairs, letting the flowers slip to the floor. She leaned over to pick them up and hand them to me. "I don't know what to say except I'm so sorry."

THURSDAY, JULY 27 – FRIDAY, AUGUST 4

I made a gingerbread cake for the night nurses and one for the day nurses. And yes, it was a bribe. I hoped the nurses would be more receptive to letting me and Marvin stay longer or come earlier than simple visiting hours. It worked. For the next two days, Marvin and I sat with Dessie, talking to her, encouraging her. Truth be told, the nurses came to appreciate our help. As Dessie got better, we were able to feed her, sponge her, change her nightie and keep her sheets from bunching up. On the third day, Dr. Abraham told us if she continued to improve the way she had been, she'd be able to go home by Sunday. He wanted her off IVs for a spell to make sure she kept improving before he'd release her. But he did say I was such a good nurse, Dessie would probably mend at home as well as she had in the hospital. He sure made me feel good. I was going to bake him a cake too. Might even add a pie to thank him.

Marvin wasn't able to stay as long as I could because Sam Clay asked us to handle his son's funeral. Marvin had his hands full organizing it. Sam played the saxophone at the local juke joint and wanted a New Orleans style funeral. Said his band would lead the procession. Word was the whole black community would be coming to show their respects. Small donations had already started pouring in to pay for a casket befitting the occasion. Luckily, Sam was in no hurry to say good-bye to his son. He knew we were struggling through our own ordeal with Des. He said he'd like the funeral to be the Saturday after Dessie got home. What a kind man, to be in such grief and still think of others. I tucked that way of behaving into my heart's pocket.

Like the doctor said, Dessie was doing pretty good. By Sunday she was eating, talking, and most important, according to the nurses, going to the bathroom like she should. Mmmm.

Anyway, by the time the hospital filled out all the paperwork, ordered all the medications, and had us sign all the release forms, they let us take her home around seven in the evening.

Granny Simms must have been peeking out of her curtain, watching for us because the minute we drove up, she was standing by the front porch. "Let me see how she's doin'," Granny insisted, almost pushing me completely out of the way.

Dessie laughed and let Granny help her to her room. When Granny sniffed the air as she folded the blanket gently around Des, I was glad I'd washed the sheets with the four drops of rosemary oil like she told me. But my pleasure was short-lived.

"I don't like that air-conditioning in here. She needs fresh air," Granny said, turning to the window and seeing the unit. Once she realized she couldn't open the window, she growled, "Ain't right." Handing me a bottle of pills, she commanded, "You give her one of these if she starts to feel bad. She's to put it under her tongue, not chew on it."

I remembered those magic pills, but I had a snakebite not a concussion. I said yes, but thought no. As if Granny could read my mind, she said, "These ain't the same pills I gave you. You needed a painkiller. Dessie needs a mind builder." I said "yes" with enough confidence Granny backed off and said she'd be back in the morning.

The week was packed with me taking care of Dessie, helping Marvin and entertaining well-wishers who brought food. I wouldn't let anyone be near Dessie in case they might pass germs. I wasn't taking any chances. I did have to go to a Head Start meeting to catch up on the plans for the opening day in four weeks. Found out the rooms were ready and Father

Bob's congregation at St. Michael's was contributing extras like a television and a record player with children's records.

By Friday, I was tired but felt confident Dessie was going to heal up and be her old self again. She wanted to go to Junior's service, but I was really reluctant to let her. Who knew what colds or contagions people had. As usual, Dessie begged Marvin. I could have cried when he said she could sit in the side room with the family if Sam agreed. Which, of course, he did.

SATURDAY, AUGUST 5

Junior Clay's service was set for one o'clock. We set out all the chairs we owned, so many they spilled out into the entry room. Because of the New Orleans style march to the cemetery after the service, the programs were thicker than usual. They included a map with the route to the plot where Junior would be laid to rest in the black cemetery. We chose the shortest route so older folks wouldn't have to walk too far in the heat.

Pastor Turner turned up around ten to help with last minute preparations. He knew the whole community was rallying around Sam, wanting to participate in a traditional, yet not often used, funeral procession. Pastor Turner brought some pictures of Junior he had taken at the voter registration meetings and yearbooks he got from the high school documenting Junior's freshman, sophomore and junior years. Pastor asked me to help him set them up. Together, we arranged the pictures and placed the yearbooks next to the two guest books on the table we'd set up in the breezeway.

Pastor Turner was right. People started coming at eleven. By noon, the chapel was full. I was surprised at the number of white people who came too. I knew Reverend Larson, Rabbi Silberman and Father Bob would come. I was pretty sure Vickie would come, just didn't expect her to bring her husband, although I must say, I was pleased to meet him.

But I was completely taken aback when I saw Chief Carter standing along the back wall. Even the Mayor who had never supported the black community was present. Did he come because he finally realized the son of a Klansman had overstepped? Or did he want the black vote now that so many were registered? I was suspicious, but I greeted everyone with the same care.

The service was lovely. I have to say Pastor Turner honored Junior with kind and comforting words. He praised the work the teens had done for voting rights and said the legacy of registering Blacks would live forever. But in the end, it was the procession to the cemetery that moved me the most.

As I watched Sam pick up his saxophone and start playing *Amazing Grace*, joined note by note by a trumpet, a trombone, a tuba and drums, I started to cry tears I'd been holding back for days. When the six young men chosen as pallbearers, lifted the casket and took their haunting step to the right, pause, step to the left, pause, following the band out on to the street, I had to leave by the back door to gather myself I was sobbing so hard. All I could think was, there for the grace of God could have been my Dessie. I felt guilty and blessed at the same time.

Marvin followed the procession in the hearse just in case someone needed carrying what with the heat and all. He planned to go to the reception too. I stayed home with Des, making her go to bed. Once I got her settled, I went back to the mortuary and started putting chairs away. I really expected a bigger mess considering how many people attended, but I was surprised. Usually, unwanted programs littered the floor and the yard, but maybe because this was such a special funeral, mourners wanted to keep them. Regardless, I was thankful there seemed so little to clean up. I collected the pictures and yearbooks for Pastor Turner and wrapped the guest books in tissue to give to Sam. With only vacuuming left, I took a break to get something to drink. As I passed from the mortuary to the back door, I heard the crunching of the gravel in the driveway. Believing it was Marvin returning from the reception, I didn't think too much about it and went on into the kitchen to get some sweet tea. I poured a glass and drank it down, quenching a mighty thirst. As I put the glass in the sink, fully planning to wash it later, I glanced out the window. I stopped short. I couldn't see a face, but I saw someone climbing back into an idling white truck and take off.

Chapter Sixteen

old on Blue. That wasn't a Mississippi license plate. I couldn't tell for certain, but I thought I saw four, one, three or was it an eight? It was kind of beat up, so it was hard to tell. I stood frozen at the window, looking out, wondering what to do when I saw Granny Simms come sneaking out her door holding a long pole like a sword. She inched up to our mailbox. Standing back, she unlatched the clasp to the cover with the end of the pole. Her head ducked left and right, up and down as she peered into the box. She stuck the pole in the box and rattled it around. I couldn't stand it anymore. I ran out to find out what was in there.

"Is there another snake in there, Granny?" I asked, standing behind her to see what she saw, swallowing hard to keep the bile rumbling up from my stomach. I could hardly look I was so terrified.

"I saw that varmint drive up 'n put somethin' in your mailbox. I apologize for lookin', but I didn't want no more snake bites," Granny said. Stopping to put the pole down, she added, "That was a mighty fine service you put on. I enjoyed it, 'specially the band playin'. I'd a like to have gone to the grave, but I had some important herbs brewin'. Couldn't take the time."

"Thank you for checking, Granny," I said. "I don't think I could have taken it if there were another snake in there," nodding my head towards the mailbox.

"No, but he put somethin' in there. Best check. I'll be your witness," Granny said.

Knowing she was curious, I reached in and felt around. My heart was racing. When I felt a slip of paper, I held my breath as I lifted it out of the box. I was so filled with fear, it took me a minute to focus my eyes.

Yur next

I knew that handwriting. Same as what Lester had given me from the motel. I was right about no one being safe until that sneaky little varmint was caught. How had he known where I lived? Although I was mad and scared, I was beginning to realize our community was focused on the rights of people to feel safe, to learn and to vote whereas the Klan was focused on hatred, fear and criminal activity.

Seemed like an eternity waiting for Marvin to get home. I really wanted to talk to the Chief, but there was no way that was going to happen. Foolishly, I tried calling Pastor Turner and Reverend Larson and wasn't surprised when no one answered. Waiting. Oh, how I hated waiting. Nerves took hold of me as I started imagining all sorts of horrible scenes. I looked in on Dessie two times before I decided to cook to calm myself down. Comfort food. That's what I'd make. Fried chicken, biscuits and gravy, beans sautéed in bacon drippings, and vanilla cookie pudding. I whacked a chicken into pieces, tossed it in my specially seasoned flour, buttermilk and more flour then plopped it in hot melted Crisco. The crackling sound calmed my nerves, the fragrant smell of hot salty grease improved my mood.

I about jumped out of my skin when Marvin said, "You are not going to believe what happened."

"Mercy, you scared me. I didn't hear you drive in," I said. "You're not going believe what happened here either." I pointed to the note on the table. He picked up the note, read it, stuffed it in his pocket and headed out the door before I could say, "Wait."

By the time he got back, Dessie was up watching TV. Biscuits were ready to put in the oven, and the table was set.

"Where'd you go so fast?" I asked.

"Took the note to the Chief. Not sitting on any information any more. It's been an extremely busy day for everyone," Marvin said, loosening the knot of his tie and pulling it off. "Let me go change and then I'll tell you all about it."

I heard him tell Dessie she might want to hear what happened at the internment. Needing no encouragement, she was sitting at the table in no time.

"Well?" Dessie and I said together as Marvin came back in the room.

"Took about an hour for everyone to complete the procession and circle round the gravesite. Sam and his band kept playing the whole time. Initially they played the traditional hymns like *Amazing Grace* or *Just a Closer Walk with Thee* and somber dirges, but once they got closer to the cemetery, they cut loose and launched into songs like *When the Saints Go Marching In* and *Didn't He Ramble*. I tell you, the ladies were keeping tempo with their parasols swinging back and forth, children started dancing to the rhythms and even the white folk got caught up in the joy of how to celebrate a young man's life. I've decided it's what I want when I pass."

"Papa! Don't even think it," Dessie moaned, but I could tell Marvin meant what he said. Safe to say, we had seen a lot of funerals and memorials, so if Marvin thought this was special and wanted it, that's what I'd do. Course, that's if I was still around.

"Don't you worry none. I don't plan on it happening soon," Marvin said reassuringly. "Anyway, once everyone was gathered 'round, and Pastor Turner started the burial rites, it was quiet. Until—guess who showed up, drunk?"

"No," I said, down deep hoping my guess would be true.

"Not Steve Conrad?" Dessie said, a smirk spreading over her face.

"Yep...And the Chief saw the whole thing. The boy drove past in his truck, his two friends sitting next to him. He yelled out his usual and tossed something at the crowd. People scattered, making him laugh and call out 'look at all them chicken niggers try to fly.' Then he sees the Chief. I wish you coulda seen the expression on his face. The Chief saw me sitting in the hearse. I anticipated his need, turned on the engine and stepped outta the way so he could put chase on that good-for-nothin' boy."

I could not believe my ears. *Hallelujah. Praise the Lord.* Junior rose out of his casket and pointed to his killer. Not the justice of the courts, but maybe a little justice from the grave.

"If you don't think the reception wasn't one big party, think again," Marvin said. "All the talk was how Junior showed up. People were laughing and crying all at the same time. No one cared whether the Chief caught Steve, they were simply rejoicing that the Chief saw what a snake that boy was. Along with the note you gave me..."

"What note?" Dessie asked, confused.

"When you were asleep, someone put a threatening note in our mailbox," I said, no longer hiding any truths from Dessie. "When your papa came home, I gave it to him."

"I took it right down to the station," Marvin broke in. "Maybe the law will start to believe Blacks are under constant threat. Two events in one afternoon should confirm how relentless the intimidation is."

"Was the Chief there?" I asked.

"Not yet, so I kept the note. Don't want it to be mysteriously misplaced. I signed the logbook though. Hopefully it won't disappear," Marvin said. "Let's eat. All I want to do is relax with my family and watch a little TV."

Although I wanted to hear all about the reception, I agreed with Marvin. Once the food was put on the table, we joined hands and bowed our heads as Dessie said a prayer of thanks. Her words moved me deeply. I was so grateful she was alive. But her last line choked me up just about as much as the music at the funeral.

"And, God, thank you for my mama and my daddy. They are the heart and soul of our family. Please keep them safe during these troubled times. I know everything they're doing, they're doing for me."

We were all settled in watching reruns of the Jackie Gleason show, only because we were too lazy to get up to change the channel. White people laughed a lot at him, but I didn't think he was funny. He was always so mean to his wife Alice, always threatening to hit her. I didn't get it. Anyway, Dessie and I were lying head to foot on the sofa, and Marvin was snoozing in his lounge chair when I heard a tap, tap, tap on the front door. I lifted up on my elbow to listen, not sure I heard right. *Who'd be tapping instead of ringing the doorbell,* I wondered.

"Marvin, wake up. I think there's someone at the door," I said, reaching over to shake him. He snorted awake, looking a little dazed.

The tapping turned into a louder rapping, as though someone was in trouble.

"I'm coming. I'm coming," Marvin grunted, running his hand over his face to wipe away sleep, while shuffling to the door. Once again, I wished we had a peephole. Bet Marvin was sorry now too. He unchained the lock and deadbolt but only opened the door a sliver. Immediately, he flung the door wide.

"Mayola? What are you doin' here?" he said, surprised. Soon as I heard who it was, I was up in a flash and at the door. Dessie wasn't far behind.

"Can I come in?" Mayola asked, looking over her shoulder, her lips and chin quivering.

"Come in," I said. Dessie on one side, me on the other, we guided her into the kitchen. While I assisted her sitting down, Dessie poured her a glass of water, putting it down on the table. Mayola started to pick it up but her hands were shaking so bad, she clasped them together to settle them down.

The three of us stood watching her for a spell, whispering calming words, "It'll be all right. Give yourself a minute. You're safe now."

Slowly, she calmed down enough to take a big swallow of water. I could see her eyes start to refocus and her breathing slow down.

"What in the world happened?" I asked.

"This was the worst night of my life," Mayola started. "I was getting supper ready when the doorbell rang. I answered it like I always do. It was Chief Carter. He was in one serious mood. He wanted to talk to the Conrads. They were in the parlor havin' their before dinner cocktails. Mr. Conrad came out and said one of his usual, 'and to what do we owe the pleasure of the Chief of Police coming to visit us?' Phony greetings he always makes. Truth be told, he doesn't like the Chief. I've heard him plenty of times bad mouthin' him. But Mr. Conrad led the Chief into the parlor, so I went back to the kitchen to finish fixin' dinner. Pretty soon I started to hear yellin'. Mr. Conrad sayin' the Chief was a liar and turned into a nigger lover, and how he'll make sure the town'll vote him out of office come the next election. More nasty words passed between the two. Somethin' about Steve being out of control…sure wished I coulda added to that…I woulda backed up the Chief because I hardly see that boy sober anymore. The Conrads have a blind eye when it comes to that boy."

Dessie reached over and grabbed my hand. I knew this was difficult for her, but she told Mayola to go on with her story.

"Next thing I know, the Chief leaves, and suddenly Mrs. Conrad comes stormin' into the kitchen and says to me, 'Mayola, you are not to associate with those Howard Negras anymore. They've been passing around horrible rumors about my son. They are evil. I forbid you to talk to them. The Howard woman is nothing but trouble. Thinks she's so high and mighty with her funeral parlor airs. Going to Washington so Negras can vote. Worse yet, running schools here in Mississippi for Negra children. You hear me. I forbid it.' Well, that was the last straw for me. Nobody's gonna tell me who my friends can and can't be. Especially no miserable bigots like the Conrads. I'd worked for them for years puttin' up with their nonsense, and I'd had it. No more. I took off my apron, put it on the table and walked out the back door. I didn't say a word, just walked out. Musta taken her a minute to figure out what I'd done because I was halfway down the driveway before I heard, 'You come back here Mayola. If you don't, I'll see to it you never work in this town again.' So here I am. I stopped by home and got my essentials. They're out on the front porch. Millie, I can't stay in this town no mo'. Who knows what they'd do? They know where I live. I'm afraid Mr. Conrad is going to turn the Klan on me." Mayola stopped and held up her glass. Dessie rushed to fill it with water.

I was dumbfounded. I didn't know what to say. For over fifteen years Mayola had worked for the Conrad family. Washed, cooked, ironed, cleaned, polished silver...tended to them when they were sick...practically raised Steve until he went to school. She couldn't even go to the service today because she only gets Sunday off. Only reason she was at Tuesday night voting rights meetings was they thought she was going to *Bible* study.

"What are you going to do, Mayola?" Marvin asked. "Mrs. Conrad'll make good on her promise. She'll see to it you never work in this town again."

"I know that. But I've got a surprising amount of money saved. And I've got a cousin in Seattle who keeps telling me to come stay with her. She says there's plenty of work out there," Mayola said.

"How are you gonna get there?" I asked.

"That's why I'm here. I got to leave tonight. Could you drive me to a Greyhound station over yonder? I don't want them to track me from here. But, looky," She pulled out a greyhound pamphlet, "Past few years I been thinkin' 'bout this, so I've been picking up time schedules. This one is up-to-date." She opened it and laid it on the table, smoothing the creases. "Says here, a bus leaves for Seattle tonight at 10:30 p.m. from two towns over." She used two fingers to show how time and place met. "I know it's askin' a lot, but I didn't know who else to turn to."

Bless Marvin. Even though I knew he was tired, he jumped right in, "Sure Mayola. It's the least we can do. I'll get dressed, and we'll go. I'll fill you in on why the Chief was at the Conrad's' tonight. You're gonna love the story. And, if it means anything to you, I think you've done the right thing."

"Mayola, let me pack you some food for the trip. We've got plenty leftovers," I said.

"That'd be nice. I'd like that," Mayola said.

While I made two ham sandwiches, wrapped three pieces of cold fried chicken and scooped a generous portion of vanilla pudding into a paper cup, covering it with sticky wrap to prevent spillage, I noticed Mayola rummaging around in her purse. She found what she wanted, looked it over and said, "I have one more favor. If you don't mind, would you call my cousin in Seattle? Her name's Dottie Jones. Tell her I'm due in Monday afternoon at two o'clock. I know it's a long-distance call, but I'd really appreciate it." She put a dollar on the table.

"Put your money away, Mayola. I'd be happy to do it. Consider it another reason Mrs. Conrad wouldn't want you to talk to me," I said, laughing.

"Papa's waiting," Dessie said, looking out the window.

Mayola stood. We hugged, tears welling. I handed her the bag of goodies I hoped would sustain her on her journey.

"Write when you get settled," were my final words to my lifelong friend. Little did she know she got out of town just in time.

"I feel so bad for Mayola," I said to Dessie as I cleaned up from making her food.

"Not your fault, Mama."

"Yes, I know. I'm gonna miss her though. We've been friends longer than you are old," I said, harkening back to the day I first met her. "When I came here to apprentice with your papa, I boarded with the Anderson family. You probably don't remember them. They moved a couple of years ago."

"Didn't they have a boy named Jessie?" Dessie asked.

"That's them," I said, surprised she remembered. "Anyway, they attended St. James AME. I was lookin' for a church to call home, so they invited me to a gathering of churches St. James was participatin' in on the upcoming Sunday. Turns out it was a picnic, the likes of which I'd never seen before. Tables set up with hams and smoked wild game and fried fish. Others set up for salads and greens cooked so many different ways, you coulda made a whole recipe book just for collards. And the desserts, I didn't know where to start. I'm piling on my plate a piece of pecan pie, a heapin' spoonful of vanilla puddin', a healthy slice of carrot cake, and trying to make room for some peach pie."

"Mama, you didn't," Dessie exclaimed at the amount I was describing.

"I did," I said proudly. "Then I hear this voice say, 'All those sweets make any fat in your body tingle with joy, don't they?' I turned to see this skinny dark woman, a little older 'n me, loading up her plate, too. Turned out she went to First Primitive Baptist Church and talked me into joining her. Never regretted my friendship with Mayola or my choice of church. She always made me laugh, and I'm going to miss her powerful bad."

After we cleaned up, Dessie and I pretended to watch a little television. I say pretended because I know neither of us cared a hoot about *Hogan's Heroes* or *Petticoat Junction*. We were lost in our own thoughts. Seemed to me Blacks took two steps forward and two steps back while whites, especially this new group called Hippies, got away with singing *All You Need Is Love* and smoking pot. Mmm-hmmm.

"Whatcha thinkin' about?" I asked Dessie.

"I was thinkin' how much I'd miss Josey if she left. We've been friends as long as I can remember. I guess that's how you feel about Mayola. I'm sorry for you," Dessie said.

"Let's call it an evening," I said—too tired, or maybe too sad, to want to talk about it. "No tellin' when your papa will get home." Dessie agreed and disappeared into her room.

I locked the front door but left the back open for Marvin and turned on the back-porch light. I decided I'd stay up until Marvin got home so he could tell me if Mayola really was okay with her decision. Changing into my summer pj's, I settled onto our bed and took out my *Bible* to find comfort. I started to doze off when I heard tires crunching on the gravel in the driveway. A sense of relief passed over me that Marvin was home so soon. He must have dropped Mayola off, made sure she had a ticket and then headed on home. I heard the creak of the backdoor hinge and waited for Marvin to come into the bedroom.

Five minutes later, when he didn't appear, I tossed back the sheet, slipped out of bed and started for the bedroom door to find out where he was. I stopped when I heard the backdoor slam shut. *That's weird*, I thought. A chill ran down the back of my spine and hair stood up on my arms.

What's that smell? Smoke. Not the warm, woody smell from burning logs in a fireplace. More an acrid smell from something not meant to burn. The terrifying whoosh of air being sucked out of the room issued a final warning. For a moment, I stood paralyzed, unable to comprehend what was happening. Suddenly, a terrifying realization dawned on me as I watched wispy tendrils of smoke circle up from around the door. Someone had set fire to our home. Fear, hidden deep in my brain, tumbled out, overriding any good sense I might have had. *Think. What did they say to do? Oh, Lord, why can't I remember?*

Flames licked at the door scorching the white paint until it bubbled and hissed. I tried to calm myself by breathing deeply, but the heat seared my lungs. *Where was Dessie? I have to save Dessie.* Instinctively, I reached for the brass doorknob. Like a hot iron, it scorched my hand adding the smell of burning flesh to the sickening stench of danger. I had to think of a different way to save my daughter.

Stumbling through the blinding smoke, I held my breath, reaching out to find the end, then side of the bed. Using it to guide my way, I made it to the window. Pushing the sill upward, I gasped for air. That's when I saw him. Wrapped in the white garb of the Klan, a figure raced across the lawn, whooping in the joy of his fiery success, until the billowy drape of his gown ensnared his legs, throwing him to the ground. He kicked and squirmed like a fish flopping on the bank of a river, swearing at his mistake. Untangling himself, he staggered to his feet. In a final gesture of loathing, he swore words of condemnation at my daughter, then dove into the safety of a waiting pickup truck. As he and his gang sped off into the veil of darkness, I could hear their shrill laughter pierce the night air. "*Cowards*," I hissed.

I didn't care about anything but saving Dessie. I ran around to her window to see her holding onto the sill as she backed out.

"*Praise the Lord*, you're safe," I cried as I reached up to help her down. She jumped back almost knocking me over, turned and caught me before I fell. We hugged, tight, protecting each other from the horrors of evil.

"Run," yelled a voice, breaking us away from our frozen embrace.

We turned to see Granny Simms beckoning us from across the yard. We heard a window explode as the fire took over and realized we were still in danger. We ran towards her. Then, like a gift from the heavens, huge drops of rain started to pour down on us. I looked up, raised my arms to the sky and praised the Lord.

"Hurry. Come into the house before you get soaked," Granny commanded. We followed her like obedient children. As we climbed her steps, I was relieved to hear sirens approaching. I turned to see a fire engine pull up. Watching the men swing into action, hooking up the hoses and their water joining the pouring rain, gave me hope not all would be lost.

"Let me take a look at that hand," Granny said, gently taking my hand in hers. "Ooh child, you burned your hand good. Wait here."

She disappeared and reappeared with a whole aloe plant in her arm. She broke off a leaf, spreading the gooey gel generously over my hand. I had forgotten what a miracle aloe was to burns. The easing of the pain was immediate.

"Any place else?" Granny asked. "Dessie? How about you?" Once she was satisfied we were properly taken care of, she said, "I saw the whole thing. I saw that Conrad boy get outta his truck. He kinda' struggled with gettin' that stupid hood on. Made me think he mighta been drinkin'. But he finally did. Then he reached in his truck and hauled out a gas can and staggered to the back door. After a few minutes he come running out. Saw him fall. Hope he hurt hisself."

I'd been so busy listening to Granny, I didn't see the fireman come walking over. A tall figure of a man wearing oversized yellow slicker pants and jacket, goulashes, and a hard hat, he was an imposing presence. Sweat from the heat of the fire and the humidity ran down his soot streaked face.

"It's almost out. We kept the fire from spreading to the mortuary. Which is about the only good thing I can say. You were lucky you got out when you did. We're pretty sure an arsonist is at work since two fires broke out in the same black neighborhood. Lots of similarities. The fires spread rapidly, started in the back of the house, and very hot. Yours was hot enough it blew through the rafters. That's why the rain helped. We won't know for sure until we investigate, but if you have any ideas, it sure would be helpful…" he said. He didn't have a chance to finish his thoughts when Granny let him have an earful about what she saw. When she was finished, I told him my story.

"Hmm. Seems someone's been busy tonight," he said.

"Two fires?" I asked suddenly, his words echoing in my head. "Was the other house Mayola Allen's house?"

"How'd you know? You wouldn't happen to know where she is, would you? We went to the Conrad's, but they said she no longer worked for them," the fireman said.

Not wantin' to give Mayola's secret away, I shrugged my shoulders and kept my face blank. Out of the corner of my eye, I saw a figure running across the lawn towards us. With fear creeping up my spine, I started backing through Granny's doorway. When I realized the figure was Marvin, I took off down the stairs to hug him, Dessie right behind.

☙Chapter Seventeen❧

A fter the firemen left, we sat in the van talking about what happened and what to do. We finally settled on spending the night in the mortuary. Its familiarity seemed as though it would be comforting. Granny had offered her place, but we needed to be alone as a family. She understood and was probably relieved. Instead she gave us three pillows and some lightweight blankets for sleeping. As we carried what little we had into the lobby, I almost broke down. I looked around. Blankly at first, but possibilities appeared with surprising clarity.

"Marvin, I do believe we could move the desk out of my office and make a right comfortable room for ourselves. As of this moment we don't have many belongings so it's not like we need a whole lot of space. My desk could be moved right here in the lobby, so I could greet folks when they come in. Dessie, we could take the family grieving room to the side of the chapel, close it off and make you a nice bedroom. And when there isn't a viewing, we could make that our parlor. We even have a shower and sink in the morgue. It'll do until we get rebuilt. Only problem is no kitchen. We could get a toaster oven, a hot plate, a crockpot…" I heard myself babbling.

"Millie, it's one in the morning. Let's get some sleep and figure this all out in the morning," Marvin said, gently. "For now, we'll settle down right here in the lobby."

And that's exactly what we did. And, you know what else? We slept deep and long. All three of us passed out, like all that had happened over the past few weeks was too much for our brains to process so we simply shut down.

Not sure who heard the knocking on the doors of the mortuary first, but we sat up together and looked at each other as if to say, *what's going on?* Then we slumped back down when we remembered what had happened. Unwanted tears spilled down my face. The knocking continued, only louder. Marvin reluctantly got up to find out who was so insistent.

I listened, hearing Pastor Turner say, "Where are Millie and Dessie? They need to get presentable. The whole town'll be here soon. We had service this morning and instead of my usual inspirational sermon, I inspired folks to come help you out. You are going to see the Lord's work in action in a short time."

People were coming? At this hour? I looked at the clock on the wall. Eleven o'clock? I checked my watch. Yep, eleven. I could not believe it. We had slept ten hours straight. The tears stopped as I jumped up, pulling Granny's blanket around me. I looked around for my clothes with the sinking realization that all I had were the pajamas I was wearing. My throat ached as I tried to swallow tears of frustration, humiliation, and panic. Then I remembered the spare clothes in the closet in my office in case of an emergency. I shuffled into the office, careful not to trip on the too long blanket, grabbed the first dress I saw and waddled back out to go to the Ladies Room. Dessie was right behind me.

"Mama, what am I goin' to wear?" she whined, a note of panic sitting on the edge of her voice. "I don't fit in any of your clothes."

Dear Lord, I've asked for a lot lately, but please help my child. She doesn't deserve this.

"Why don't you go into the preparation room and see if you've got something in there you can wear?" I suggested.

"Oh Mama, that's a great idea. Last time I helped Papa I left a dress on the hook next to the shower when I changed into coveralls," Dessie shouted out, disappearing down the hall.

Thank you, Lord.

I didn't have much time to change or clean up. With no toothbrush, I did my best with what was available. And, for the first time, I congratulated myself for providing special touches of hand cream, mouthwash, deodorant, lipsticks and powder for our grieving clients. When I first put those items in the bathroom, Marvin had questioned my sanity, but I told him, "When people are grieving, they sometimes forget to take care. No telling when they realize they don't smell too good or their eyes are all puffy or they need lipstick." He just shrugged. Wait until I reminded him now. He was going to be glad I put deodorant and mouthwash in the Gentleman's Room, too.

I floated through the day. If I remember correctly, a group of ladies brought in enough food to feed an army, presenting me with a new coffee pot, two pounds of Maxwell House coffee and two different sizes of cured wrought iron skillets. But the perfect gift was a list of meals provided for August—every day, breakfast and dinner, with a promise of a similar list for September. How'd they get so many sign-ups so fast? Tears welled again and again, such generosity. Seemed everything was making me cry.

"Got to tell you, Millie," Ella May said, "We're all mighty suspicious about your house and Mayola's goin' up at the same time. Has anyone seen her?"

A chorus of "No" and "I hope she wasn't burned to death in her home," answered Ella May's question. I felt guilty I didn't say anything, but I wanted to make sure she got to Seattle safe and sound before I told what I knew.

"We want to help her too," Ella May said. "We got to stick together during hard times."

If that wasn't enough, the ladies had brought clothes, pants and suits for Marvin, and for Dessie and me, dresses, undies, bras, shoes, sundries. They filled the lobby with kitchen utensils, plates and glasses. A few friends could only give one glass or one plate, but that glass or plate often meant someone in the family had to share. Speaking of people of little means, I looked over to see Marvin talking to Mr. Brown and another man I didn't recognize. The two men and Marvin were deep in discussion.

As the day wore on, I realized Pastor Turner was right. Black folks kept coming. Men brought their trucks and loaded them with the charred remains of our lives - the broken frame of our bed, a melted television screen, a glob of metal that once was silverware, skeletons of possessions, some meaningful, some not. I watched with a strange detachment. I wasn't prepared for what happened next.

I looked over to see Marvin standing alone, drinking water. I walked over to caution him about doing too much. He'd been working as hard as anyone to remove the charred debris.

"You best take it easy, Marvin," I cautioned. "You're going to wear yourself out."

"You're right," he said, pouring out another glassful of water and drinking it down. "How are you doin' Millie?"

"Honestly? I'm numb." I looked down at the burned flesh on my hand. I was surprised I had no pain. "That aloe Granny gave me really worked. Look," I said, holding my hand out. "You'd hardly know I burned it." I decided I wanted aloe plants in every room of the house. That was, once our house was rebuilt. "I was surprised to see Mr. Brown here. You seemed to be deep into something with him."

"Yeah. Seems he and his cousin, Dewayne Brown, both been outta work. Because we hired Mr. Brown when we went to D.C., he asked if I would give him and his cousin a chance to help rebuild our house. Said the two of them together would make a good team. Just because his arm was bad, he could still use it, and his other arm was strong. He said they wouldn't charge but for one man. Two for the price of one. All they wanted was a chance to show they could work. Millie, I couldn't say no, so they'll start tomorrow. That means we got to decide what we want," Marvin said.

"That's no problem. I want exactly what we had," I said, starting to cry. "Thank you, Marvin. Knowing we're going to start rebuilding right away fills me with hope."

Giving Marvin a hug, I didn't notice two white men getting out of a shiny black sedan. What caught my attention was Pastor Turner walking over to shake hands with each of the men.

"Who's that?" I asked, pulling away from my hug.

"I don't know, but let's go find out," Marvin said, taking my hand to lead the way.

Turned out to be Fire Chief Brandt and the fireman from last night, Captain Jorgenson. The two men were extremely fit. I guess wearing all that heavy gear and toting those hoses around keeps a person looking fine. The Chief was well over six feet tall and maybe in his fifties, crew cut hair. Handsome man until he opened his mouth to talk, the sour breath from chew insulted my nose. Maybe he was so desensitized by the smell of smoke, he didn't know how bad his breath was.

"Sorry for your loss," Chief Brandt said, after the introductions. "We came to do our preliminary investigation of suspected arson. We been over at Mrs. Allen's house. Can't seem to find her. You wouldn't happen to know where she is, would you?" He looked directly at Marvin and me.

There it was again. Questions about Mayola's whereabouts. Marvin and I didn't say anything, just shook our heads. If we didn't say anything, nobody could say we were lying.

"What did you find at Mrs. Allen's?" Pastor Turner asked as he walked up to the group, thankfully redirecting the conversation.

"Sure as shootin', looks like arson," the Chief said. Then looking at all the people dragging rubble out of our house, he added, "Looks like you've made our job a little harder. You shouldn't have moved anything. If it's arson, it's a crime scene."

"Sorry, Sir, we didn't know that," Marvin said.

"Maybe you didn't want to know," the Chief said, with a note of warning in his voice. "Cuz if it's arson, you know your insurance won't pay you a penny. Maybe you're cleaning up so fast cuz you want to hide the evidence."

"I do believe Chief Brandt thinks we set our own house on fire on purpose just to get insurance," I said to Marvin once we were alone.

"The Chief doesn't know it, but his threat warned us how hard it's going to be to collect on insurance we've been paying for all these years. He as much as said it would be his word against ours," Marvin said. I could see him fighting the anger gnawing at his awareness of injustice. "Doesn't make any sense two Blacks would set fire to their houses, but no white jury would ever believe us against him, and he's made up his mind."

Fighting back tears, I asked, "How will we be able to afford rebuilding?"

"We'll figure a way. I might be able to take out a loan. We got the $2000 we been saving for others. We'll have to use it for ourselves. It's a start," Marvin said. "Nothing we can do about it tonight. Let's try to straighten up all these donations and then get some sleep."

We decided let Dessie go to Josey's house for a while with the understanding she was to rest. Josey's mom assured us she would care for her as her own. So, we spent the next two hours organizing and figuring out where to put things. We made enough progress to feel if we had any funeral business, the clients wouldn't think they'd invaded a home.

"It's livable," I said as I spread a sheet over a mattress someone gave us.

The next few weeks I walked around in a haze. I know I continued to organize household goods, helped Marvin run the business, went to meetings for Head Start and instructed new voters. But for the life of me, I can't remember doing any of it. Pastor Turner later told me it was grief. Sure didn't feel like grief. I didn't really have a word for how disconnected I felt. Not sure I would have pulled out of my stupor if it hadn't been for the children.

TUESDAY, SEPTEMBER 5 – FIRST DAY OF HEAD START

I set my alarm for 6:00 am. I'd been sleeping a lot lately and was afraid I wouldn't get to St. Michael's on time to help cook breakfast. Dessie came home from Josey's because she wanted to help with first day of school activities. Since her classes didn't start until the next day, I said, "Yes, but don't get overtired..." I stopped when she gave me the "mother look." I wonder where she learned that.

We needn't have bothered about setting the alarm. We were up at the crack of dawn and out the door by 7:30.

By the time we arrived at St. Michael's, the place was buzzing with activity. Vickie was in charge of the breakfast and had planned bacon, sausage, scrambled eggs, country potatoes, grits, sweet rolls, orange juice, pineapple juice, milk and hot chocolate. She said she'd been reading articles about poor children being protein deprived, so she wanted a good protein breakfast. Dessie and I looked at each other. Seemed like awful heavy fixings for children used to grits and porridge for breakfast, but we didn't say anything.

Dessie and I set to work decorating tables with first day favors like finger puppets, brightly colored placemats, and name tags. We'd made name tag necklaces for each of the children, name tags for tables and name tags for hangers in the closet. Vickie thought it was a way to teach them to recognize a few letters from the alphabet and maybe even their names. I hoped such good intentions worked.

Sister Doris, Sister Lydia and Sister Leona were busy in the two classrooms making sure each child would have a toothbrush, toothpaste and a box of crayons. The rooms were beautifully arranged according to a particular activity: bean bag chairs placed on a rug surrounded by low bookcases filled with picture books and preschool books for reading; three easels set up with paper, brushes and red, blue, yellow and white paints for artists; an assortment of large and small blocks, pieces of cardboard and chunks of wood for the builders; tables set with paper and crayons for drawing; toys and other items for free play.

One of the cleverest ideas was to cut out shoe prints from contact paper and stick them to the floor as a pathway to the bathroom. Most of the children had never seen indoor plumbing. Knowing where to go once they were taught how to use the sink, faucet and flush toilet would be most important. All in all, I rejoiced in the work the team had done, especially considering three months ago we didn't know where the school would be after the bombing at the Temple.

While we were busy preparing for the day, Reverend Larson and Mr. Reasoner were picking up some of the children in the new VW Bus. Pastor Turner and Rabbi Silberman were picking up others in a church bus. Because we had two large vehicles, all the children would arrive at about the same time.

"Here they come," Vickie shouted out. I think she might have been crying. She was so excited the moment had finally arrived. We gathered together to greet the children. Even though I had signed up seven of the incoming students, I had forgotten how young they were. As the two vehicles pulled up, eyes peeked out over the windows of the buses. When Reverend Larson and Pastor Turner opened the doors, none of the children moved. Vickie moved to jump on the bus to welcome the children, but Sister Doris held her back.

"Let Sister Lydia and Sister Leona do it. Miss Vickie, these children are scared to death. They've never been separated from their families, and they've never seen what they're going to see today," Sister Doris said. "Your heart is in the right place, but you got a white face and oft times a white face means danger to these young'uns."

Vickie took Sister's words better than I thought she would. She stepped back, smiling and nodding her head in understanding.

Slowly, with gentle guidance, four little boys jumped off the step of the bus in a frog leap from the bus to the sidewalk. Not knowing any different, each child mimicked the jump and within minutes, they were playing follow the leader into the lunchroom. Looking at those little faces, bravely overcoming their fear, moved my spirit. Their courage was an inspiration. I felt a warmth of healing and renewal slowly lifting the haze of the past few weeks.

Once the children were seated, Sister Doris welcomed them and said, "A special friend of Jesus wants to say something to you."

"Welcome, boys and girls," Father Bob said. "We thank the Lord for your presence here today. You are going to have a fun day. Amen."

Hallelujah. Thank goodness his blessing was short and sweet because the children had no idea what was going on. They brightened up when the servers brought out plates full of food. Heads turned to see if they were next for what appeared to many as more food than they had seen in their lifetime. But full stomachs did not change the shyness of most of the children. One or two sat up straighter but only a few. Quietly, they waited for whatever came next.

I was standing by Dessie as she tried to cheer a particularly shy little girl by slipping a puppet on her finger and saying, "My name's Dessie. What's yours?" But the child only looked down and wrung her hands in worry. I recognized her as one of the Brown's children, one I had signed up. Dessie looked up at me and shrugged as if to say, "I'm trying." I wasn't worried. I knew this particular child, Linda, would come around. She was one of the few I knew wanted to be here.

I felt bad for Vickie. She was having no luck. Each child she approached recoiled from her and flinched as if she approached them with a switch in her hand, fixing to whip them. I watched her as she tried over and over until, soundly defeated, she stood in the back of the room and dabbed her eyes with a napkin she'd found on a table.

Just as I was heading over to her, Sister Doris took charge. Holding up a toothbrush and toothpaste, she announced, "Children, this is a toothbrush. And this is toothpaste. Each one of you is going to get your own toothbrush and toothpaste. Be careful not to lose them," she said, nodding her head at the rest of us to hand them out. "After breakfast, I will take four of you at a time, that's one, two, three, four," she said counting on her fingers, "and teach you how to use your toothbrush and toothpaste. While I'm doing that, the rest of you will get to know each other."

Sister Doris led the first four children to the bathroom, making a game out of stepping on the footprints, teaching each child how to use them to find their way. Later, Sister told us once the children got over being amazed by running water, most loved brushing their teeth. Standing on little stools, they brushed with the toothpaste until beards of foaming paste dripped off their chins into the sink. Some of them started to giggle as they saw how funny each other looked. This delighted Sister tremendously. Then they washed their brushes under the faucet and sucked the water from the bristles.

She let each group play for a while before she showed them the flush toilet. Some of the children had toilets at home, so they knew what to do. Those who only had outhouses were terrified the whirlpool of the flush could suck them down. The boys figured out how to handle their fear. They'd pee and simply not flush. But the girls didn't want to put their little bottoms on the seat which explained the wet pants and tears of embarrassment throughout the day.

While Sister Doris was teaching bathroom skills, teachers and volunteers led the other children towards the classrooms. Their eyes grew wide when they saw the pretty rooms filled with colorful books and art supplies and pictures on the walls. They seemed most delighted by chairs that were just the right size for them. They kept sitting down and standing up, turning and looking at the chairs. The pleasure they took from the simplest things was beautiful to watch.

Sister Leana and Sister Lydia divided the children into two groups, calling them by the colors on the tags they wore. Once each Sister had an equal number of children, they seated their students on rugs in the different rooms for story time. The first book they read aloud was *Hi, My Name is Holmer*. Most of the children had never been read to. They were captivated. After the story was finished, the Sisters read the names on the tags, one at a time, asking each child to say something about themselves. Once a few of the children caught on to the idea, others followed. But one or two stayed curled up in tight little balls of fear only registering interest occasionally.

Watching the Brown children, Linda, Grace and Jerimiah, was of particular interest to me. Standing in the back of the room, I thought immediately they were going to need extra time and support to feel safe enough to participate. The gap of experience, of exposure to the modern world, between these children and the others, was so wide I wondered if it could ever be bridged.

My stomach flipped when Linda, the oldest, was separated from her brother and sister for the toothbrush experience. I decided to follow her and watch how she did. I declare, I was surprised by her change in confidence. She was curious about where the faucet water came from, where the flushed water of the toilet went. She asked question about the germs Sister Doris taught them about. What were germs? Are all germs bad? That child was six years old. Where did she get her curiosity from? All I knew was her life, all of their lives, would be limited significantly by the poverty they lived in without the Head Start program.

Just before lunch, Vickie sidled up to me. "Millie, I am so sorry."

"Why are you sorry Vickie?" I asked.

"I guess I came bouncing in here thinking I knew what was best for these children, that I knew how to run a preschool. All my stupid lesson plans. I really had no idea. Why didn't someone say something to me?"

"Miss Vickie," I started to say.

"Call me Vickie. Please." She saw me blink because she added, "You can't do that, can you?"

When I didn't reply, she pushed, "Try…. say it…. Vickie."

"Vickie," I said. I thought I would choke but actually, it rolled off my tongue easier than I thought. I realized if she could find it in her heart to apologize to us, we should be able to call her what she wanted. Maybe her lesson plans didn't work for the children, but she had taught me something I thought I'd never learn.

At three o'clock the buses were lined up outside to take the children home. As they boarded, we gave them each a paper bag filled with their crayons, nametags and finger puppets plus an apple to take home. You would have thought it was Christmas. I hoped they wouldn't be so scared when they came back the next day.

"How'd it go?" Marvin asked as Dessie and I walked in the back door of the mortuary.

"Mixed," I said, setting my purse and keys on the table we used for the guest book during funerals. "It's going to take a week or so to get some of the children to open up and not be afraid. What was your impression, Dessie?"

"I don't know. They seemed pretty good to me. A little shy, but I can remember how weird the first few days of school were when I was little. I hated my teacher because she pointed me out for not putting my chair on the desk right. I didn't want to go the next day, but you made me," Dessie said.

"I did?" I said. Always amazed me how different Dessie and I remembered the same event. I thought she loved school, and I was the one suffering because my baby was growing up.

"What'd you do today?" I asked Marvin, changing the subject.

"Worked on the house with Mr. Brown and his cousin. By the way, finally asked him his first name. It's Solomon," Marvin said. "Went and bought more supplies. Mr. Giannini at the hardware store has been giving me a generous discount. Said when he heard what had happened about no insurance, he was none too happy because he knew we didn't set our house on fire. He's got some strong feelings about the person who did. He made it clear he knew all about Steve Conrad and the Klan. He even cursed them for settin' Mayola's house on fire. Couldn't believe the boy would do such a thing to the woman who'd taken such loving care of him and the family for so long. As far as Mr. Giannini was concerned, settin' fires were the last straw. Said plenty of people in town were gettin' fed up with the reputation the Klan was givin' Mississippi."

I cringed when I heard Mayola's name. I still felt guilty about not calling Mayola's cousin the night she left. Took a couple of days before I finally remembered I'd promised to call. What prompted me was the fire. I had to tell her about how our houses burned down, and who set the fires.

She laughed. "Don't tell nobody I left. I like the idea they're wonderin' if I'm lurkin' to get revenge. It'll make that Conrad family sweat good. I shoulda done this years ago. My cousin Dottie has quite a business goin'. She cleans people's houses. Works regular hours, white peoples' hours and gets one dollar and forty cents per hour. Can you imagine? She's already found me more jobs than I can handle. I miss my friends though. You especially. But I don't miss feelin' abused all the time."

"Speakin' of meals," Marvin said, drawing my attention back. "Mrs. Ainsworth dropped off a lasagna and salad right before you got home. Said we best eat right away if we want hot food. Smells fine and I'm hungry so I set…"

Is this my husband? I couldn't believe what I was hearing. Marvin set the table?

We sat down to eat, and wouldn't you know? The phone rang. After all that'd been happening, I held my breath. We all did. Marvin held up his finger and answered, listening. I saw his face relax.

"Sure, Pastor. We're eating dinner right now, but we'll be there," Marvin said.

"We'll be where?" I asked when he sat down.

"We'll go to the voter meetin' tonight. I know you're tired and school starts tomorrow for Des, but Pastor Turner wants us to come. Says he has somethin' important for us," Marvin explained.

I was confused. I thought we had canceled the Tuesday voter meetings what with school startin' and all. We finished up and took off for the church. Dessie really wanted to stay at home because somehow, she knew Anthony wasn't going to be there. But no way were we letting her. Unh-unh. I no more trusted the Klan to leave us alone than I trusted a cottonmouth not to bite me.

When we drove up to the parish hall, there were hardly any cars in the parking lot. Only one I recognized was Chief Carson's police car.

"What's goin' on?" I said, knowing Marvin didn't know any more than I did.

"I don't know, Millie," Marvin confirmed.

We walked into the parish hall, and sure as shooting, there wasn't a meeting going on. The three of us stood, looking around, clearly confused, when Pastor Turner came out of his office to greet us.

Reaching out to shake Marvin's hand, he said, "I know you're confused, but Chief Carter thought this was safest way to meet. Come on in. He's in the office with Rabbi Silberman."

As we entered, Chief Carter greeted us, "Sorry about the deception. But I think you're going to like the reason."

He motioned for us to sit down. But first, I greeted Rabbi Silberman.

"We missed you at school today. I thought you'd be there," I said.

"I wanted to, but as I'm sure you're learning, the business of rebuilding takes constant attention. How was the opening?" he asked.

"I'd say, as well as could be expected." I looked to Dessie for support. She smiled at me showing approval with my answer. But I was still baffled. "Are we here to talk about Head Start because you couldn't come today?"

"No," the Chief said. "Rabbi's here to give you something. Remember when you gave us those papers from your source at the motel?"

"Yes," I said, hesitantly.

"Well, if you remember correctly, you kept feeding us information. That information led to stopping the Klan from making good on their threat to assassinate Rabbi Silberman. They tried and would have succeeded, but we got word from you and put our plan into action in time. You and your source saved his life," he said with emphasis, "Equally important, the license number you gave us led to the arrest of one Randy Randall two days ago while he was committing a robbery at a gas station. That beat up white truck is not going to bother anyone again."

Hallelujah. One driver of a white truck caught. If they could only catch the driver of a '67 white Chevy truck, I would feel a whole lot better.

"So," interrupted Rabbi, "I met with our board of trustees. They, with the blessing of the president of the congregation, want to award you $20,000 of the reward money with one condition. We would like a portion to go to your source."

"I'm not sure I heard you right," Marvin said, tilting his head as if to hear better. "Did you say twenty thousand…dollars?"

"I know the reward was for $25,000 but the board wants $5000 of the reward to go to the undercover agents who did some great detective work," Rabbi Silberman said, misinterpreting Marvin's question.

I sat, trying to get my head around what I was hearing. I must have looked like a zombie or something because Rabbi Silberman said, "Mrs. Howard, are you all right?"

I started to open my mouth to say "thank you" but burst into tears instead, covering my face and leaning over so as not to faint. Relief swept through my body like the warmth of the sun rising in the morning. The darkness of the past months lifting.

"She's fine, Rabbi," Marvin said. "She's just overwhelmed by your generosity, as am I," lifting his hand to his heart, "and Dessie, here," placing his hand on Dessie's shoulder. "We'll never be able to thank you enough."

"Nonsense," Rabbi Silberman said. "Your courage saved my life."

After many thanks and hugs, we headed back to the mortuary.

"How much do you think we should give Lester?" I asked once we got back and started to get ready for bed.

"If it weren't for Lester, we'd never gotten any of the reward. I say we share it, half 'n half," Marvin said. "Not only that, she risked more than we did. Well, until our house was burned down, and you got bit by a snake. And the accident."

"All of those things happened because of our participatin' in the voter registration and Head Start. And from what Mayola told us because we went to Washington. I don't think the Klan knows we had anything to do with figurin' out what they were up to. In fact, if it hadn't been for Lester, you're right Marvin, we wouldn't have," I said. "This morning we were figurin' out ways to rebuild without the reward. Ten thousand is such a blessing for us. Think of what it'll be for Lester."

"I vote for giving her half," Dessie yelled from the "family viewing room" in the front where we'd set up a mattress and some hangers for her. I looked at Marvin, grimacing, realizing Dessie could hear everything we said. Hmmm. Might have to be more careful if I were to get frisky with Marvin.

"I'll tell Pastor Turner tomorrow," Marvin said, smiling with perfect understanding, but continuing because he wanted Dessie to hear. "I don't want anyone to see us with Lester and put two and two together. Might get her and us in deeper trouble than we already are. Better to let Pastor Turner deal with it. In fact, we really shouldn't talk about the reward to anyone. Hear that Des?" he called out, "Talk to no one…" then added, "We can build one fine house for ten thousand dollars."

"Amen," I said. The day had been one of the oddest days in my life. Full of ups and downs. I will say it ended on such a positive note I had trouble getting to sleep thinking about the house, the children, Lester, and the reward. For the first time in a long time, I had real hope.

ᐸᔆᐅChapter Eighteenᐸᔆᐅ

WEDNESDAY, SEPTEMBER 6

I wish I could say the next day lived up to my expectation of hope. I dropped Dessie off at school early so she could talk to the counselor about taking six classes. She had improved so quickly and so miraculously since the accident, I was certain she wouldn't have trouble handling the load. Truth be known, the challenge would be good for her. Keep her busy and focused.

My plan for the day was to stop by Head Start to pick up the medical forms and fill in names, ages and addresses to have everything ready for Dr. Rothman when he came next week. He'd scheduled his first session with the children a week into the program figuring they'd be less afraid. After yesterday and seeing how scared those children were, I sure hoped he was right, but I wasn't convinced.

By the time I arrived at St. Michael's, breakfast was over, and the children were in their classrooms listening to their teachers reading a new book called *Brown Bear, Brown Bear, What Do You See?* I was about to step into the room where the children were when Jill Larson, Reverend Larson's wife, came out of the kitchen wiping her hands on her apron.

"Just the person I wanted to see," Mrs. Larson said, leading me to the "crying room" which was turning into a sort of office, dispensary, storage room, you name it. She picked up a packet, starting to shake out the contents. "This came yesterday from Stennis's office. He is doing everything in his power to try to stop the program. Look at this garbage," she said disgustedly. "He's hoping to overwhelm us with paperwork to account for every penny we spend. One mistake and he'll stop the money. I'm sorry. This is turning out to be more work for you. Luckily, we've got all the receipts."

I must admit I wasn't very pleased with the prospect of more forms, but the expression on the Reverend's wife's face was so worried and sad, all I said was, "I've seen worse." Which wasn't true, but what else could I say?

"If you give me the receipts, I'll start working on them today. I'm glad I stopped by. How are the children doing today?" I asked.

"Maybe a little better. They ate a good breakfast, and most brushed their teeth with no help. For many, using the toilet is still an issue. Our big job, for now, is to get them over being so afraid. Until they feel safe, they aren't going to want to be here, much less learn."

"That's the truth. I guess I best get started on all this paperwork," I said pointing to the mess on the table. "Think it'd be okay to work here? Where are you going to be in case I have questions?" I asked.

"I'll be here all day." Smiling, she touched me lightly on the shoulder, turned to walk out of the room and with a wave of her hand said, "Good luck."

The work turned out to be more tedious than difficult. I shook my head in disbelief when I read under food—*fill in dates of purchase, list amounts and cost. Be careful to categorize proteins, fruits, vegetables, snacks, starches, desserts.* I wondered if the person who wrote these forms had taken lessons from the writers of the literacy tests? Who thinks this stuff up?

They made the same demands and arbitrary categories for school supplies, healthcare items, cleaning products and donations. Ridiculous. Once I got started on the forms, my competitive nature took over. Uh-huh, I was not going to be outsmarted by the folks who wanted to destroy this program.

I made a rough draft. Thank goodness, because my first go-through was a mess. Looking it over, I found items in the wrong place. Or I had to guess if they wanted cookies in snacks or desserts. One significant receipt from Winn-Dixie for twenty-five dollars and forty-six cents fell off the table. I might never have known if Vickie hadn't seen it on the floor when she brought me lunch. I had to go back through each column and make adjustments. But I worked until I finished the whole packet. Leaning back in my chair, my final copy looked really good—no erasures, totally organized, and neatly transcribed. So much for self-satisfaction. When I looked at the clock, I panicked. In fifteen minutes, I was supposed to pick Dessie up from school.

"Mrs. Larson," I said, poking my head into the kitchen. "I left the packet and attached receipts on the table in the 'crying room.' I have to pick up my daughter. I'll be back tomorrow to check if you think it's ready for signatures." And off I went.

One look at Dessie's pursed lips and hunched body, I knew her day had not gone well. Walking over to the van, pulling open the door and tossing her backpack onto the floor, she slumped onto the front seat, crossing her arms over her body with a "Humph."

Turning on the engine, looking over my shoulder to see if there were any oncoming cars, I pulled away from the curb. "Okay, what happened?" I asked.

Silence. No answer. I wasn't surprised. She clams up when she's really mad. Could be because we don't allow temper, but we've been through too much lately as a family to keep the same pattern going.

"Dessie, I can't help you if you don't tell me what happened," I said.

"My counselor won't let me take six classes. Said if she changed me, she'd have to change a whole bunch of people, and she hasn't got time," Dessie mumbled. "I told her about visiting Howard this summer. All she said was 'Oh, that explains all the packets.' No encouragement, no 'what a great school,' just blah, blah, blah. No move to help. I coulda tore her framed Ole Miss diploma right off the wall."

"Huh," I scoffed. "Want me to talk to her?"

"Naw. Won't do any good. But that wasn't what really set me off," Dessie said through clenched teeth.

I waited.

"My locker. When I opened my locker, there was poop smeared all over the inside." She started to cry, tears of humiliation and fury.

For the first time in my life, I left rubber on the tarmac as I wheeled a U-turn and headed back to the school.

"Mama. No. Don't. Please. It'll make things worse," Dessie begged.

"Worse? Worse than what? You almost being killed? Our house set on fire? Worse? I don't think so, Dessie." I pulled up to the school, pulled on the brake and told her to wait. She melted down into the seat so no one could see her.

"I'd like to see the principal," I said in the sweetest most servant-like voice I could muster to the secretary at the front counter.

"Mr. Clarkson is busy," the secretary said, but I knew she was lying because I had seen him duck in his office when he saw me.

"Too busy to talk to a parent of one of his students," I said, still sweet as could be.

"I'm afraid so. It's a busy day," she said while pretending to straighten some papers on the counter.

I asked if I could use the telephone.

"I'm afraid it's only for school business," she said, patting the phone protectively.

"This is school business," I said. I'll admit, I was getting a little edgy.

"I'm not sure I like your tone, Mrs... I didn't catch your name."

I turned around, walked out and drove right to Head Start. Luckily, Vickie was still there.

"I need your help," I said. She took one look at me. That's all she needed. Grabbed her purse and followed me out. I explained what happened as we drove back to the school. She clarified a few things with Dessie, like, "Did anyone clean up the locker?" "No." "Did they assign you another locker?" "No." "Did anyone follow through with any of your issues?" "No."

As we pulled up to the school, Vickie said, "Wait here." For a brief moment I felt like Dessie must have felt a half-hour ago.

I looked over to Dessie and she said "I sure wish I could be a fly on the wall. I'd love to see what was goin' on in there."

I started to laugh, "Well, someone's gonna' get a lesson they won't forget. Not sure if it'll be Vickie or Mr. Clarkson."

"Or the secretary," I added after a few minutes.

An hour went by before we saw Vickie push through the double doors of the school and bound down the steps towards the van. I felt my heart start to pound and my breathing accelerate. I looked over at Dessie who was no better off than I was. She looked like she was going to burst into tears any minute.

"Relax," Vickie said as she slid in beside Dessie, pushing her over closer to me.

"Well?" I said, hesitantly.

"Well, everything is taken care of. Dessie, here's your new schedule," Vickie said, handing Dessie an official schedule. "Six classes. I made sure you had five solid and one easy. The sixth class is typing. I can honestly tell you, I use typing more than anything I ever studied in high school." Then handing her another half sheet, she said, "And this is your new locker with your new combination."

I didn't know what to say, but Dessie did. "I can't thank you enough. How'd you do it? I mean in one hour you got everything I needed. Thank you, thank you, thank you," Dessie gushed.

"And, if there's any backlash from that snippy secretary, you let me know," Vickie said.

"Really? You thought she was snippy too?" I asked. "How did you manage all of this?"

"The threat of public humiliation for not complying with the Civil Rights Act made Mr. Clarkson cave pretty quickly. He's not the type of man who wants a black mark on his reputation."

I had no idea what she was going on about. What did public humiliation have to do with Dessie?

"I guess you don't know, but I went to this very school," she continued. "My parents moved here from California when I was a freshman in high school. At the time the school was all-white, and quite frankly, I didn't think a thing about it. In fact, I loved it. It's where I met my husband John. We were high school sweethearts. John had lived here all his life, and I thought he was the sexiest guy alive. I loved his accent. So charming.

Dessie and my eyes grew wide and our mouths opened just a touch. We had never heard a white woman talk so familiar, like we were friends. Genuine friends. This is how Mayola and I talked with each other. My goodness, that woman was so innocent. She continued on without a clue how special this was to Dessie and me.

"Anyway, in our junior year, the Brown decision came down from the Supreme Court. Within one day, we saw a different side of many of our so-called friends. U-G-L-Y. John and I decided we didn't want any part of it. We looked for a university as far away as possible and thought UCLA sounded perfect, so we applied. When we were accepted, we moved to LA and never looked back. It was great. We graduated, got married and had kids. Pretty soon it dawned on us that the children would never really know their grandparents. When John's magazine offered him an assignment to cover the civil rights movement and now the upcoming trial of some Klansmen, we decided we could handle living here for maybe two years. We figured that would be enough time for the kids to bond with our folks. My dad is pretty political and ran for school board to try to expedite the integration process. He won. Maybe you've heard of him..."

My mind started to drift. I realized how little I knew about Vickie, much less the upcoming trial. I'd heard rumors about the government taking on an Imperial Wizard and a sheriff accused of killing some civil rights workers. But black folks only heard what white folks wanted them to hear. The local white newspaper sure didn't paint a fair picture, and the black newspaper only ran a paragraph or two about the story. Maybe they were afraid if they wrote too much, the trial wouldn't happen because it gave black folks hope. Then again, if what Vickie was saying was true, it would be the first time anyone took on the Klan. I sure hoped they could find enough evidence to prosecute that Conrad boy and his father.

"That's amazing. Don't you think so, Mama," Dessie asked, bringing me back to the present.

"I'm in shock about all of this," I said, trying to cover why I wasn't paying attention. Truth be told, if I'd thought I'd ever call on a white woman to help my family, I'd have told Marvin to lock me in a room and throw away the key on account of how crazy I was thinking.

"Oh, ye of little faith," Vickie said, laughing, then looking at her watch, said, "Oh golly, I need to get home. My kids are probably worried, wondering where I am."

Once I got my kitchen back, I decided I would make Vickie a gingerbread cake. We were both so grateful to her for what she had done, and I know she felt good about it too. Despite my gratitude, I couldn't help but wish I had been the one who was able to do this for my daughter. Maybe someday soon.

THURSDAY, OCTOBER 5

After I finished attaching the physical examination reports to the proper forms and readied them to send off to Senator Stennis, I straightened up the desk in what had become my office on Tuesdays and Thursdays, Dr. Rice's office on Monday mornings, and Dr. Rothman's office on Wednesdays. We were considerate of one another, leaving the room clean and neat.

Dr. Rice's reports reflected his surprise at how cavity-free most of the children's teeth were, attributing the health to little or no sugar in their diets. He was concerned about swollen gums but thought the daily brushing and a better diet might improve the problem. His follow-up plan was to check the gums of the children each week. If he could see no improvement, he would consult with Dr. Rothman about possible physical reasons for the disorder.

On the other hand, Dr. Rothman's reports were full of alarm at the number of runny noses, allergies, asthma, infections and insect bites prevalent throughout the children, especially from the poorest areas. He also observed diminished energy. He originally planned to volunteer on

Wednesday mornings only, but quickly changed to an all-day regime, at least for the first four weeks. He spent his first afternoon planning a vitamin-rich menu, with a particular emphasis on vitamin C and D. He suggested orange juice and sliced oranges at every meal. He implied a lack of citrus in the diet was probably responsible for many of the symptoms.

On a weekly basis, he treated the infections and bites with samples the pharmaceutical people gave him. But mainly he used calamine lotion. He didn't want to prescribe medicines families might not be able to afford, but he did check into what the new Medicaid program provided. His hope was underprivileged children would get the help and medicines they so badly needed. Rabbi Silberman had found us a gem of a doctor in this man. Far as I was concerned, he was as good as Dr. Starke. High praise from a black about a white.

I was putting on my coat to go pick up Dessie when Sister Doris peeked in.

"Got a minute? I want to show you something," Sister said.

"Sure do," I replied.

Sister led me to one of the classrooms where the children were singing *The Wheels on the Bus* in preparation for boarding their buses to go home. After the song, they collected their possessions. Some went to the coat hangers to retrieve sweaters or coats, some wanted to take their art projects home, and one or two selected a book to take home. I was pleased to observe after only four weeks, all of them looked healthier and happier. Then, quite unexpectedly, Linda Brown, the Linda I had signed up and thought would adjust the best, broke out in tears.

"What's the matter, Linda?" Sister Lydia leaned over, embracing the sobbing child.

"I...I... don't want... to go home," Linda said between sobs. "I want to spend the night here."

"That's not possible. We all go home so there wouldn't be anyone here to take care of you," Sister Lydia explained.

"I don't care. I can take care of myself," Linda said, clinging her book to her chest.

"Pastor Turner is waiting for you, and he'd be sad if you didn't get on his bus," Sister Lydia said, trying to guide Linda toward the open door.

"What if I finish this book? I won't have anything to read," Linda said, stalling and twisting away from Sister.

"You're such a good reader, I'll let you take three books home. That way you can pretend you're at school, but you'll be in your own bed," Sister Lydia said.

Sister Doris beckoned to Pastor Turner to honk his horn. He tooted three quick times, then waved to Linda, calling, "It's time to go so the wheels on the bus can go 'round and 'round."

Linda tightly clutched the three books Sister Lydia had given her, then sprinted onto the bus.

Praise the Lord, I wasn't wrong about her. She was a bright child who would never have blossomed if it hadn't been for the Head Start program.

In fact, I really couldn't believe these were the same children who four short weeks ago were so shy and frightened. But I couldn't stay any longer either. I needed to pick up Dessie, get home, check on the progress being made on our home, make dinner and get to the voter meeting by seven. Days like this made me wonder why I'd taken on so much.

I guess I shouldn't complain. Marvin was doing more than his share too. Preparing all the things that had to be done for funerals without much help from me or Dessie. Along with funeral work, Marvin was supervising and helping with the rebuilding of our home, making all the decisions on what should go where. Once the roof was back on, Marvin started in on the kitchen while Solomon and Dewayne worked on the rest of the house. Marvin figured we could always sleep in the mortuary, but with no kitchen, we were dependent on other people for our food.

Truth be told, I rather liked people delivering our meals to us every night, not having the worry of what to cook. But I knew it wouldn't last forever, so I took one day to go pick out the appliances I wanted. I went to Sears to make my selections. I thought it was going to be easy. Oh my, appliances had changed over the years. There were so many choices, I hardly knew where to begin.

After much consternation, I picked out the latest color, avocado green, for my new countertop stove, double oven and refrigerator. Ooh wee, it was going to be so pretty. Then, out of the corner of my eye, I could see all sorts of bathroom ideas one aisle over from the kitchen department. I couldn't resist looking.

Turned out, I couldn't resist ordering. I decided to keep the bathroom basins, counters, and self-sticking, linoleum tiled floors white, but loved pink for my bathroom walls and shower curtain. I knew it was going to be months before the house was finished, but I convinced myself ordering now only made it easier later.

Luckily, Marvin didn't mind. He was so satisfied with Solomon and DeWayne, he was sure it wouldn't be long before we would be moving in. Said they took pride in their work, often taking initiative to present ideas for better ways of doing things. Dewayne suggested a new type of closet built into the length of the room rather than the small closets we had. I loved that idea.

Even Dessie was working to full capacity. Unfortunately, studying and getting good grades branded her as a goodie two-shoes, but she didn't seem to mind because she "had a dream." In fact, she said she felt sorry for the kids who would be stuck in town because they didn't know any better. The six classes challenged her study habits but not her abilities. I told her it was a matter of time management. Learning how to organize what to study and when would only benefit her at Howard. She agreed and as time passed, she realized it became routine to spend two to three hours per night on homework.

Still, she made time for the voter registration meetings. Ever since Washington, she was passionate about civil rights. In fact, she and Anthony designed an extremely clever comic book instructing newly registered voters what to expect. I thought it was so good it should be published. But maybe that was a mother's pride speaking.

ᴄ✒Chapter Nineteen✑つ

I f I thought meetings had been full before, the next meeting was packed. Folks felt the possibilities swirling in the air. For once, the volunteers thought they could make a difference. Everyone was energized. When Pastor Turner rang his bell for people to take their seats, he had to ring it again to get them to quiet down.

"Hallelujah praise the Lord," Pastor Turner sang out.

The crowd answered, "praise the Lord."

"We are blessed tonight to have one of our favorite speakers," Pastor Turner said to the crowd, who collectively held its breath in anticipation. Pastor looked down at his notes on the podium and hesitated, and then with a grand gesture of sweeping his arm to the right, he announced "Buddy Murray."

The room exploded with a standing ovation as if we were in Las Vegas watching James Brown belt out the first notes of *Say it Out Loud! I'm Black and I'm Proud.*

Mr. Murray walked out to the podium, standing straight, acknowledging the applause.

I declare, the ladies of the congregation were swooning over him almost to the point of fainting. Ella Mae, who was sitting right next to me, took my hand and squeezed it so hard I thought it might break in two.

"Millie," she crooned. "He is the most handsome man I've ever seen. Every time I hear him speak, I get goosebumps all over my arms."

Rhoda Roberts, who was sitting behind us, leaned forward and whispered, "He's as handsome as Kennedy was. He should be the first black president of the United States."

"Humph," I said. "That'll never happen."

Took Pastor Turner ringing the bell again to settle the crowd down.

"Ladies and Gentlemen," Buddy opened, "I am so honored to be speaking before you again. A short four months ago I encouraged you to register fifty percent of the black population. You did better than that. Your hard work signed up sixty percent of the population of your town."

To say cheers broke out would be an understatement. The audience went wild.

"Mississippi..." he paused, letting the crowd settle down, "is the poorest state in the union. Its population is thirty-six percent black, the highest of any of the fifty states. Resistance to the civil rights movement has been as deadly and intense here as anywhere. As you know, state and local officials have led some of the resistance, erecting many obstacles to prevent black people from voting. Some of your brothers and sisters went to Washington to protest and obtain injunctions against some of those obstacles."

Many in the crowd looked at me and Marvin, nodding their heads with awareness of our trip. A chorus of "Mm-hmm," "praise the Lord," and "amen" echoed throughout the room sending chills down my spine. I looked across the room and saw Anthony hug a very embarrassed yet proud Dessie.

"Because of their courage, polls will be open in black communities on voting day."

Again, our friends whooped and hollered and applauded.

"Because of their courage, brothers and sisters, the polls will be open all day, so you can vote."

He paused again. I felt the ache in my throat that comes from holding back tears.

"Because of their courage, federal observers will be sent to your county to observe elections, thus ensuring all rights granted in the Voting Act of 1965 are honored. In a further attempt to disenfranchise the black voter, the state legislature has changed a number of the laws to limit your influence. In your county, they have changed the method of selecting key county officials from voting them into office to appointing them in an attempt to silence your voice. Those in power in Mississippi are afraid of you. They fear your vote. That is why they try to intimidate, to incite fear, to instigate terror. They will stop at nothing to prevent you from voting."

I felt like Mr. Murray was talking directly to me. I had a burned-out house as a testament to what he was saying. I wondered how many of my brothers and sisters felt the same way. I was so filled with hope and possibility.

"You must not allow them to dissuade you from exercising your rights as a citizen of the United States. On Tuesday, November 7th, I hope every eligible person in this room who is registered to vote exercises their right to cast a ballot for the candidates of their choice. Together we can change the injustices that have plagued us for hundreds of years. Together we can overcome."

I swear, the man was a genius. He made us forget the dangers and filled us with dreams of possibilities. I'd never heard Dr. King in person, but I doubted he could be any better than Mr. Buddy Murray.

Took Pastor Turner five minutes to calm the crowd.

"I thought I could move the spirit. But after Buddy's speech, I realized all I do is nudge it a little," Pastor Turner said.

People laughed, still glowing with enthusiasm.

"We have a lot of work to do between now and November. I posted a list of candidates we should support, who are backed by the National Association for the Advancement of Colored People and the Interdenominational Ministerial Conference. We can bring freedom to our county if you help elect Henry Hunter the first Negro Deputy Sheriff. We have the votes to do it. But to get the job done, we need your dollars. We have already raised $1,600 for our Henry Hunter. We are halfway to our goal. Help us with reach our goal by opening your wallets and purses and contributing to our candidate. Let's make this happen."

The reality of the election in the form of a plea for money sure quieted the group down. Then, in the twinkling of an eye, my blessed Marvin stood up and pledged ten dollars. Everyone knew our house had been burned and saw his gesture as a real sacrifice. Applause broke out. Brothers quickly started passing the hat for the donations of pennies and dollars. Pastor Turner started singing *Oh, Happy Day*. His voice inspired me to start singing and clapping. Others joined in and soon the whole room was swaying and clapping. I could feel the promise returning. Maybe, just maybe, we could make a difference.

The rest of the evening was social. Although some newly registered voters were meeting with volunteers to make final arrangements for transportation on election day, most of us were chatting and congratulating each other on a job well done. I was helping myself to some cookies and punch when Ella May sidled up.

"Have you heard any word from Mayola? They didn't find her remains in the ashes so all I can figure is she's still alive. That Mrs. Conrad is circulating horrible rumors about her being a drunk and a thief, so she fired her," Ella May said, worry lines creasing her forehead.

"Please tell me you don't believe her, Ella May," I said, avoiding having to tell where Mayola was when she asked me not to.

"Of course not. But I am worried about her," Ella May said.

"Tell me. Who'd Mrs. Conrad get to work for her?" I asked. "I'd be more worried about her than Mayola."

"What're you sayin'?" Ella May asked, picking up on my insinuation right away.

"I'm just sayin', worry about the poor new maid," I said. "Don't you worry about Mayola."

"Thank you, Millie. I won't worry any more. I feel a whole lot better," Ella May whispered. "I know you'll tell me all about it when you can." And with that, we started talking about the election.

"Will you excuse us, Ella May?" the breathless, almost apologetic voice of Lester Ball interrupted as she took my arm.

I looked and shrugged at Ella May as Lester dragged me into the Ladies room. Here we were again, looking under doors to make sure no one was present. Satisfied we were alone, Lester broke into tears.

"You are the most generous...uh, uh...wonderful person...uh, uh...in the world," Lester blurted out, trying to catch her breath between sobs.

"Lester, stop crying. I can't understand you when you cry so hard," I said.

"Thank you for sharing the reward. Do you know what this means to me? I don't have to work at that disgusting motel any longer. I can go back to school. People think I'm stupid because I got a limp. Why do folks think a handicap affects a mind too? I want to be a teacher. I love little children," Lester said.

"That sounds wonderful. You deserve the best. You risked a lot and it's paid off in all sorts of ways. Lester, you don't need to thank me. Marvin, Dessie and I want to thank you," I said.

She burst into tears and gave me a hug. After she calmed down, I said, "Just be careful how you proceed. Don't want to be too obvious about coming into money."

At that moment, Mrs. Wilkins pushed open the door of the Ladies Room. Seeing us, she said, "Isn't this the most wonderful night you've been part of?"

"Yes indeed, it sure is," I said.

WEDNESDAY, OCTOBER 25

News traveled fast. Considering I hardly knew about a KKK mucky-muck being arrested until Vickie told me her husband was a newsman writing about the trial of the big

Imperial Wizard, I was surprised how quickly I became fascinated by what transpired. Dessie and I started to follow stories in the paper. But it wasn't enough. I asked Marvin to buy us a TV so we could follow the story on the evening news. I pointed out he'd been missing some of his sports' programs. He agreed he was feeling a little off not being able to relax at night watching some of his favorite programs. He suggested we go out the next day while Dessie was in school and buy a new TV.

We drove down to the appliance store and ended up buying a Motorola color TV console. Can you beat that? Color. And a console, not a tabletop. Our first piece of furniture for when our home was ready. Marvin said it was the wave of the future.

That night, we started watching the news. The Imperial Wizard, who was from our town, was on trial for the murder of a black man. I held my breath with anticipation when a TV anchorman said Blacks were prospective jurors. The next day I heard none of the black people made it through the selection process, but as Dessie said, "Small steps, Mama. Small steps." She was right of course.

The jury took two weeks before they had a verdict. When the anchorman came on the TV news to announce the all-white jury had convicted an Imperial Wizard of the White Knights of the KKK, Dessie and I hugged each other, half-laughing, half crying.

Marvin came into the lobby, saw us and asked, "What's all the hugging about?"

When we told him, he shook his head, smiled, and said, "Well, I'll be. Wonders never cease. Maybe that's why the little coward confessed."

"Confessed? I don't think the Wizard confessed. They simply had a lot of evidence against him," I explained to Marvin since he hadn't been following the trial.

"No, no. You're right about that. See, I was at Gidding's place getting gas when Chief Carter drove up. Told me he was on his way over to the mortuary. Wanted to talk to all of us, but said I'd do fine. I guess I saved him a trip because he took me in the back. Told me Randy Randall, the guy…"

"We know who Randy Randall is," I interrupted.

"I sure do," Dessie said, shivering in disgust.

"Well, apparently Randy was in a plea-bargaining mood. I'm thinkin' he heard about what was happenin' to the Wizard and decided he'd better cut a deal so as not to spend the rest of his life in prison. He confessed to his part in the bombings of the Synagogue," Marvin said.

Dessie threw her hand to her mouth, and I hissed, "That weasel."

"I'm not finished yet," Marvin said. "Maybe you best sit down."

Marvin waited until we did, and then said, "He signed a statement naming Steve Conrad as the person who set fire to our house and to Mayola's."

For the first time in my life, I could not think of one thing to say. Seemed like the same for Dessie. We sat, speechless, mouths dropped open, eyes wide.

"I should tell you news like this more often. Maybe then I'd have peace and quiet," Marvin joked, then turned serious. "Chief cautioned the Conrad boy would probably get off, scot-free. Mr. Conrad's lawyer wouldn't have any trouble pittin' a two-bit crook like Randy against an upright, reputable family like the Conrad's."

"But I saw him, and Granny Simms saw him," I pleaded.

"Millie, you think a lawyer wouldn't tear you apart? It was dark. All you saw was a person in a robe running from the house," Marvin said.

"Mama, he's right," Dessie interjected, trying to control her anger.

"Humph." I wasn't down for the count yet.

"Where's Vickie?" I asked, walking into the kitchen at St. Michael's.

One of the volunteers nodded to the dining area, saying, "She's cleaning up from lunch."

I grabbed a cup of coffee and headed into the auditorium. When she looked up from wiping the tables and saw me, she said, "What brings you here on a Wednesday?"

"Special congratulations to you and your husband," I said. "Aren't you pleased about the trial?"

"Of course. But we had nothing to do with the outcome. All my husband did was report what was happening," Vickie said. "The lawyers are the ones who deserve all the credit. Brave men. They were the ones who put their reputations on the line and gathered all the evidence. They've been building their case for years from what I understand."

"Ummm," I mumbled, suddenly realizing all this time I was watching the trial and celebrating the verdict, I had thought somehow Vickie influenced the outcome. Since she had helped my daughter, I had come here today hoping she could help me convict Steve Conrad.

"You look serious," Vickie said, finishing the last bit of cleaning. "Anything I can help you with? That school secretary isn't giving you any trouble, is she?"

"No, it's not that," I said and proceeded to spill out all the details of the trouble we'd had with Steve and my new hope he'd be prosecuted.

Vickie listened, placed her hand on mine, and said, "I'm sorry, but I have to agree with Marvin and Dessie. This is one time I can't help. I wish I could, but the cards are stacked against you. What kind of friend would I be if I held out false hope? I suspect the Randy guy is in trouble, but the Steve boy... maybe he'll sweat a little, but he'll get off."

"Really? Why couldn't you threaten to humiliate the family publicly like you did Mr. Clarkson?" I asked.

"Millie, if the boy has been arrested, the family is already humiliated," Vickie said, pointing out the obvious.

She was right, of course. I so appreciated how honest Vickie was with me. She truly was a friend. With fifteen minutes before the children got out of school, we sat down at the table and shared our perspectives about the trial over a cup of coffee. She even refilled my cup. Imagine. A white woman severing me.

As she talked, I drifted off to thinking about how I thought the Head Start and Voting committees were going to be a burden, and how I thought Vickie was a clueless white lady who didn't understand our situation here in the south. I realized I had my own biases and, just like the times, I needed to start changing.

ᘓᐤ᧰Chapter Twenty᧰ᐤᘚ

TUESDAY, NOVEMBER 7 — ELECTION DAY

Mississippi turns pleasant around the first week in November, and this year was no different. No need for air conditioning or furnaces or wood burning stoves. With a high of seventy-one degrees, the air felt cool and refreshing. For that first week, we opened windows and didn't worry about humidity creating mildew on our shower curtains or on the bottom of our shoes in the closet.

For the voters who had to walk from their jobs to the polls, the weather was perfect. No rain or blistering heat to get in their way. And for those who needed assistance, an army of volunteers was ready to drive would-be voters to the polls.

I'd spent a good portion of the night sitting at my desk, map spread out, figuring out the most efficient way to drive the folks who had signed up with Marvin and me to the polls. I had a list for Marvin and another for me. All in all, we had about twenty-five folks we'd help vote for the first time.

Marvin had spent his day washing and polishing the hearse for him to drive and the van for me. I figured each of us could comfortably handle five people per trip. Marvin probably could have gotten a whole lot more in, but we already thought we were pushing our luck delivering voters to the polls in a hearse. I suggested decorating the vehicle with flags, but Marvin said, "No, no, no. We've had enough trouble. Puttin' an American flag on a hearse on votin' day would attract too much attention."

I had to agree. Not one of my better ideas. Nonetheless, we were excited. Dessie wanted to take the day off from school to go with us, but we pointed out she would be using up a precious place in one of the cars. Disappointed, her spirits picked up when I suggested she ask Anthony to pick her up to take her to school. Now that was one of my better ideas.

We went to bed early, setting our alarm for 5:00 a.m. Needn't have worried, we were up by 4:30.

"I sure will be glad when our kitchen is done. I miss your good breakfasts and the smell of bacon cookin' on the stove. Makes getting up easier," Marvin said, staring at a spoonful of cold cereal.

"How much longer do you think it's gonna be?" I asked, knowing all that was left to do was install the appliances I ordered. Although I loved the breakfasts our friends had been making, I had to agree with Marvin. I was beginning to miss frying bacon and mixing my special sweetbreads.

"I wanted to surprise you, but since you asked, I'm hoping by the end of the week," Marvin said, breaking into a big smile.

"If it is, we'll have one of the tastiest breakfasts I ever made," I said. "But we best get going." Standing up, I collected our empty cereal bowls, kissed Marvin on his forehead and went to the Ladies room to rinse out the dishes.

Our first trips were to pick up people who had to be to work by 8:00 a.m. Seems we weren't the only ones excited. As I drove up to the first home on my list, Abby and Jonas Foster bounded down the stairs and greeted me with broad grins.

"We been so nervous, I don't think we slep' a wink las' night," Jonas said, opening the door of the van, letting Abby slip in beside me.

"I got my list of people I'm gonna vote for," Abby said. "I don't wanna get confused when I get in that booth."

"You're going to do just fine," I reassured them.

As we drove, Abby checked her purse three times to make sure the list was there.

"Abby, you gonn' work the clasp right off that purse if you do that any mo'," Jonas said, teasing her.

Next on the list was old man Joshua Paquette.

"Hope you haven't been waiting long," I said as I pulled up slowly, having seen him standing on the curb. The temperature was not much warmer than the 52 degrees when I left the mortuary.

"Ms. Millie, I been waitin' all my life for this moment. I ain't cold. I'm rejoicin' inside," Josh said, nodding his head saying, "Mornin," to the Fosters.

Turned out I didn't have to wait for anyone. Little Hank Holt and Granny Arnett were waiting out front of their houses too.

"Hope you didn't have to wait long in the cold," I said, more as conversation than anything else, as I picked them up.

"Oh, don't you worry none about a little cold. It's a beautiful day," Granny said, and climbed into the back and squished in beside Little Hank.

I carefully stopped in front of their polling place, Shirley Lansing's Beads and Beauty Shop. I could see Shirley looking out over the logo painted on the front window. But, much to my surprise, there was a reporter from one of the major networks standing out in front too. He had a microphone in his hand and a cameraman waiting at his side, ready to interview any willing voters as they headed into or out of the beauty shop.

"I see a newsperson is here," I said to my group. "I admit, I was not expecting this. I'll distract him if you want to vote first."

They looked at each other, fear replacing smiles.

"Look at it this way. If the press is here, the Klan sure won't be," I said, sputtering out the only thing I could think of. But it worked. They nodded in agreement, and their smiles returned.

"That's the truth. Never thought of it that way," Granny said. "Let's go vote."

We piled out of the van. True to his profession, the reporter rushed over and tried to stick a microphone in Jonas' face.

"Is this your first time to vote?" he asked.

"Sir," I interrupted. "These people have to get into the polls to vote and then get to work. Why don't you go over to city hall for interviews," I said, trying to divert him, but he'd been snubbed by better than me.

Relentlessly, he shoved the microphone back. This time it worked, but I don't think he was expecting what he got.

"Young man," Granny said. "Please respect our right to vote without harassment."

Huh, that'll teach him. Once inside, they each signed the register, and Shirley gave them their ballots to take into the booth. Before they did, I said, "I've got more people to pick up. By the time I get back, you'll be finished, and I can drop each of you off at work."

When I walked out, the reporter was gone, but I noticed a man sitting in a Buick sedan parked across the street. As I started the van, looking over my shoulder for oncoming cars, our eyes met. He nodded ever so slightly. I wasn't sure what to think. Who was he? Wasn't anyone I'd ever seen before.

I didn't have time to ponder about a strange man. I had to pick up my second group. They were the same as the first—waiting, nervous, excited. In fact, almost the same conversation took place inside the van.

As I pulled up to Beads and Beauty to let out my second group, Jonas, Abby, Josh, Granny and Little Hank stood proud as peacocks waiting for me. They opened the van, greeted the departing passengers, reassured them with pats on the back and, "It was just like we were taught," "You won't have no trouble." "Easy as sweet potato pie," "It's a wonderful feeling."

Once I took the second group to work, I realized I was free until six o'clock when I was supposed to collect three people from their workplace and take them to vote before the polls closed. As I sat in the van wondering what on earth I was going to do with all this time on my hands, it occurred to me, I hadn't voted yet. Wouldn't that have been one for the books. Made myself laugh out loud with that one.

Took me no time at all to get back to Shirley's. I stood in line with a dozen others, all eager to cast our ballots. I was so proud to be voting for Henry Hunter. I sure hoped he'd win. I also enjoyed voting for Chief Carter. If the Chief and Henry won, Blacks were going to be a lot safer. Or, that was my hope. Whatever the outcome, I felt proud to vote my conscience at the ballot box.

After I voted, Shirley said, "Why don't you stay awhile. I expect the big rush is over."

"Quite a day, isn't it?" I said, not really expecting an answer. Then I remembered the man sitting out front earlier. "You aren't worried about any trouble, are you?"

"No. Why do you ask?"

"I saw someone out front when I was driving the first group this morning," I explained.

"Good eye. That was agent Preslik. He's one of the federal observers sent to make sure all the polls are open from 7:00 a.m. to 7:00 p.m. He introduced himself this morning. Said he'd be driving around town checking polling places all day. Gotta admit, he made me feel safe," Shirley said.

I felt relieved too. Another bonus from our trip to Washington.

By the time I got home from driving the last voters to their homes, I was tuckered. Wasn't from doing much. More from being wound up all day. The minute I walked through the mortuary doors, I felt the tension I'd been holding start to melt from my shoulders and slip out through my fingertips. And bless Dessie's heart, she had set up the table with the dinner Granny Arnett provided. I noticed four settings on the table. Didn't take long to see Anthony and Marvin had parked the folding chairs in front of our new TV.

"Papa said it was okay if Anthony stayed for dinner," Dessie said, anticipating the question she knew was coming. "Said he could watch the returns with us."

Why didn't I think of that? Watching election results sounds fun.

"Come on over here," Marvin called. "Results are starting to come in."

"Maybe we should pull the table over closer to the TV, so we can eat and watch," I said to Dessie because I was really hungry. I hadn't eaten anything but cold cereal since early this morning. Anthony saw us start to lift the table and rushed to help. Now that's what I call a gentleman. I liked this boy.

We ate in silence watching the local commentator read county by county results. The big news was Holmes County. A black schoolteacher, Robert Clark, was running against a white incumbent, J. P. Love, for a seat in the Mississippi state legislature. Mr. Love was not only an incumbent but the chair of the House Education Committee. However, results were slow to come in. So slow, when the clock turned 8:00 p.m., the "regularly scheduled programs" resumed.

"Guess we're not going to know anything until tomorrow," Marvin said.

Wednesday, November 8

When I got up, I tied my robe tight and tip-toed out to pick up the paper. I was sorry I hadn't put on my slippers because it was so cold if you milked a cow, you'd get icicles.

The paper wasn't worth the effort. Apparently, they had to go to press before some of the close races had been settled. The minute I came back in, I gathered my clothes and went into the prep room to take a hot shower. Once I was finally warm again, I dressed, went into the lobby and turned on the TV, hoping the morning news had more up-to-date results. Good news was Clark had won. Certainly encouraging, but I still heard nothing about Henry or the Chief.

I decided I'd call Shirley at her shop, on account of she opened at seven. Considering she was an official polling location, I thought she might know something.

"Beads and Braids Beauty Salon," Shirley said, sounding professional but warm and inviting.

"Hi, Shirley, Millie here. Two things. Uh, I think I'd like to do cornrows. Do you have any appointments today?" I asked, stunned at myself. Where did that come from? Me with cornrows?

"Why, yes I do. I'm so surprised. Why didn't you say something yesterday?" she asked.

"Because I…I had no idea I wanted them," I said, laughing. Dessie and Marvin were going to think I was going mad.

"Why don't you come in around ten? It takes about an hour the first time."

That was sooner than I bargained for. But at least it gave me no time to back out. "Okay. That's good."

"What was the second thing?" Shirley asked.

"Have you heard any results about Henry or the Chief?" I asked.

"Why yes. They both won."

Down I went as Shirley stepped on a bar to lower the swivel chair.

"Don't look until I'm all through," Shirley commanded. "Hope I'm not hurtin' you. I really enjoy your doing this. If you're willin' to do it, maybe other ladies in town will follow your lead."

Hard not to take a peek at what she was doing what with the life-sized mirror right in front of me, but I honored her request. "What do you think I should do about a hat. You know, I don't feel properly dressed if I don't have a hat," I said.

"You might not want a hat when you see what I've done," Shirley said with pride.

"Shirley, I love you, I really do, but me without a hat is like apple pie without any cheese," I said.

"My cousin Addie might be able to help you. She's made some mighty fine hats for ladies. Always lookin' for new customers," Shirley suggested.

"Oh, really? Where does she show her hats?" I asked.

Shirley stopped what she was doing, walked to her phone, and called her cousin. Explaining my request given my new hairdo, I heard her say, "Uh-huh...Uh-huh...take me about half-hour more...Okay...we'll be here."

"What?" I asked.

"She's bringing some hats over," Shirley said.

"You don't waste any time, do you?" I said.

"Neither do you, my friend," she said. We both burst out laughing.

While she finished, I asked her what the best part was of running a polling place. She thought a moment and said, "Millie, I think it was the best day of my life. Watching our brothers and sisters step into the booth, knowing they were casting their votes, some for the first time, gave me goosebumps all day long. I was so proud to be a part of it. Then to find out Henry won was like the powdered sugar on one of your gingerbread cakes."

THURSDAY, NOVEMBER 23 — THANKSGIVING DAY

To celebrate with praise and thanks for the recent voting successes, the pastors of four black churches in town planned a gathering of churches for Thanksgiving Day. Pastor Turner inspired most of his flock to forsake their usual family traditions to participate in the festivities. Naturally, I offered to bring my special gingerbread cake. Dessie wanted to bring some greens and Marvin volunteered to help with the clean-up committee. Truth be told, we all know clean-up was most people's least favorite thing to do. Anyway, the dinner was planned for 2:00 p.m.

Marvin had been true to his word. He finished my new kitchen the weekend after elections. It was so beautiful. The contrast of avocado green appliances with the white Formica counters framed by the dark walnut cabinets took my breath away. Sort of the same reaction Marvin and Dessie had to the cornrows patterned around my head—perhaps a slight exaggeration.

On Thursday morning we were up early to start cooking. Breakfast first, of course, then the cake and the collards. Dessie and I were busy in the kitchen when Marvin opened the back door, leaned in and said, "Come see. The Macy's Thanksgiving Day Parade is on TV in color," and disappeared before we could say, "No, we're busy cooking."

"I'll be so glad when our living room is ready, so we can move back and forth with ease instead of having to go back and forth from the mortuary to the house," I said to Dessie as we rushed to get our food cooking in order that we could join Marvin. Seeing the parade in color was amazing. I predicted people would start watching the parade in the warmth of their homes now it was in color.

At one o'clock, we started to get dressed. If Dessie and Marvin were surprised with my cornrows, they were going to be blown away by the hat Shirley's cousin had designed specially to show off my new do. Feathers swirled as did the rows, held together by a gorgeous broach. I also bought a new outfit from Penny's with just the right earrings.

Marvin looked handsome in his dark suit, and Dessie was a picture of youthful perfection in a dress she'd found at a new type of store where rich people brought good clothes they didn't wear anymore but got money for them. Didn't make no mind of difference, it had been a long time since I felt so fine about me and my family. We surely had much to be thankful for.

After a final dusting of the gingerbread cake with powdered sugar, I wrapped it in Saran wrap. Dessie donned potholder mitts and lifted her pot into a box Marvin had found for her. We put on our coats and headed out to the van where Marvin was waiting for us with the heat on and the door open.

"Last time I went to a gathering like this was just before your papa proposed to me," I said more to Marvin than to Dessie.

"You're as beautiful now as you were then." Marvin winked at me, taking my hand with a little squeeze.

"Really? I hope you don't act like this at the gathering," Dessie mumbled, embarrassed by our show of affection.

The event was at St. James AME parish hall. With the largest congregation, they had the accommodations to handle the number of people expected. The hall was across town. Marvin was driving slowly so as not to upset the pot of collards when, hearing sirens, he looked in his rearview mirror and saw the flashing lights of a fire engine followed by police cars. He pulled over to let them pass.

"Uh-oh. Looks like they're headed in the same direction we are," Marvin said as he eased back onto the road. He stayed back. He didn't want to look like an ambulance chaser. But he was right. As we neared St. James, we saw it. Ominous as always—a cross burning in the lawn and a scarecrow mannequin hanging from a tree.

"Oh, dear Lord," I said, grasping Dessie's hand and leaning against Marvin. "Will it ever end?"

Epilogue

MONDAY, JANUARY 16, 2017

If I knew I was going to live this long, I would have taken better care of myself. I know old people say that a lot, but I'm ninety-years-old, and I really mean it. With so much behind me and so little ahead, I spend a good deal of time reflecting, grateful for the extraordinary lessons I've learned along the way. The uncomfortable moments and dangers forced me to change, to grow. As Marvin used to say, "Why would we change if everything is going our way?"

Speaking of Marvin, I miss him every day. He was always so good to me. I'll never forget that morning twenty years ago. We had finished breakfast. He went back to our room to get ready for the day, still going strong as the head mortician for our business. We had hired an assistant to help him a few years before, but he was the go-to man everyone wanted to supervise their loved ones passing. I was washing the dishes when I heard the thud, a sound so distinctive, so clearly a notice of disaster, I knew my Marvin was gone. Only blessing was he didn't know he died. It's hard on those of us left behind, but a better path to the other side for those who depart. He wanted a New Orleans style funeral like he'd seen years before for a young boy, and that's what Dessie and I gave him.

Dessie, my sweet little girl, isn't so little anymore. She's a grandmother. Married Franklin Tucker, a man she met during her first semester at Howard University. Never thought we'd be able to afford four years of a college education plus three more for her PhD in African Studies until some insurance money we never thought we'd see came through. With the help of Mr. Reasoner, the lovely man we met when we went to Washington, D.C., the insurance company finally accepted that we had not set fire to our own house and reimbursed us the $10,000 we spent to rebuild. Dessie is a professor at Howard, and Frank works as a lawyer for the Southern Poverty Law Center. They've worked hard. They gave me two wonderful grandchildren who are starting families of their own. I never thought I'd live long enough to see great grand babies.

See, I told you I live with my memories. They flutter through my brain like birds, sometimes pecking at me, sometimes just passing over. Pastor Turner and Reverend Larson led a flock off into the horizon years ago. Come to think of it, I expect Rabbi Silberman and Father Bob did too, but I lost track of them. Didn't lose track of that vulture Steve Conrad. He ended up caged by the bottle in a prison of his own making.

On a happier note, there's Vickie. She's like a hummingbird. Flits in and out of my life with phone calls or cards. She's out in California in some retirement community. Keeps asking me to come visit her. I say I will, but I know I won't. I'm too old to go gallivanting around. Maybe that's her on the phone now.

"Hello," I say, hitting the speaker on the smartphone the kids gave me for Christmas two years ago. I do that because I'm a little hard of hearing.

"Mama. How you doin'?"

I feel joy hearing the familiar voice of Dessie. "Good. How about you?" I say.

"Well, I had an interesting day. You sittin' down?" she asks. I never like the sound of that, but I sit down anyway.

"I am now. Tell me what happened."

"You are not going to believe it. Today is Martin Luther King's birthday," Dessie says.

"I had plumb forgotten that," I say.

"It is. And in keeping, as my final gift to the university," she says...

"Your what?"

"I'm retiring Mama. I'm sixty-eight years old," Dessie reminds me, as if I didn't know how old my own daughter was. "Anyway, I planned a speaker to commemorate the day, someone who could talk about the lasting influence of Dr. King in the twenty-first century. I heard about a teacher in Virginia who was Teacher of the Year last year for the whole state. Heard she has a spectacular unit for Black History Month. I invited her. She was a small woman, but she was the most dynamic speaker I've ever heard. When she talked about her early childhood in Mississippi, I really perked up. You know who she was?"

"No, Dessie. I don't," I say. "How would I know?"

"Think back to the day you signed up your first children for Head Start," Dessie said.

I doubt I'll ever forget that day. "You mean the day when all those ticks tried to suck out my blood? If we hadn't gotten them all off, I might not be here today," I laughed.

"That's the one, Mama. And my speaker was one of the first children in the Head Start program," Dessie said.

"You don't mean?" I asked, feeling my eyes well up with tears as I remembered a little girl begging to go to school.

"I do. You recollect her name?" Dessie asked.

How could I ever forget? I knew she was special.

"Linda Brown."

Millie's Special Gingerbread Cake

Grease a 10" x 10" pan and turn oven on to 350°

3 cups flour sifted

1 tsp cinnamon

1 tsp ginger

1 tsp cloves

1 tsp baking soda

1 cup brown sugar

½ cup melted shortening

1 cup molasses

2 eggs

1 cup boiling water

Sift flour, spices and soda together.

Stir brown sugar into melted shortening, add molasses and unbeaten eggs. Beat well.

Add sifted ingredients and hot water a little at a time, beating thoroughly after each addition.

Pour into pan, cook for about 25 minutes.

If I took it to a gathering or to a friend, I dusted it with powdered sugar. Sometimes, for really special occasions, I whipped the cream I skimmed from the top of our milk bottles and put dollops on the top.

Marvin said, "Five minutes out of the oven. That's when it's best. Doesn't need anything." Dessie just liked licking the bowl.

About the Authors

Sheryl Williams graduated from University of D.C. where she earned an Associate Degree in Health and Sciences. She worked as a mortician for several years and then for the United States Postal Service for 38 years. Retiring in 2003, she moved from Washington D.C to DeLand, Florida, where she now resides, plays viola with the Orange City Orchestra and raises chickens.

email: Sherylj1946@gmail.com

Martha Eddleman (the M of M.K.) graduated from University of Pacific with Bachelor of Arts degree in United States history and English literature. She lives in California where she writes, makes art, plays Bridge and follows the Giants.

email: mkeddleman65@gmail.com

Katie Eddleman (the K of M.K.) graduated from Fresno State University with a Bachelor of Arts degree in Theater. Later she earned a M.Ed. from University of Phoenix and M.S. from University of Arizona. She and her husband live in Arizona where she teaches Science and writes.

Email: mkeddleman65@gmail.com